Bibliographies of Mo
ISSN 0749-47
Number O

G000075644

£15-95.

C73231

The Work of
COLIN WILSON

An Annotated Bibliography & Guide

by
Colin Stanley
University of Nottingham

Edited by Boden Clarke

R. REGINALD
The Borgo Press
San Bernardino, California ◻ MCMLXXXIX

"The answer seems to be in achieving a
certain state of mind called 'vision'...
the moment of great insight in which
the purpose of all life is seen.
Ultimately, this is the only thing
worth achieving."
Colin Wilson—*Religion and the Rebel*

*For Colin, of course,
And for "Outsiders" everywhere*

Library of Congress Cataloging-in-Publication Data

Stanley, Colin, 1952-
    The work of Colin Wilson : an annotated bibliography & guide /
by Colin Stanley ; edited by Boden Clarke.
        p. cm. -- (Bibliographies of modern authors, ISSN 0749-470X ;
no. 1)
    Includes index.
    ISBN 0-89370-817-8 : $29.95. -- ISBN 0-89370-917-4 (pbk.) :
$19.95. -- ISBN 0-89370-010-X (signed, ltd. ed.) : $49.95.
    1. Wilson, Colin, 1931- —Bibliography. I. Title. II. Series: Bibli-
ographies of modern authors (San Bernardino, Calif.) ; no. 1.
Z8976.487.S7 1989   84-11181
[PR6073.I44]
016.823'914--dc19   CIP

Produced, designed, and published by R. Reginald and Mary A. Bur-
gess, The Borgo Press, P.O. Box 2845, San Bernardino, CA 92406 USA.
Cover design by Highpoint Type & Graphics; cover photo by Anna de
Courcy.

FIRST EDITION——September, 1989

CONTENTS

ACKNOWLEDGMENTS

My thanks to Colin and Joy Wilson, Gail Stanley, and Howard F. Dossor of La Trobe University, Melbourne, Australia, for allowing me to use the catalogue of his collection to fill some of the gaps in this bibliography.

Also, my appreciation to Brenda Marshall of the College of Psychic Studies; Jerry Drost of the State University of New York at Buffalo; K. Gunnar Bergström of Uppsala University, Sweden; Professor Bruce McQuarrie; and Tom Greenwell of *The Yorkshire Post*.

And: to Jeff Kwintner, Virginia Hackett, and my colleagues Hilary Newton, David Young, Tony Barker, Glenis Pickering, and Gordon Johnston.

Finally, thanks to Boden Clarke of California State University, San Bernardino, for "polishing" the manuscript.

NOTE

In the Books Section, citations under "Secondary Sources and Reviews" to Bendau, Bergström, Campion, Tredell, and Weigel reference those authors' critical monographs on Wilson's work; full citations are provided in Section H—About the Author.

4

INTRODUCTION

The Quest for Colin Wilson

"...At the end of the Second World War, the literary critics scanned the horizon for an upsurge of literary talent...nothing happened. In England highbrow critics—like Cyril Connolly—got into the habit of remarking that the novel, as a literary form, was probably at the end of its life span...What was expected—and what stubbornly failed to materialize—was a 'movement'...."[1]

This was Colin Wilson's own assessment of the platform onto which he, and several other loosely connected writers, were thrust in the mid-1950s when his first book, *The Outsider*, was published to tremendous critical acclaim:

—"A major writer—and he's 24."[2]
—"*The Outsider* is the most remarkable book upon which the reviewer has ever had to pass judgement."[3]
—"Mr. Wilson's book is a real contribution to our understanding of our deepest predicament."[4]
—"...one of the most remarkable books I have read for a long time."[5]

He became a celebrity overnight, part of the "Angry Young Men" movement created by the media to fill the literary vacuum that then existed, and which was destroyed soon afterwards by the same hands. But out of the ruins emerged a writer and thinker who, some thirty years and ninety books on, must now be considered one of the foremost of our time.

"Who is Colin Wilson?" asked Philip Toynbee in his famous review of *The Outsider*, and indeed, even today, with all the wealth of material we have at our disposal, this is a difficult question to answer. When his first biography was published in 1962,[6] he commented:

"I would prefer that it completely ignored the biography and concentrated on my work. Why should anybody be interested in the biographical facts about any man under the age of eighty?"[7]

His own "preliminary autobiography"[8] bears this out—being more of a philosophical statement than a record of a life. Arguably, this can reveal more about a man than a conventional listing of dates, places, personalities, and events, but, in truth, the "real" Wilson will never come to light until his meticulously kept journals are published. The tantalizing extracts which appear in Sidney Campion's biography would seem to confirm this.

In the meantime, for the purposes of this essay, a few superficial facts are required in an attempt to paint some sort of picture of the man behind the writings...

He was born on June 26, 1931 in the East Midlands city of Leicester—the first child of Arthur and Annetta Wilson. At the age of eleven he attended Gateway Secondary Technical School, where his interest in science began to blossom. Even at this early age he seemed to be blessed with the self confidence and optimistic belief in his own genius that later was often mistaken for arrogance:

"Secretly I admired Newton, for I imagined him as occupying a place in the hierarchy—Archimedes, Galileo, Newton, Planck, Einstein—which would one day include myself."[9]

By the age of 14 he had compiled a multi-volume work of essays covering all aspects of science entitled *A Manual of General Science*. But by the time he left school at the age of sixteen, his interests were already switching to literature. His discovery of George Bernard Shaw's work, particularly *Man and Superman*, was an important landmark. He started to write stories, plays, and essays in earnest—a long and intricate "sequel" to *Man and Superman* made him consider himself to be "Shaw's natural successor." After two unfulfilling jobs—one as a laboratory assistant at his old school—he drifted into the Civil Service, but found little to occupy his time:

"Being a good Civil Servant consists in knowing how to look busy when you have nothing to do."[10]

He began openly to bring books into his office to read. Then, in the Autumn of 1949, he was drafted into the Royal Air Force, but soon found himself clashing with authority. Frustrated and bored, he finally invented a story that he was homosexual—in order to be discharged. Upon leaving the R.A.F. he took up a succession of menial jobs, spent some time wandering around Europe, and finally returned to Leicester in 1951. There he married his first wife, Betty, and moved to London, where a son, Roderick, was born. But the marriage rapidly disintegrated as Wilson drifted in and out of several unrewarding jobs. During this traumatic period Wilson was continually working and reworking the novel that was eventually published as *Ritual in the Dark*. He also met two young writers who eventually became close friends—Bill Hopkins and Stuart Holroyd. Another trip to Europe followed, and he spent some time in Paris with Bill Hopkins attempting to sell magazine subscriptions.

Returning to Leicester again, he met Joy Stewart—later to become his second wife—who accompanied him to London. There he continued to work on *Ritual*, receiving some advice from Angus Wilson (then Deputy Superintendent of the British Museum's Reading Room), and camped in the open on Hampstead Heath to save money.

On Christmas Day, 1954, alone in his room, he sat down on his bed and began to write in his journal. He described his feelings as follows: "It struck me that I was in the position of so many of my favourite characters in fiction: Dostoevsky's Raskolnikov, Rilke's Malte Laurids Brigge, the young writer in Hamsun's *Hunger*: alone in my room, feeling totally cut off from the rest of society. It was not a position I relished...Yet an inner compulsion had forced me into this position of isolation. I began writing about it in my journal, trying to pin it down. And then, quite suddenly, I saw that I had the makings of a book. I turned to the back of my journal and wrote at the head of the page: 'Notes for a book *The Outsider in Literature*'...."[11]

Thus was *The Outsider* conceived. He continued to work on it at a furious pace and..."One day I typed out the introduction, and a few pages from the middle, and sent them to Victor Gollancz with a letter giving a synopsis of the book. He replied within 2 days, saying he would be interested to see the book when completed...."[12]

It was eventually published on Monday, May 28, 1956, to the aforementioned critical acclaim, and Wilson was immediately the center of a great deal of media attention, much of it damaging to his reputation and those of his fellow "Angry Young Men." This reached a peak of absurdity when Joy Stewart's father—having read and misunderstood Wilson's journals (which contained notes about a sadistic sex murderer intended for inclusion in *Ritual in the Dark*)—threatened his future son-in-law with a horsewhip. The story appeared in all the scandal-oriented newspapers the next day. Wilson and his future wife were forced to escape from London to avoid the constant attention of the press. They moved to Cornwall, where they have remained ever since. But the overexposure was damaging to his reputation as a serious writer, and his second book, *Religion and the Rebel*, was savaged by the critics when it appeared in 1957. Victor Gollancz advised him to give up writing until the fuss died down.

Fortunately and typically, Wilson ignored this advice and continued producing book after book, completing his important "Outsider Cycle" in 1966. Works of non-fiction were accompanied by a string of novels—each entertaining in its own right, but also blatantly using various genres to put his philosophical ideas into practice. These books, which appeared in a steady stream throughout the Sixties, were usually either given dismissive reviews by the critics, or, worse still, totally ignored. In an interview with his friend and fellow-writer Dan Farson,[13] Wilson summed up this very frustrating period:

"Book after book of mine disappeared, like throwing stones down a well. Not even a splash."

Ironically, this was Wilson's most important sustained period of creative writing to date—a fact that is now appreciated by some enterprising publishers who have set about reprinting those early books. In 1971, however, the tide turned when he published a massive volume entitled *The Occult*:

"The reviews had a serious and respectful tone that I hadn't heard since *The Outsider*... As if conveying the blessing of England's literary establishment, Cyril Connolly and Philip Toynbee...produced lengthy and thoughtful reviews... Apparently all was forgiven."[14] Since then a number of important (and many secondary) works have appeared. Among the former are: *New Pathways in Psychology*, a book about Abraham Maslow, in 1972; *The Craft of the Novel* (1975); *Mysteries* (an equally bulky sequel to *The Occult*) in 1978; *Frankenstein's Castle*, on the "double brain," in 1980; *Access to Inner Worlds*, an important book that should be seen as a pendant to the "Outsider Cycle," in 1983; and the immensely impressive *Criminal History of Mankind* (1984). In 1985 two important retrospective collections of essays appeared: one edited by Wilson himself entitled *The Essential Colin Wilson*, and a second edited by Howard F. Dossor called *The Bicameral Critic*, both essential reading for the growing numbers of students of his work.

My own interest in Wilson began in 1970 when, at the age of eighteen, just out of school, I came across *Ritual in the Dark* in a bookshop in Exeter, and then went on to read *The Glass Cage*. Although I was impressed, I was more interested in the subject matter than the author himself, and over the next ten years "strayed" to other writers. But a series of coincidences led me back to Wilson's work, and when (in 1980) I was offered a position as a library assistant at Nottingham University Library, I decided to make use of the considerable resources at my disposal to construct a bibliography and guide. I wrote to him suggesting this, and he replied promptly and enthusiastically, inviting me to his home and putting his library at my disposal. Thus began what has been (for me, at least) a very fruitful association with Wilson and his family. This book is the direct result of that association.

Section A is complete to 1988, but Sections C and D (or this bibliography itself) will never, I fear, be finished, for Wilson is such a prolific writer that even *he* cannot keep track of all the articles, reviews, and introductions he has produced over the years. It goes without saying that the size of this book owes much to my being able to browse through Wilson's personal library, and having the added benefit of being able to consult the author himself. Much of the material listed would have been impossible to trace using conventional reference sources. Its publication is timely, since Wilson's books are now beginning to appear on university reading lists. And if this bibliography is essential to the student of Wilson's work, so too is the sourcebook of critical essays which I began compiling during the summer of 1985, collecting essays from friends, colleagues, and scholars worldwide, and moulding them into a volume called *Colin Wilson, a Celebration* (London: Cecil Woolf, 1988). Publication of both works will lay a very firm base for future Wilson scholars to build upon.

In the meantime, Wilson continues to produce. 1990 will, I confidently predict, see him once again restored as a bestselling author when his three-volume fantasy novel, *Spider World*, is finally completed. As with all of his major fiction, it can be read purely for entertainment, for its philosophical message—or both. For here again we find the theme that runs through all of Wilson's work—the quest for the essential "Self," a quest that can only be achieved through individual Effort and Will, pushing beyond the bounds of everyday consciousness to a new stage in the evolution of Man: "If we have any sense of a destiny, we won't waste our time wandering around and doing nothing or feeling sorry for ourselves, but go straight for the object."[15]

—Colin Stanley
Nottingham University Library
April 1, 1989

NOTES

1. From Colin Wilson's introduction to *Interviews with Britain's Angry Young Men*, edited by Dale Salwak. San Bernardino, CA: The Borgo Press, 1984, p. 5.

2. Title of John Connell's review of *The Outsider* in *London Evening News* (May 26, 1956): 4.

3. Kenneth Walker's review in *The Listener* 55: 767.

4. Philip Toynbee, in *The Observer* (May 27, 1956).

5. Cyril Connolly, in *The Sunday Times* (May 27, 1956): 5.

6. Campion, Sidney. *The World of Colin Wilson*. London: Frederick Muller, 1962.

7. *Ibid.* Colin Wilson's introduction, p. xiv.

8. *Voyage to a Beginning*. London: C. &. A. Woolf; New York: Crown Publishers, 1969.

9. Colin Wilson's autobiographical introduction to *Religion and the Rebel*, p. 14. London: Victor Gollancz, 1957.

10. *The World of Colin Wilson*, p. 32 (quote by Wilson).

11. Wilson's introduction to the Picador edition of *The Outsider*, published in 1978: "The Outsider, Twenty Years On," p. 9-10.

12. *Voyage to a Beginning* (U.K. edition), p. 117.

13. "Coming in from the Outside," by Daniel Farson, in *The Sunday Telegraph Magazine* no. 219 (Dec. 7, 1980): 30-36. Reprinted in *Colin Wilson: A Celebration* (London: Cecil Woolf, 1988).

14. "The Outsider, Twenty Years On," p. 18.

15. *Interviews with Britain's Angry Young Men*, p. 83.

A COLIN WILSON CHRONOLOGY

1931   Colin Henry Wilson born June 26th in Leicester, England, first child of Arthur Wilson (a shoemaker) and Annetta Jones.

1942   Passes his scholarship examination and attends Gateway Secondary Technical School, where, despite a generally unremarkable academic career, his interest in science flourishes.

1944   Wilson pens a multi-volume work of essays, *A Manual of General Science* (unpublished).

1946   Hears a radio broadcast of George Bernard Shaw's *Man and Superman*, which has an enormous impact on him; begins writing stories, plays, and essays in earnest, including a long sequel to Shaw's play (not published).

1947   Leaves school at the age of sixteen, and begins working at a series of unrewarding jobs, including laboratory assistant at his old school.

1948   Contemplates suicide, but becomes aware that what he wants is *more* life, not less, an important discovery that eventually becomes the core of all his later literary and philosophical work.

1949   Joins the Civil Service, but is then drafted into the Royal Air Force. Begins writing a short story, "Symphonic Variations," which later forms the basis of his novel, *Ritual in the Dark*.

1950   Discharged from the R.A.F., and takes on a succession of menial jobs. Spends some months wandering through Europe.

1951   Returns to Leicester, where he meets and marries his first wife, (Dorothy) Betty Troop (divorced 1973). They move to London, where his first child, Roderick Gerard, is born (November 23rd). Drifts in and out of a series of exhausting but unrewarding jobs.

1953   Remains in London while Betty and Roderick return to Leicester. Meets a young poet, Bill Hopkins, who becomes a great influence and close friend. Travels abroad again, and then back to Leicester, where he meets (Pamela) Joy Stewart—later to become his second wife—and returns with her to London.

1954   Begins working in earnest on *Ritual in the Dark*, writing in the British Musuem, and sleeping, at times, in the rough on Hampstead Heath. In December begins *The Outsider*.

1955   Completes *The Outsider*, which is accepted for publication by Victor Gollancz Ltd.

1956   *The Outsider* is published to enormous (unexpected) critical acclaim (May 28th). Wilson becomes an instant celebrity at 24.

1957   Moves to Cornwall with Joy Stewart. His second book, *Religion and the Rebel*, is savaged by the critics. Gollancz advises him to give up writing for a while.

1959   Publishes *The Age of Defeat* (released as *The Stature of Man* in the U.S.), and moves to his present home at Gorran Haven, Cornwall, England.

1960   Second child, Sally Elizabeth, born August 15th. His first novel, *Ritual in the Dark*, is finally completed and published, eleven years after conception.

1961   Embarks on a ten-week tour of American universities and colleges. *Adrift in Soho* and *Encyclopaedia of Murder* published.

1962   *The World of Colin Wilson*, by Sidney Campion, is published, the first full-length critical study of Wilson's work. Although Wilson himself revised part of the manuscript prior to publication, he still expressed reservations about the final product. The projected sequel to this book was never published. Publishes *The Strength to Dream*, fourth in the "Outsider Cycle."

1963   His controversial novel, *The Sex Diary of Gerard Sorme* (*Man Without a Shadow*) published; also, *Origins of the Sexual Impulse* and *The World of Violence* (*The Violent World of Hugh Greene*).

1964   *Brandy of the Damned: Discoveries of a Musical Eclectic*, released, with *Necessary Doubt*, a novel, and *Rasputin and the Fall of the Romanovs*.

1965   Completes the important "Outsider Cycle" with *Beyond the Outsider*. Also publishes *Eagle and Earwig*, his first collection of essays. Third child, (John) Damon, born August 4th.

1966   *Introduction to the New Existentialism* is published ("If I have contributed anything to...twentieth century thought,...here it is"), in addition to *Chords and Discords*, *The Glass Cage*, and *Sex and the Intelligent Teenager*. Wilson is Writer-in-Residence at Hollins College in Virginia.

1967   Serves as Visiting Professor at the University of Washington in Seattle. *The Mind Parasites*, Wilson's first venture into fantasy, is published. R. H. W. Dillard's pioneering critical essay on Wilson's work appears in *The Hollins Critic*.

1969   Publishes *Voyage to a Beginning* (an autobiography), *Bernard Shaw: A Reassessment*, *A Casebook of Murder*, *Poetry and Mysticism*, and the novel, *The Philosopher's Stone*.

1970   The novels *The God of the Labyrinth* (*The Hedonists*) and *The Killer* published, plus *Poetry & Mysticism* (expanded version), and *Strindberg* (a play).

1971   Fourth (and youngest) child, (Christopher) Rowan Mark, born May 26th. Publishes *The Occult*, an immense work in which the concept of "Faculty X" is developed in depth for the first time. The book is generally well-received by the critics, and becomes the first in a long line of lesser works on the subject. Also publishes *The Black Room*, a novel. The author's play, *Strindberg*, is performed on stage.

1972   Pens *New Pathways in Psychology*, on the life and work of Abraham Maslow, whose ideas had always run parallel to Wilson's own, and whose writings are much quoted by Wilson in his later work. Also writes *L'Amour: The Ways of Love*, a sex manual, and *The Order of Assassins: The Psychology of Murder*.

1973   Serves as Writer-in-Residence at Rutgers University in New Jersey. Publishes *Strange Powers* and *Tree by Tolkien*. Marries Joy Stewart.

1974   Wilson's *A Book of Booze*, on wine, beer, and other spirits, is released, plus the critical essays, *Hermann Hesse*, *Hesse—Reich—Borges*, *Jorge Luis Borges*, *Wilhelm Reich*, and *Ken*

Russell, and the novels, *The Return of the Lloigor* and *The Schoolgirl Murder Case*.

1975   Publishes *The Craft of the Novel*, *Mysterious Powers*, and *The Unexplained*. John A. Weigel's full-length assessment of Wilson's work, *Colin Wilson*, published by Twayne. Arthur Wilson, Colin's father, dies.

1976   Two occult titles released, *Enigmas and Mysteries* and *The Geller Phenomenon*, plus the science fiction novel, *The Space Vampires* (later *Lifeforce*).

1977   Edits *Colin Wilson's Men of Mystery*.

1978   In *Mysteries*, the sequel to *The Occult*, Wilson writes of the series of "panic attacks" he had recently suffered, and which has led him to speculate about the possibility of a "ladder of selves." Also publishes *Mysteries of the Mind* (with Stuart Holroyd) and *Science Fiction As Existentialism*.

1979   *Colin Wilson: The Outsider and Beyond*, by Clifford P. Bendau, is published by Borgo Press, as is Wilson's own essay, *The Haunted Man: The Strange Genius of David Lindsay*.

1980   Publishes *Frankenstein's Castle*, a book on split-brain psychology, *Starseekers*, *The War Against Sleep: The Philosophy of Gurdjieff*, and *The Book of Time* (edited with John Grant).

1981   Produces several books on the occult, *The Directory of Possibilities* (edited with John Grant), *Poltergeist!*, *The Quest for Wilhelm Reich*, and *Witches*, plus his collection, *Anti-Sartre, with an Essay on Camus* (Borgo Press).

1982   Nicolas Tredell's *The Novels of Colin Wilson*, the first book-length assessment of the author's fiction, is published.

1983   *An Odyssey to Freedom*, K. Gunnar Bergstrom's thesis on Wilson, is published in Stockholm. Wilson himself produces the important book, *Access to Inner Worlds*, which gives practical advice on the inducement of peak experiences, and *Encyclopaedia of Modern Murder, 1962-82* (with Donald Seaman).

1984   Publishes *A Criminal History of Mankind*, another important milestone, and *The Janus Murder Case* (a novel), *Lord of the Underworld: Jung and the Twentieth Century* (biography), and *The Psychic Detectives* (occult).

1985   Two important retrospective collections of essays are released: *The Essential Colin Wilson*, edited by the author, and *The Bicameral Critic*, edited by Howard F. Dossor. The novel *The Space Vampires* is filmed as *Lifeforce* (and the novel is reprinted under that title). Also publishes *Afterlife*, *Rudolf Steiner*, and *The Personality Surgeon*.

1986   Embarks on a major lecture tour of Japanese and Australian universities. Publishes *An Essay on the "New" Existentialism*, an important condensation of his philosophical ideas, *G. I. Gurdjieff: The War Against Sleep*, *The Laurel and Hardy Theory of Consciousness*, *Scandal!: An Encyclopaedia* (with Donald Seaman), and co-edits *Book of Great Mysteries* (with Christopher Evans) and a book of political essays, *Marx Refuted* (with Ronald Duncan).

1987   The first two volumes of Wilson's impressive new fantasy novel, *Spiderworld* (*The Tower* and *The Delta*), are published in England (the books are broken into several volumes each for American publication). Also publishes *Encyclopedia of Unsolved Mysteries* (with Damon Wilson), *Jack the Ripper* (with Robin Odell), *The Musician As "Outsider,"* and *Aleister Crowley: The Nature of the Beast*.

1988   *The Misfits*, a controversial book on sexual outsiders, achieves a great deal of media attention. The festschrift, *Colin Wilson, a Celebration*, edited by Colin Stanley, is published in England; also released is *Beyond the Occult*, *Autobiographical Reflections*, *The Mammoth Book of True Crime* (edited by Howard Dossor), *The Magician from Siberia*. Wilson gives a series of lectures in California in October.

1989   Publishes *Existentially Speaking* (a collection of essays), *The Decline and Fall of Leftism* (political science), *Written in Blood* (crime), and *The Untethered Mind* (edited by Howard Dossor). *The Work of Colin Wilson: An Annotated Bibliography & Guide*, by Colin Stanley, the first comprehensive guide to the author's work, is published.

A.

BOOKS

A1. **The Outsider.** The Outsider Cycle, Book 1. London: Victor Gollancz, 1956, 288 p., cloth. [philosophy]

    b. Boston: Houghton Mifflin Co., 1956, 288 p., cloth.

    c. London: Pan Books, 1963, 316 p., paper.

    d. as: *Al-Lamuntami.* Beyrouth: Dar Al-Ilm Lilmalayin, 1965, 328 p., cloth (?). Translated by Anis Hasan. [Arabic]

    e. New York: Delta Books, 1967, 302 p., paper.

    f. London: Pan Books, 1967, 332 p., paper. Includes a new postscript.

    g. as: *Al-Lamuntami.* Beyrouth: Dar Al-Adab, 1969, 336 p., cloth (?). Translated by Anis Hasan. [Arabic]

    h. London: Pan Books, 1978, 317 p., paper. Includes a new introduction, "The Outsider, Twenty Years On."

    i. Los Angeles: J. P. Tarcher, 1982, 308 p., paper.

    j. as: *El Disconforme.* Buenos Aires: Emece, n.d., 317 p., cloth (?). Translated by Carmen Castro. [Spanish]

    k. as: *L'Homme en Dehors.* Paris: Gallimard, n.d., 359 p., cloth (?). Translated by Les F. van Hoy. [French]

    l. as: *Sivullisen Engelma.* Helsinki: Otova, n.d., 363 p., cloth (?). Translated by Kristina Kivivuori and Tuomas Anhava. [Finnish]

    m. as: *Der Outsider.* Stuttgart: Scherz & Goverts, n.d., 336 p., cloth (?). Translated by Lisolotte and Hans Rittermann. [German]

    n. as: *Lo Straniero.* Milano: E. M. Lerici, n.d., 378 p., cloth (?). Translated by Aldo Rosselli and Enzo Siciliano. [Italian]

    o. as: *Autosaida.* Tokyo: Kinokuniya Shoten, n.d., 333 p., cloth (?). Translated by Tsuneari Fukuda and Yasuo Nakamura. [Japanese]

    p. as: *Autsaideo.* Seoul: Beomusa, n.d., 431 p., cloth (?). Translated by Lee Geong Gyu. [Korean]

    q. as: *De Buitenstaander.* Baarn: In Den Torn, n.d., 313 p., cloth (?). Translated by E. Straat. [Dutch]

    r. as: *Utenfor Sirklene.* Oslo: Cappelen, n.d., 344 p., cloth (?). Translated by Colbjörn Helander. [Norse]

s. as: *Outsider*. Krakow: Wydawn Lterackie, n.d., 476 p., cloth (?). Translated by Maria Traczewska. [Polish]

t. as: *Outsidern*. Stockholm: Bonnier, n.d., 275 p., cloth (?). Translated by Nils Holmberg. [Swedish]

u. as: "The Country of the Blind (*The Outsider*)," in *The Essential Colin Wilson*. London: Harrap, 1985, cloth, p. 22-34. A reprint of the first chapter from the original volume (see also C14), collected into a volume consisting largely of excerpts from Colin Wilson books.

In addition to the above, Gollancz has kept the original book in print through at least another eighteen printings (1986), with over 45,000 copies sold in this cloth edition; these have not been separately listed.

An examination of the Outsider theme in literature. Dedication: "For Angus Wilson, with gratitude." The introductory quotation is taken from George Bernard Shaw's *John Bull's Other Island*, Act IV.

ANALYTICAL TABLE OF CONTENTS:
1. The Country of the Blind: Henri Barbusse's *Hell*, H. G. Wells, Jean-Paul Sartre's *Nausea*. 2. World Without Values: Albert Camus' *The Outsider*, Ernest Hemingway, Harley Granville-Barker's *Secret Life*. 3. The Romantic Outsider: Hermann Hesse, with particular reference to *Steppenwolf*; Henry James. 4. The Attempt to Gain Control: T. E. Lawrence's *Seven Pillars of Wisdom*, Vincent van Gogh, Waslaw Nijinsky. 5. The Pain Threshold: William James, Franz Kafka's "Fasting Showman," T. S. Eliot, Friedrich Nietzsche's *Thus Spake Zarathustra*. 6. The Question of Identity: Leo Tolstoy, Fyodor Dostoyevsky. 7. The Great Synthesis: *The Brothers Karamazov*, with particular reference to "The Grand Inquisitor," "The Recollections of Father Zossima," and "Ivan's Vision." 8. The Outsider As Visionary: George Fox, William Blake. 9. Breaking the Circuit: Sri Ramakrishna, Gautama Buddha, Georges Gurdjieff, P. D. Ouspensky, T. E. Hulme.

COMMENTS: Colin Wilson's first book made him famous overnight (for further details, see the relevant chapters in *Voyage to a Beginning* and Sidney Campion's *World of Colin Wilson*). One of the most unusual books ever to reach the bestseller lists, *The Outsider* captured the imagination of the popular market. Its notoriety was almost certainly due to an unusual confluence of events, including the literary mood of the times (which was ripe for change), the publicity surrounding Wilson when it was discovered that he had slept out on Hampstead Heath while compiling the book, the author's age (he was just 24 when it was published), and the sense of freshness, vitality, and enthusiasm which pervades the book itself. See also: "The Faust Outsider" (C24) and "Country of the Blind" (C14).

SECONDARY SOURCES AND REVIEWS:

1. *American Scholar* 26 (Spring, 1957): 250.
2. Amis, Kingsley. "The Legion of the Lost," in *Spectator* 196 (June 15, 1956): 830-831.
3. Arvin, Newton. "Our World, Not Theirs," in *New York Times Book Review* (Sept. 9, 1956): 6.
4. Ayer, A. J. *Encounter* 7 (Sept., 1956): 75.
5. Baker, Roger. *Times* (July 1, 1978): 7.
6. Bendau, p. 30-31.
7. Bergström, Chapter 1, Part 2.
8. *British Book News* no. 192 (Aug., 1956): 470.
9. Campion, Chap. 16.
10. Castillo, Arthur. *Chicago Review* 10 (Winter, 1957): 91-97.
11. "Chosen Few." *Times Literary Supplement* no. 2832 (June 8, 1956): 342. See also p. 393, 749, and 765 (a letter by Wilson).
12. Connell, John. "A Major Writer—And He's 24." *London Evening News* (May 26, 1956): 4.
13. Connolly, Cyril. "Loser Take All." *Sunday Times* (May 27, 1956): 5. See also: H26.
14. Cooper, William. *Nation* 183 (Aug. 25, 1956): 162.
15. *Current History* 31 (Nov., 1956): 310.
16. Gannett, Lewis. *New York Herald Tribune* (Sept. 4, 1956): .
17. Hartt, J. N. *Yale Review* n.s. 46 (Winter, 1957): 288-294.
18. Henderson, Archibald. "The Outsider—Integrity or Integration?" in *Southwest Review* 42 (Spring, 1957): 162-165.
19. Hogan, William. *San Francisco Chronicle* (Sept. 4, 1956): 21.
20. Hook, Sidney. "Sense & Salvation," in *Commentary* 22 (Nov., 1956): 479.
21. Krutch, Joseph Wood. *Saturday Review* 39 (Sept. 8, 1956): 37-38.
22. Lancour, Harold. *Library Journal* 81 (Sept. 15, 1956): 1999.
23. *The Listener* 55 (June 7, 1956): 767. Includes the famous quote: "*The Outsider* is the most remarkable book upon

which the reviewer has ever had to pass judgement." See also: H26.

24. Malcolm, Donald. *New Republic* 135 (Nov. 5, 1956): 18.
25. McDonald, Dwight. *New Yorker* 32 (Oct. 13, 1956): 187.
26. McLaughlin, Richard. *Springfield Republican* (Oct. 14, 1956): 10C.
27. *Modern Fiction Studies* 2 (Winter, 1956-1957): 245.
28. Muller, H. J. *New York Herald Tribune Book Review* (Sept. 2, 1956): 5.
29. Nieman, Gilbert. *New Mexico Quarterly* 29 (Spring, 1959): 119-121.
30. Peel, Robert. "Outsiders and Their Young Spokesman," in *Christian Science Monitor* (Sept. 6, 1956): 4.
31. Priestley, J. B. "Thoughts on the Outsider," in *New Statesman* 52 (July 7, 1956): 10-11. See also: H26.
32. Rolo, Charles J. *Atlantic* 198 (Oct., 1956): 96.
33. Scrutton, Mary. *New Statesman* 51 (June 16, 1956): 700.
34. *Time* 68 (July 2, 1956): 80.
35. Toynbee, Philip. "Unlucky Jims." *Observer* (May 27, 1956): . See also: H26.
36. *Twentieth Century* 160 (July, 1956): 82.
37. Wagenknecht, Edward. *Chicago Sunday Tribune* (Sept. 9, 1956): 3.
38. Warner, Rex. *London Magazine* 3 (no. 9, 1956): 54-56.
39. Weigel, p. 32-39.
40. Williams, Raymond. "The New Party Line?" in *Essays in Criticism* 7 (Jan., 1957): 68.

A2. **Religion and the Rebel.** The Outsider Cycle, Book 2. London: Victor Gollancz, 1957, 333 p., cloth. [philosophy]

b. Boston: Houghton Mifflin Co., 1957, x, 338 p., cloth.
c. as: *Suqut al-Hadarah.* Beyreuth: Dar Al-Ilm Lilmalayin, 1964, 399 p., cloth (?). Translated by Anis Zaki Salih. [Arabic]
d. Westport, CT: Greenwood Press, 1974, x, 338 p., cloth.
e. Bath: Ashgrove Press, 1984, xii, 352 p., paper.
f. Salem, NH: Salem House, 1984, xii, 352 p., paper.
g. as: *Shukyo To Hankonin.* Tokyo: Kinokuniya Shoten, n.d., 296 p., cloth (?). Translated by Yasuo Nakamura. [Japanese]
h. as: "An Autobiographical Introduction (*Religion and the Rebel*)," in *The Essential Colin Wilson.* London: Harrap, 1985, cloth, p. 35-61. A reprint of the introductory essay from this book, collected into a volume consisting largely of excerpts from Colin Wilson books.

An examination of the Outsider theme in religion. Dedication: "For Negley and Dan Farson." No introductory quotation. Includes bibliographical notes and a good index.

ANALYTICAL TABLE OF CONTENTS:
Autobiographical Introduction. The meaning of life seems to lie "...in achieving a certain state of mind called 'vision,' the moment of great insight in which the purpose of all life is seen. Ultimately, this is the only thing worth achieving." PART ONE. 1. The Anatomy of Imagination: The outsider's development; Shaw's *John Bull's Other Island*; The outsider and pain; Two visionaries: Rainer Maria Rilke and Arthur Rimbaud, F. Scott Fitzgerald; The need for a new religion in our time. 2. The Outsider and History: Oswald Spengler's *The Decline of the West*; Arnold Toynbee's *A Study of History*.
PART TWO: Introduction: The making of Christianity. The need for a sense of purpose; The essence of Christ's teaching: to become God-like; Human beings lack the application or desire to achieve this; St. Paul changes Christ's message from "redeem yourself" to "let me redeem you," a proposition more acceptable to the majority; Christian church is established; Christianity spreads; Religious outsiders and the Reformation; The scientific age; The outsider today stands midway between science and the church; Is the outsider strong enough to create his own religion? 1. Jacob Boehme: "the greatest Protestant mystic." 2. Nicholas Ferrar: "[he chose] one way out of the outsider's dilemma; he had set his own little corner of the world in order, and lived in that corner as if the rest of the world did not exist." 3. Blaise Pascal: "In all things he excelled...It is difficult, in our age of dilettantism and specialisation, to comprehend his greatness." 4. Emanuel Swedenborg: "A man of scientific genius who is known to posterity by his religious genius." 5. William Law: "One of the greatest and most powerful minds ever produced by the Church of England." 6. John Henry Newman: "If the twentieth century could produce even a few men of Newman's stature, the whole course of history might be changed." 7. Søren Kierkegaard: "A man of superb intellect, and great spiritual strength, but a lopsided, tragic figure." 8. Bernard Shaw: "[He] touched on the outsider problem at almost every point, and came closer to providing a complete solution than any other thinker." 9. Wittgenstein and Whitehead: "Wittgenstein failed because he could never resist the temptation of intellect. [Nevertheless,] he is one of the most important European thinkers since Descartes." "[Whitehead was] one of the broadest and most profound minds

19

since Plato." Conclusion: the outsider as a rebel against the established church. A call for completeness, in a balance of the intellectual, emotional, and physical centers of man.

COMMENTS: *Religion* suffered greatly from the publicity backlash surrounding the initial overreactions to *The Outsider.* Reading it today, however, it is difficult to see what all the fuss was about. In many ways this is a better book than its predecessor: more carefully planned, clearly argued, better structured, elements scarcely sufficient to attract such vitriolic criticism. Particularly interesting is the introductory chapter to Part Two, "The Making of Christianity," and the autobiographical introduction, which was later expanded to form *Voyage to a Beginning.* The 1984 editions are slightly revised, and include a new "Retrospective Introduction" on pages viii-xii.

SECONDARY SOURCES AND REVIEWS:

1. Aldridge, John W. *New York Times Book Review* (Nov. 17, 1957): 18.
2. Allsop, Kenneth. "Is This the Voice of Young Europe?" in *Daily Mail* (Oct. 19, 1957):   .
3. Ayer, A. J. *Spectator* 199 (Oct. 15, 1957): 550
4. Bendau, p. 31-32.
5. Bergström, Chapter 1, Part 2.
6. Campion, p. 161-169.
7. Cohen, Ralph. *Kenyon Review* 20 (issue 2): 488.
8. Cranston, Maurice. *London Magazine* 4 (no. 12, 1957): 58-62.
9. Henderson, Archibald, Jr. "Hagiography of Outsiders," in *Southwest Review* 43 (Winter, 1958): 82-84.
10. *Kirkus Reviews* 25 (Oct. 15, 1957): 786.
11. Kirsch, Robert. *Los Angeles Times* (Dec. 2, 1957):   .
12. Krutch, Joseph Wood. *Saturday Review of Literature* 40 (Dec. 14, 1957): 16.
13. Lunn, Sir Arnold. "The Infallibility of Colin Wilson," in *Month* (Nov., 1961): 278-286.
14. Mankowitz, Wolf. "Outsider Turned Inside-Out," in *News Chronicle* (Oct. 23, 1957):   . This article is typical of the responses of many critics, who extended their criticism to the so-called "Angry Young Men" in general. Mankowitz notes: "From now on the phrase 'Angry Young Men' will not be used on this page in any context whatsoever."
15. Miller, Perry. *New York Herald-Tribune* (Nov. 24, 1957): 10.

16. Mortimer, Raymond. "Not Angry Enough," in *Sunday Times* (Oct. 20, 1957): .

17. Murdoch, Iris. *Manchester Guardian* (Oct. 25, 1957): 6.

18. Nieman, Gilbert. *New Mexico Quarterly* 29 (Spring, 1959): 119-121.

19. Peel, Robert. *Christian Science Monitor* (Nov. 14, 1957): 7.

20. "The Price of Admission." *Times Literary Supplement* no. 2904 (Oct. 25, 1957): 640. See also page 657 for a letter by Colin Wilson.

21. Rolo, Charles. *Atlantic* 200 (Dec., 1957): 168.

22. Smith, J. A. *New Statesman* 54 (Oct. 26, 1957): 536.

23. *Time* 70 (Nov. 18, 1957): 122.

24. *Times* (Oct. 24, 1957): 13.

25. "The Tohu-Bohu Kid," in *Time* 70 (Nov. 18, 1957): 122-123.

26. Toynbee, Philip. "Unhappy Sequel," in *Observer* (Oct. 20, 1957): .

27. Wagenknecht, Edward. *Chicago Sunday Tribune* (Nov. 24, 1957): 13.

28. Weigel, p. 39-47.

A3. **The Age of Defeat**. The Outsider Cycle, Book Three. London: Victor Gollancz, 1959, 157 p., cloth. [philosophy]

b. as: *The Stature of Man*. Boston: Houghton Mifflin Co., 1959, 171 p., cloth.

c. as: *The Stature of Man*. Westport, CT: Greenwood Press, 1968, xiv, 171 p., cloth.

d. as: *Haiboku No Jidal*. Tokyo: Shincho-Sha, n.d., 205 p., cloth (?). Translated by Saiichi Tani. [Japanese]

A further development of Wilson's examination of the outsider. Dedication: "For Eve and Negley with affection." Introductory quotation taken from Strindberg's Legends. Not indexed.

ANALYTICAL TABLE OF CONTENTS:
Introduction: The vanishing hero. Part One: The evidence of sociology. Inner-direction and other-direction; Inner-direction and insanity; Other-directed religion; The American child; The pattern of violence; The psychology of violence; Conclusion. Part Two: The evidence of literature. The defeated hero; The English scene; Conclusion. Part Three: The anatomy of insignificance. What is a hero?; The old hero and the new; nothing to be done: the romantic dilemma; Some nineteenth-century heroes; The last stand of the romantic hero;

Literary faking; A European hero in the twentieth century. Part Four: The fallacy of insignificance. A philosophy of inner-direction; Existential psychology; What is to be done?; The contribution of Camus; Conclusion. Part Five: The stature of man. Three types of "commitment"; Towards a new existentialism; Existentialism and the hero; The absurd man; A god or a worm; Conclusion. Postscript.

COMMENTS: The American version contains no analytical table of contents, and also lacks the autobiographical section. Some of Wilson's comments on communism were deleted, and the introduction is abridged.

SECONDARY SOURCES AND REVIEWS:

1. Bendau, p. 32.
2. Bergström, Chapter 1, Part 2.
3. *British Book News* no. 231 (Nov., 1959): 733.
4. Fuller, Edmund. *Saturday Review* 42 (Dec. 19, 1959): 35.
5. Gardiner, Patrick. *London Magazine* 7 (no. 3): 75-78.
6. Henderson, A. *Southwest Review* 45 (Winter, 1960): 99-101.
7. Howe, Irving. "Where Are the Heroes?" in *New York Times Book Review* (Nov. 15, 1959): 6.
8. Jones, Jack. *Western Mail* (Sept. 10, 1959): .
9. Lunn, Sir Arnold. *Month* (Mar., 1960): 142-146.
10. "The Non-Conformist," in *Church Times* (Sept. 11, 1959): .
11. O'Donnell, D. *Spectator* 203 (Sept. 4, 1959): 307.
12. Peel, Robert. "A Time Without Heroes?" in *Christian Science Monitor* (Dec. 24, 1959): 7.
13. "A Pious Hope." *Times Literary Supplement* no. 3001 (Sept. 4, 1959): 503.
14. Raven, Simon. "Teach Yourself Heroism," in *Punch* 237 (Sept. 23, 1959): 218-219.
15. Ross, T. J. "Is There a Hero in the House?" in *New Republic* 142 (Feb. 1, 1960): 18-19.
16. *Times* (Sept. 3, 1959): 13.
17. Walsh, Chad. *Chicago Sunday Tribune* (Dec. 13, 1959): 2.
18. Weigel, p. 47-50.

A4. **Ritual in the Dark.** London: Victor Gollancz, 1960, 416 p., cloth. [novel]

b. Boston: Houghton Mifflin, 1960, 442 p., cloth.
c. New York: Popular Library, 1961, 383 p., paper.

d. London: Pan Books, 1962, 415 p., paper.
e. as: *Le Sacré de la Nuit*. Paris: Gallimard, 1962, 468 p., cloth, novel. Translated by Odile de Lalain. [French]
f. as: *Ritueel in het Donker*. Amsterdam: Contact, 1972, 473 p., cloth (?). Translated by Jean A. Schalekamp. [Dutch]
g. Bath: Cedric Chivers, 1974, 416 p., cloth.
h. as: *Ritual en la Oscuridad*. Barcelona: Luis de Caralt, 1976, 401 p., cloth. Translated by Francisco Elias. [Spanish]
i. London, New York: Granada, Panther Books, 1976, 416 p., paper.
j. Chicago: Academy Chicago, 1982, 416 p., paper.
k. as: *Ritual i Morke*. København: Fremad, n.d., 2 v., cloth (?). Translated by Elisabeth and Knud Rasmussen. [Danish]
l. as: *Der Schacht zu Babel*. Stuttgart: Scherz, n.d., 511 p., cloth (?). Translated by Hans Flesch-Brunningen. [German]
m. as: *Riti Notturni*. Milano: E. M. Lerici, n.d., 559 p., cloth (?). Translated by Aldo Rostagno and Diamante Medici. [Italian]
n. as: *Ankoku No Matsuri*. Tokyo: Shincho-Sha, n.d., 419 p., cloth (?). Translated by Yasuo Nakamura. [Japanese]
o. as: *Ritual i Morket*. Oslo: Cappelen, n.d., 469 p., cloth (?). Translated by Per Wollebaek. [Norse]

Dedication: "For Bill Hopkins." No introductory quotation. The first novel of the Gerard Sorme trilogy.

COMMENTS: Wilson's first novel was penned initially in 1949, but rewritten extensively prior to publication (see Campion's study for further details). For Wilson's own comments on the writing of the novel, see pages 232-236 of *Craft of the Novel*. Many critics regard this as the author's best work of fiction. All of Wilson's interests are reflected here, and shaken and stirred about to generate just the right blend of action and ideas. Subsequent novels, while perhaps more disciplined, can still be seen merely as a filtering-off or expansion of one or more of the themes first examined in *Ritual*. More detailed assessments can be found listed below.

SECONDARY SOURCES AND REVIEWS:

1. Adams, Phoebe. *Atlantic Monthly* 205 (Mar., 1960): 114.
2. Allen, Walter. *New York Times Book Review* (Mar. 6, 1960): 4.
3. Allsop, Kenneth. "2 Cheers for Mr. Wilson," in *Daily Mail* (Feb. 29, 1960): .
4. Baro, Gene. *New York Herald Tribune* (Mar. 6, 1960): 5.
5. Bendau, p. 32-34.

6. Bergström, p. 59-67.
7. *British Book News* no. 237 (May, 1960): 372.
8. Bryden, Ronald. *Spectator* 204 (Mar. 4, 1960): 329.
9. Campion, Chapter 18, plus other references.
10. Carr, John Dickson. *Kenyon Review* 22 (no. 3, 1960): 509.
11. Dempsey, David. *Saturday Review of Literature* 43 (Mar. 12, 1960): 20.
12. Dillard, p. 4-7.
13. "Dionysiac Delights." *Times Literary Supplement* no. 3027 (Mar. 4, 1960): 141. "Mr. Wilson, writing a novel for the first and, conceivably, for the last time..."
14. Georgi, Charlotte. *Library Journal* 85 (1960): 1619.
15. Gilman, Richard. *Commonweal* 72 (Apr. 1, 1960): 20.
16. Gorn, L. H. *San Francisco Chronicle* (Mar. 13, 1960): 20.
17. Hughes, Riley. *Catholic World* 191 (May, 1960): 120.
18. Kermode, Frank. *Encounter* (June, 1960): 81.
19. *Kirkus Reviews* 28 (Jan. 15, 1960): 58.
20. Lehmann, J. *Chicago Review* 14 (Summer, 1960): 123-126.
21. Lister, Richard. *Birmingham Evening Chronicle* (Mar. 2, 1960): .
22. Miller, Karl. *The Observer* (Feb. 28, 1960): .
23. Price, R. C. G. "Rank Outsider," in *Punch* 238 (Mar. 16, 1960): 398.
24. Quinton, Anthony. *London Magazine* 7 (no. 5, 1960): 78-81.
25. Shrapnel, Norman. *Manchester Guardian* (Mar. 4, 1960): 8.
26. *Time Magazine* 75 (Mar. 7, 1960): 102.
27. *Times* (Mar. 3, 1960): 15.
28. *Times Literary Supplement* (Mar. 4, 1960): 141.
29. Towney, Tom. *John O'London's* 2 (Mar. 3, 1960): .
30. Tredell, Chapter 4.
31. *Twentieth Century* 167 (June, 1960): 575.
32. Walsh, Chad. *Chicago Sunday Tribune* (Apr. 10, 1960): 12.
33. Weigel, p. 66-71.
34. West, Anthony. *New Yorker* 36 (Aug. 20, 1960): 105.
35. West, Paul. New Statesman 59 (March 5, 1960): 342.
36. Young, Kenneth. *Daily Telegraph* (Mar. 4, 1960): .

A5. **Adrift in Soho: A Novel.** London: Victor Gollancz, 1961, 224 p., cloth. [novel]

  b. Boston: Houghton Mifflin Co., 1961, 229 p., cloth.

c. as: *Bohemiens in Soho.* Amsterdam: Contact, 1962, 224 p., cloth (?). Translated by Jean A. Schalekamp. Reprinted in 1970. [Dutch]
c. London: Pan Books, 1964, 172 p., paper.
d. as: *Soho à la Dérive.* Paris: Gallimard, 1964, 236 p., cloth. Translated by Odile de Lalain. [French]
e. as: *A la Deriva en el Soho.* Barcelona: Luis de Caralt, 1964, 279 p., cloth (?). Translated by Rafael Nadal Guasp. Reprinted in 1976. [Spanish]

The dedication reads: "For James." No introductory quotation.

COMMENTS: A semi-autobiographical novel written in conjunction with another writer's manuscript (see Campion, p. 234), incorporating several scenes from Wilson's early play, *The Metal Flower Blossom.* As in *Ritual in the Dark,* the plot revolves around the hero (in this case, Harry Preston, a young man new to London). Wilson's characters are beautifully delineated; one in particular, Ricky Prelati, an artist, achieves overnight fame in a manner parallelling Wilson's own rise to literary stardom following publication of *The Outsider.* Intended as an English "beat" novel, the book lags somewhat at the end (Wilson has admitted, on page 236 of *The Craft of the Novel,* that he was at a loss for a proper conclusion). Out-of-print since the mid-1960s, *Adrift* is now one of the most difficult of Wilson's books to find, bringing high prices on the secondhand market.

SECONDARY SOURCES AND REVIEWS:

1. Adams, Phoebe. *Atlantic* 208 (Nov., 1961): 185.
2. Bendau, p. 34-35.
3. Bergström, p. 67-68.
4. *Booklist* 58 (Nov. 15, 1961): 193.
5. *Bookmark* 21 (Nov., 1961): 39.
6. Bowen, Robert O. *National Review* 13 (Dec. 2, 1961): 384.
7. Bradbury, Malcolm. *Punch* 241 (Sept. 27, 1961): 479-480.
8. Bryden, Ronald. *Spectator* 207 (Sept. 8, 1961): 329.
9. Campion, p. 232-235.
10. "Cool Introduction to London's Bohemia," in *Washington Star* (Oct. 15, 1961): .
11. Daniels, Sally. *Minnesota Review* 2 (Summer, 1962): 546-557.
12. Dillard, p. 7-8.
13. Fuller, John. *The Listener* 76 (Sept. 7, 1961): 361.

14. Hogan, William. *San Francisco Chronicle* (Nov. 2, 1961): 35.
15. *Kirkus Reviews* 29 (Sept. 1, 1961): 807.
16. Kirsch, Robert. "Soho Downs Venice West," in *Los Angeles Times* (Nov. 20, 1961): .
17. Levin, Martin. *New York Times Book Review* (Oct. 15, 1961): 48.
18. *Manchester Guardian* (Sept. 15, 1961): 7.
19. Mayne, Richard. *New Statesman* 62 (Sept. 8, 1961): 315.
20. Moon, Eric. *Library Journal* 86 (1961): 3494.
21. Newman, David. "Beats Don't Change," in *New York Herald Tribune Books* (Oct. 22, 1961): 10.
22. "Outward Bound." *Times Literary Supplement* no. 3106 (Sept. 8, 1961): 593.
23. Shaw, Fred. "Let's Keep Trying to Communicate," in *Miami News* (Oct. 22, 1961): .
24. *Time* 78 (Oct. 13, 1961): 102.
25. *Times* (Sept. 7, 1961): 15.
26. Tredell, Chapter 5.
27. Walsh, Chad. "The Dickens Who Would Be Another Dostoyevsky," in *Chicago Sunday Tribune* (Oct. 29, 1961): 6.
28. Weigel, p. 71-74.

A6. **Encyclopaedia of Murder**, written and compiled by Pat Pitman and Colin Wilson. London: Arthur Barker, 1961, 576 p., cloth. [criminology]

b. as: *Encyclopedia of Murder.* New York: G. P. Putnam's Sons, 1962, 576 p., cloth.
c. London: Pan Books, 1964, 671 p., paper.
cb. London: Pan Books, 1984, 671 p., paper.
d. as: *Enciclopedia del Delitto.* Milano: E. M. Lerici, 1964, 2 v., cloth. Translated by Ettore Capriolo. [Italian]
e. as: *Satsujin Hyakka.* Tokyo: Yayoi Shobo, n.d., 230 p., cloth (?). Translated by Oba Tadao. [Japanese]
f. as: *Enciclopedia del Crimen.* Barcelona: Luis de Caralt, n.d., p., cloth (?). [Spanish]

Dedicated "To Frank Lynder." No introductory quotation. Includes a select bibliography, classified index, and general index.

COMMENTS: A fascinating book to dip into. Pitman and Wilson cover criminals both famous and obscure, including Christie, Jack the Ripper, Kurten, and Sylvestre Matushka, who could, apparently, only achieve sexual satisfaction by watching train crashes he himself had arranged. The book is arranged alphabetically, with an introductory essay by Wilson titled, "The Study of Murder," and an interesting fragment from a discarded section of *The Outsider* called "The Faust Outsider." Contains several black-and-white illustrations. The appendix by C. H. Norman discusses capital punishment. See also its sequel, *Encyclopedia of Modern Murder* (A66).

SECONDARY SOURCES AND REVIEWS:

1. Aynsley, Cyril. "The Mentality of Murder," in *Daily Express* (Nov. 17, 1961):   .
2. Bendau, p. 35.
3. *Bookmark* 21 (June, 1962): 260.
4. Cuff, Sergeant. *Saturday Review of Literature* 45 (Mar. 31, 1962): 22.
5. Gitomer, Irene. *Library Journal* 87 (1962): 88.
6. Holloway, David. "Motives for Murder," in *Daily Telegraph* (Nov. 17, 1961):   .
7. Howard, Esther. *Spectator* 207 (Dec. 22, 1961): 934.
8. *Kirkus Reviews* 29 (Nov. 1, 1961): 996.
9. Offord, Lenore Glen. *San Francisco Chronicle* (Mar. 3, 1962): 30.
10. Richardson, Maurice. "Good Murders," in *New Statesman* 62 (Dec. 1, 1961): 839.
11. Symons, Julian. "Murder," in *Financial Times* (Nov. 28, 1961): .
12. *Sunday Times* (Nov. 19, 1961):   .
13. *Times* (Dec. 14, 1961): 16.
14. *Times Literary Supplement* no. 3116 (Nov. 17, 1961): 830.
15. Weigel, p. 114-115.

A7. **The Strength to Dream: Literature and the Imagination.** The Outsider Cycle, Book 4. London: Victor Gollancz, 1962, 224 p., cloth. [philosophy]

b. Boston: Houghton Mifflin Co., 1962, 277 p., cloth.
c. as: *El Poder de Soñar*. Barcelona: Luis de Caralt, 1965, 302 p., cloth. [Spanish}
d. Westport, CT: Greenwood Press, 1973, xxiv, 277 p., cloth
e. London: Abacus/Sphere, 1976, 254 p., paper.
f. as: *Munhaggwa Sangsangiyeog*. Seoul: Beomusa, 1978, 420 p., cloth (?). Translated by Lee Geong Gyu. [Korean]
g. as: *Yumeniru Chikara*. Tokyo: Takeuchi Shoten, n.d., 326 p., cloth (?). Translated by Yasuo Nakamura. [Japanese]

Dedication: "To Dan and Jeanette Danziger with affection."
No introductory quotation. Includes a comprehensive index.

ANALYTICAL TABLE OF CONTENTS:
Acknowledgements. Preface. Introduction: The crisis in modern literature. Chapter One: The assault on rationality. H. P. Lovecraft; W. B. Yeats; Oscar Wilde; August Strindberg; Conclusion. Chapter Two: The implications of realism. Émile Zola; Nathanael West; William Faulkner; Acceptance and rejection; Evelyn Waugh and Graham Greene; Jean-Paul Sartre; The anti-novel; Alain Robbe-Grillet; Nathalie Sarraute. Chapter Three: The implications of total pessimism. Leonid Andreyev; Samuel Beckett; Conclusion. Chapter Four: The vision of science. H. G. Wells; The development of science; Utopias and anti-utopias; Wells again; Zamiatin; Science fiction and space opera; Lovecraft again; Bell's *Before the Dawn*; Popular science fiction; Conclusion. Chapter Five: The power of darkness. E. T. A. Hoffmann; Gogol; Ghosts and the supernatural; Sheridan Le Fanu and M. R. James; J. R. R. Tolkien; The gothic novel; De Sade's *120 Days*; Conclusion. Chapter Six: Sex and the imagination.   Maupassant; Wedekind; Artzybasheff; D. H. Lawrence; Conclusion. Chapter Seven: The need for polarities. "Illusion" and "reality"; Summary; The need for an existential criticism. Appendices: Existential criticism and the work of Aldous Huxley; Nikos Kazantzakis; Friedrich Dürrenmatt: heir of the existential tradition.

COMMENTS: Wilson's fourth examination of the Outsider motif has slowly become accepted as a classic in its field, which has resulted in several later printings in both the U.S. and Britain during the mid-1970s.

SECONDARY SOURCES AND REVIEWS:

1. Bendau, p. 35-36.
2. Bergström, Chapter 1, Part 2.
3. Campion, p. 235-236.
4. Carruth, Hayden. "An Important, Perhaps Liberating, Book on Books," in *Chicago Daily News* (Oct. 31, 1962): .
5. De Mott, Benjamin. *Harper's Magazine* 225 (Oct., 1962): 90.
6. Derleth, August. "Imagination in Writers," in *Capitol Times* (Oct. 25, 1962):   .
7. *Encounter* 19 (Aug., 1962): 80.

8. Gold, Arthur R. "Craving a Re-Made World," in *New York Herald-Tribune* (Apr. 11, 1962): .
9. Hope, F. *Spectator* 208 (Apr. 27, 1962): 558.
10. Hornish, Rudi A. *Bestsellers* (Dec. 1, 1962): .
11. Kirsch, Robert R. "Education of a Quiz-Kid," in *Los Angeles Times* (Jan. 29, 1963): .
12. *Library Journal* 87 (1962): 3048.
13. *Modern Fiction Studies* 9 (Summer, 1963): 193.
14. Moore, Harry T. "Assessments of Reputations," in *New York Times Book Review* (Oct. 28, 1962): 28.
15. Nye, Robert. *Western Mail* (Apr. 14, 1962): .
16. Quinton, Anthony. *Sunday Telegraph* (Apr. 15, 1962): .
17. Russell, Peter. *Aylesford Review* 5 (no. 1): 31-36. "An important attempt to relate the purpose of literature to the purpose of life."
18. "Simple Pleasures?" *Times Literary Supplement* no. 3137 (Apr. 13, 1962): 250.
19. Swanson, Roy Arthur. *Minnesota Review* 3 (Summer, 1963): 499.
20. *Times* (Apr. 12, 1962): 18.
21. Weigel, p. 51-55.
22. Young, B. A. "The Uses of Imagination," in *Punch* 242 (Apr. 25, 1962): 661.

A8. **The Sex Diary of Gerard Sorme.** New York: Dial Press, 1963, p., cloth. [novel]

b. as: *Man Without a Shadow: The Diary of an Existentialist.* London: Arthur Barker, 1963, 266 p., cloth.
c. New York: A Cardinal Giant, Pocket Books, 1964, 212 p., paper.
d. as: *L'Homme Qui N'Avait pas D'Ombre.* Paris: Julliard, 1964, 297 p., cloth (?). Translated by Pierre Kyria. [French]
e. as: *Man Without a Shadow: The Diary of an Existentialist.* London: Pan Books, 1966, 253 p., paper.
eb. London: Pan Books, 1968, 255 p., paper.
f. as: *Man Zonder Schaduw.* Amsterdam: Contact, 1972, 271 p., cloth (?). Translated by Jean A. Schalekamp. [Dutch]
g. as: *Geurimja Eom-Neun Yogmang.* Seoul: Yeoweon Munhwasa, 1979, 269 p., cloth (?). Translated by Seon Gyeol Kim. [Korean]
h. St. Albans: Panther Books, 1980, 251 p., paper.
i. as: *Il Diario Sessuale di Gerard Sorme.* Milano: E. M. Lerici, n.d., 346 p., cloth (?). Translated by Nuccia Agazzi. [Italian]

j.   as: *Garard Sorme Shi Na Sem No Nikki.* Tokyo: Futami Shobo, n.d., 367 p., cloth (?). Translated by Isomura Jun. [Japanese]

k.   as: *The Sex Diary of a Metaphysician.* Berkeley, CA: Ronin Pub., 1989,   p., paper.

Dedication: "With love for Joy and Sally." No introductory quotation.

COMMENTS: This second book in the Gerard Sorme series, following *Ritual in the Dark,* takes up where the earlier book leaves off, and ties up many of its loose ends. It can, however, be read and enjoyed as a completely separate work. Apart from many other interesting characters, Sorme meets one Caradoc Cunningham (a loosely fictionalized Aleister Crowley), who introduces him to "sex magic." Wilson comments (in *The Craft of the Novel,* p. 235-236): "Ideas tended to shape themselves into characters and events; [thus] *Origins of the Sexual Impulse* was followed by the novel, *Man Without a Shadow.*" The novel includes a preface in which Wilson expresses his opinions on the evolution of fiction.

SECONDARY SOURCES AND REVIEWS:

1.   Adams, Phoebe. *Atlantic* 212 (Sept., 1963): 126.
2.   Bendau, p. 38.
3.   Bergonzi, Bernard. *New Statesman* 66 (Nov. 1, 1963): 623.
4.   Bergström, p. 107-112.
5.   Dillard, p. 9-10.
6.   Hayes, Mary Anne. "Colin Wilson Peeks Inside the Outsiders," in *Houston Post* (May 19, 1963):   .
7.   Kauffman, Stanley. "Sorme Likes It Hot," in *New Republic* 148 (May 4, 1963): 32-33.
8.   Maurer, Robert. "More Shooting Stars from Wilson," in *New York Herald Tribune Books* (June 23, 1963): 10.
9.   Moon, Eric. *Library Journal* 88 (1963): 1905.
10. *New Yorker* 39 (May 19, 1963): 177.
11. *Newsweek* 61 (June 3, 1963): 87.
12. Nicholas, Anthony. *Tribune* (Jan. 24, 1964):   .
13. Price, R. C. G. *Punch* 245 (Nov. 6, 1963): 688.
14. "Prodigals at Large." *Times Literary Supplement* no. 3218 (Nov. 1, 1963): 881.
15. *Time* 81 (May 31, 1963): 87
16. Tredell, Chapter 5.
17. Weigel, p. 79-82.

A9. **Origins of the Sexual Impulse.** The Outsider Cycle, Book 5. London: Arthur Barker, 1963, 263 p., cloth. [psychology]

b. New York: G. P. Putnam's Sons, 1963, 263 p., cloth.
c. as: *Los Origenes del Impulso Sexual.* Barcelona: Luis de Caralt, 1964, 300 p., cloth (?). Translated by Francisco Elias. [Spanish]
d. London: Panther Books, 1966, 282 p., paper.
e. as: *Origine degli Impulsi Sessuali.* Milano: E. M. Lerici, n.d., 314 p., cloth (?). Translated by Leda Mussio Sartini. [Italian]

Dedication: "To Professor G. Wilson Knight." Introductory quotation taken from Nietzsche's *The Will to Power*, with a short quote from Hegel. Includes a comprehensive index and a bibliography, divided into three sections: Phenomenology; Sexual perversion and crime; Psychology.

ANALYTICAL TABLE OF CONTENTS:
Introductory note: Definition of aims. Chapter One: General discussion of sexual aberration. Central problem of the book; What part does sex play in man's total being?; Tolstoy and Gide; Freud and Gurdjieff; Aldous Huxley and sex; Noyes and the "karezza"; D. H. Lawrence and sodomy. Chapter Two: Promiscuity and the Casanova impulse. Gurdjieff's psychology of sex; Mann and "Faustus"; Casanova; Frank Harris; Henry Miller; The case of "M"; Artzybasheff; Female Sexuality. Chapter Three: The method of analysis. The Phenomenological method; Husserl and gestalt psychology. Chapter Four: The meaning of "perversion" (I). The sexual criminal; The Black Dahlia murder; Imitative murder; Sexual under-privilege; Sexual fulfilment and the problem of "vision"; William Blake; Introverted sexuality; Eliot and W. J. Turner; T. E. Hulme; De Sade; Kierkegaard. Chapter Five: The meaning of "perversion" (II). De Sade and boredom; Problem of frustration; Fetishism; Examples of fetishism and sex crime in literature; Musil's *Man Without Qualities*; Heirens; The case of Rodney Shires. Chapter Six: The meaning of "perversion" (III). A shepherd's case of self mutilation; Sex murder; The Christie case; Heath; Necrophilia; The case of "D.W."; Sergeant Bertrand; Homosexuality. Chapter Seven: Sadism and the criminal mentality. Existentialism and its categories; Inauthentic existence, bad faith, etc.; The Pieydagnelle case; John Cowper Powys and sadism; The Kurten case; Freud's death wish and theory of aggression; The sexual impulse in animals; Gestalt theory; Bestiality; The existential alternative to Freud; The prevention of sex crime.

Chapter Eight: Existential psychology. History of psychology; Freud, Jung, Rank; History of existential psychology; Medard Boss's case of compulsive patient; Fellini's *La Dolce Vita*; Dostoyevsky and Briussov; Summary. Chapter Nine: The theory of symbolic response. Recapitulation and conclusion. Appendix: The criminal mentality. Shaw on crime; Metaphysics of murder.

SECONDARY SOURCES AND REVIEWS:

1. Bendau, p. 37-38.
2. Bergström, Chapter 1, Part 2.
3. Connell, John. *Books of the Month* (May, 1963): 3-4.
4. *Kirkus Reviews* 31 (Apr. 15, 1963): .
5. Levine, George. "Naive Study of Sex," in *Louisville Courier-Journal* (Aug. 25, 1963): .
6. Maurer, Robert. "More Shooting Stars from Colin Wilson," in *New York Herald Tribune Books* (June 23, 1963): 10.
7. Moon, Eric. *Library Journal* 88 (May 1, 1963): 1892.
8. Richardson, Maurice. *New Statesman* 65 (May 24, 1963): 798.
9. Schaffer, Leslie. "Sex Is Not a Simple Appetite," in *Washington Post and Times Herald* (June 16, 1963): .
10. Sorensen, Robert. *Minneapolis Tribune* (July 7, 1963): .
11. *Times* (May 23, 1963): 15.
12. Weigel, p. 55-57.

A10. **The World of Violence.** London: Victor Gollancz, 1963, 272 p., cloth. [novel]

b.   as: *The Violent World of Hugh Greene.* Boston: Houghton Mifflin Co., 1963, 272 p., cloth.
c.   London: Pan Books, 1965, 301 p., paper.
d.   as: *Un Mundo de Violencia.* Barcelona: Luis de Caralt, 1970, 369 p., cloth (?). Tranlated by Ramón Coll. [Spanish]
e.   as: "Uncle Sam (*The World of Violence*)," in *The Essential Colin Wilson.* London: Harrap, 1985, cloth, p. 213-219. A reprint of a section from this volume, collected into a volume consisting largely of excerpts from Colin Wilson books.

Dedication: "For Jean and Harry and the boys in the back room at the Wolfe." No introductory quotation.

COMMENTS: Wilson's third novel has always suffered a bit from its clumsy title, which, to the uninitiated, could easily be considered as a work of nonfiction. The book is divided into two parts: One—The Outer Dark; and Two—The Inner Dark, each of which reads almost as an independent novella. The first section concerns the early life of Hugh Greene. Greene's uncles, Nick and Sam, are both not at home in this world, and they provide the young Hugh with a developing sense of perspective. A young recluse, Jeremy Wolfe, furthers his development. In Part Two the mood changes, as Hugh becomes deeply involved in a world of violence. An absorbing novel which is, according to Tredell, "an important contribution to the literature of childhood." An extract from the book was included in G. G. Urwin's anthology (see B10).

SECONDARY SOURCES AND REVIEWS:

1. Bendau, p. 36-37.
2. Bergström, p. 68-69.
3. Blevins, Winifred. "Light and Darkness," in *St. Louis Post-Dispatch* (Nov. 3, 1963): .
4. Campion, p. 237-238.
5. Colimore, V. J. *Best Sellers* 23 (Oct. 15, 1963): 260.
6. Deane, Peter. *Book Week* (Oct. 13, 1963): 16.
7. Dillard, p. 8-9.
8. Duchene, Anne. *Guardian* (June 21, 1963): .
9. "Growing and Ingrowing Pains." *Times Literary Supplement* no. 3198 (June 14, 1963): 417.
10. Jones, D. A. N. *New Statesman* 65 (June 14, 1963): 910.
11. Moon, Eric. *Library Journal* 88 (Oct. 15, 1963): 3863.
12. *New Yorker* 39 (Dec. 7, 1963): 244.
13. Pickrel, Paul. *Harper's Magazine* 227 (Nov., 1963): 128.
14. Pryce-Jones, Alan. *New York Herald-Tribune* (Nov. 2, 1963): .
15. Pryce-Jones, Alan. "Not So Violent Story," in *San Francisco Examiner* (Oct. 28, 1963): .
16. Ritalin, Thane. "In the Dark Recesses of the Human Mind," in Chicago News (Oct. 12, 1963): .
17. *Times* (June 13, 1963): 15.
18. *Times Literary Supplement* (June 14, 1963): 417.
19. Tredell, Chapter 5.
20. Wakefield, Dan. *New York Times Book Review* (Oct. 13, 1963): 47.
21. Weigel, p. 74-79.

A11. **Brandy of the Damned: Discoveries of a Musical Eclectic.** London: John Baker, 1964, 182 p., cloth. [music]

For reprints, see the expanded version, *Chords and Discords* (published in England as *Colin Wilson on Music*), item A16 in this bibliography. Dedication: "For Mark Bredin, who taught me the little I know about music, but who should not be blamed for that." No introductory quotation. No bibliography or index.

ANALYTICAL TABLE OF CONTENTS:
Introduction: Purely personal: on being a musical eclectic. Chapter One: The romantic half-century. Liszt; Wagner; Brahms; Hanslick; Bruckner; Mahler. Chapter Two: Mozart and Beethoven: a retrospect. Chapter Three: Modern music—the problem. Schoenberg; Webern; Hindemith; Stravinsky. Chapter Four: The tragedy of Bartók. Chapter Five: Two mystics: Scriabin and Bloch. Chapter Six: The nature and spirit of jazz. Chapter Seven: Delius. Chapter Eight: Some English music. Sullivan; Elgar; Holst; Butterworth; Warlock; Vaughan Williams; Bax; Ireland; Bliss; Walton; Britten; Tippett; Searle. Chapter Nine: Some notes on opera. Orff; Strauss; Modern Italian opera; Menotti; Poulenc; Janacek; Prokofiev; Modern Russian opera.

COMMENTS: An informative and readable book: Wilson's enthusiasm for the subject is readily apparent.

SECONDARY SOURCES AND REVIEWS:

1. Bendau, p. 39-40.
2. *British Book News* no. 293 (Jan., 1965): 50.
3. "The Eclectic Listener." *Times Literary Supplement* no. 3275 (Dec. 3, 1964): 1100.
4. Noble, Jeremy. *New Statesman* 68 (Dec. 11, 1964): 930.
5. Porteus, H. G. *Observer* (Nov. 14, 1965): 28.
6. Taubman, R. *New Statesman* 70 (Dec. 3, 1965): 896.
7. *Times Literary Supplement* (Dec. 3, 1964): 1100.
8. Weigel, p. 112-114.
9. Williamson, Malcolm. *Sunday Times* (Nov. 15, 1964): .

A12. **Necessary Doubt.** London: Arthur Barker, 1964, 287 p., cloth. [novel]

b. New York: Trident Press, 1964, 306 p., cloth.
c. London: Panther Books, 1966, 251 p., paper.
d. New York: Pocket Books, 1966, 239 p., paper.

e. London: Village Press, 1974, 239 p., paper.
f. as: *De Schuldvraag*. Amsterdam: Contact, n.d., 278 p., cloth (?). Translated by Johan Van der Woude. [Dutch]
g. as: *Duda Necesaria*. Barcelona: Luis de Caralt, n.d., 249 p., cloth (?). Translated by Ramón Margaief Llambrich. [Spanish]

Dedication: "To Dan and Jeanette Danziger with affection." Introductory quotation from Rilke's *Notebooks of Malte Laurids Brigge*.

COMMENTS: An intriguing and unconventional detective novel in which the hero, Professor Karl Zweig, pursues an ex-pupil, Gustav Neumann, through the English countryside, believing the latter to be a dangerous criminal. As in *Ritual in the Dark* and *The Glass Cage*, the novel reaches a climax when the protagonists finally meet. They are talking as the police close in.

SECONDARY SOURCES AND REVIEWS:

1. Bendau, p. 38-39.
2. Bergström, p. 70-71.
3. *Best Sellers* 24 (Aug. 1, 1964): 171.
4. Dillard, p. 10.
5. Fleischer, L. *Publishers Weekly* 189 (Jan. 17, 1966): 134.
6. Fuller, John. *New Statesman* 67 (Mar. 20, 1964): 460.
7. Gaines, E. J. *Library Journal* 89 (Sept. 1, 1964): 3188.
8. Goran, Lester. *Chicago Sunday Tribune Books Today* (Aug. 30, 1964): 6.
9. Hogan, William. "Colin Wilson Getting Back on the Track," in *San Francisco Chronicle* (Aug. 24, 1964):   .
10. Hoight, Charles Alva. "Wilson Excellent," in *Courier-Journal* (Sept. 13, 1964):   .
11. Kirsch, Robert R. *Los Angeles Times Calendar Section* (Sept. 20, 1964):   .
12. M., M. *Christian Science Monitor* (Sept. 24, 1964): 7.
13. *Observer* (Apr. 24, 1966): 22.
14. Sherman, John K. "Tale Has More Than Suspense," in *Minneapolis Tribune* (Sept. 6, 1964):   .
15. "A Sphinx at the Yard." *Times Literary Supplement* no. 3235 (Feb. 27, 1964): 161.
16. Tredell, Chapter 6.
17. Ware, Cade. *Book Week* (Aug. 9, 1964): 14.
18. Weigel, p. 83-86.

19. Wright, Giles E. "Philosophy Gives Mystery a Dash of Spice," in *Los Angeles Herald-Examiner* (Aug. 9, 1964): .

A13.   Rasputin and the Fall of the Romanovs.   London: Arthur Barker, 1964, ix, 240 p., cloth. [biography]

b.   New York: Farrar, Straus & Co., 1964, 240 p., cloth.
c.   London: Panther Books, 1966, 251 p., paper.
cb.   London, New York: Granada, Panther Books, 1977, 251 p., paper.
d.   as: *Rasputin y el Ocaso de los Romanof.* Barcelona: Luis de Caralt, 1967, 274 p., cloth. [Spanish]
e.   Secaucus, NJ: Citadel Press, 1967, 240 p., paper. Also reprinted in 1971.
f.   as: *Rasputin.* Tokyo: Yomiuri Shinbunsha, n.d., 310 p., cloth (?). Translated by Uchyama Tsutomu. [Japanese]

Dedication: "To C. J. P. Ionides, with whom Rasputin would have agreed that snakes are on the whole preferable to human beings." No introductory quotation. The book includes a list of leading characters, bibliography, and index.

ANALYTICAL TABLE OF CONTENTS:
Introduction: The meaning of religion to Rasputin. Short survey of other biographies. Chapter One: The possibilitarian. Early life; Second-sight; First visit to a monastery; Dissatisfaction with village life; Death of baby son; Pilgrimage—10,000 miles in two years; History of heretical sects. Chapter Two: The wanderer. His travels around Russia collecting followers; First visit to St. Petersburg; Rasputin's will to power; Personal power. Chapter Three: History as nightmare. The history of the Romanovs. Chapter Four: God help Russia. St. Petersburg: full of artistry and vice; Tsar Nicholas: no sense of reality; Tsarina Alexandra's interest in religion and mysticism; Uprisings and brutal reprisals. Chapter Five: City of dreams. Rasputin meets the Tsar for the first time in 1905; Becomes famous as a healer; Hypnotism; Husserl's phenomenology; Rasputin's positive outlook on life; His vitality recharges the Tsar and Tsarina; Gurdjieff, a contemporary of Rasputin; Rasputin's hypnotic and thaumaturgic powers. Chapter Six: The rise to power. Rasputin cures the Tsarevich; Becomes the Tsarina's spiritual advisor. Chapter Seven: The enemies multiply. Rasputin's sexual appetite used as a scandal by his enemies; Attacked by the press; Makes a pilgrimage to the Holy Land in 1911; Enemies influence the Tsar: Rasputin banished;

The Tsarevich becomes ill again and Rasputin is recalled. Chapter Eight: The storm gathers. Bolsheviks, liberals, and conservatives unite against Rasputin for various reasons; Rasputin's health deteriorates due to drunkenness and promiscuity; Strikes in Russia in 1912-13; World War I, 1914; The first attempt to assassinate the priest fails. Chapter Nine: The rain of fire. Russia in retreat, 1915; Rasputin universally hated, except by the Tsarina, who relies on him; Another assassination attempt. Chapter Ten: Rasputin as Tsar. Hvostov plans a coup; He and Yussupov plot Rasputin's assassination. Chapter Eleven: The end. Discontent widespread over Russia; Rasputin assassinated; Revolution gathers momentum; Royal family arrested and murdered. Chapter Twelve: The legend and the problem. Rasputin as an outsider. Appendix: Thaumaturgy and Pre-Vision.

COMMENTS: A book generally regarded as "pro-Rasputin," although the man's faults are there for all to see. What Wilson seems to be saying is that Rasputin was a man who possessed remarkable powers, and that he was almost certainly not the complete villain subsequent historians have made of him.

SECONDARY SOURCES AND REVIEWS:

1. Bendau, p. 39.
2. *Choice* 1 (1964): 448.
3. Dennis, Nigel. *Sunday Telegraph* (Aug. 9, 1964):   .
4. Ivsky, Oleg. *Library Journal* 89 (Oct. 15, 1964): 3952.
5. Malia, Martin. "The Holy Devil," in *New York Review of Books* 3 (Dec. 31, 1964): 20-21.
6. Mitchell, Adrian. *The New Statesman* 68 (Aug. 14, 1964): 222.
7. Payne, Robert. *New York Times Book Review* (Dec. 13, 1964): 20.
8. Peel, Robert. "Rasputin As an Outsider," in *Christian Science Monitor* (Dec. 17, 1964): 9.
9. Raymond, John. *Sunday Times* (Aug. 9, 1964):   .
10. "Russian Eminence." *Times Literary Supplement* no. 3264 (Sept. 17, 1964): 857.
11. Stanley, Donald. "Rasputin Analysis," in *San Francisco Examiner* (Oct. 29, 1964):   .
12. *Times* (Aug. 27, 1964): 13.
13. Weigel, p. 117.

A14. **Beyond the Outsider: The Philosophy of the Future.** The Outsider Cycle, Book 6. London: Arthur Barker, 1965, 236 p.,
cloth. [philosophy]

b. Boston: Houghton Mifflin Co., 1965, 236 p., cloth.
c. London: Pan Books, 1966, 256 p., paper.
d. as: *Outsider o Koete.* Tokyo: Takeuchi Shoten, n.d., 262 p.,
cloth (?). Translated by Yasuo Nakamura. [Japanese]
e. as: *Ma B'ad al-Lamuntami.* Beyrouth: Dar Al-Adah, n.d.,
280 p., cloth (?). Translated by Y. Shruru and 'Umal 'Iq.
[Arabic]
f. as: "The Strange Story of Modern Philosophy (*Beyond the Outsider*)," in *The Essential Colin Wilson.* London: Harrap,
1985, cloth, p. 84-101. A reprint of a section from this volume, collected into a volume consisting largely of excerpts
from Colin Wilson books.

Dedication: "To Bob Ardrey with affection and admiration."
Introductory quotations taken from Wilson's novel *Necessary
Doubt* and H. G. Wells' *The Croquet Player.* Includes subject
bibliography and detailed index.

ANALYTICAL TABLE OF CONTENTS:
Preface: The "Outsider" Cycle explained. Reactions of the
critics; "St. Neot Margin." Introduction: The "age of meaning-
lessness." Chapter One: The sound barrier. The inconsistency
of nihilism; The indifference threshold; The spirit of romanticism; The failure of romanticism; The failure of language; The
new romanticism: existentialism; The sound barrier. Chapter
Two: The strange story of modern philosophy. The treason of
the intellectuals; From the Greeks to Galileo; The source of
confusion: Descartes; After Hegel. Chapter Three: The new
foundation. Whitehead proposes a solution; Origins of phenomenology: Brentano; Intentionality; Husserl's development;
Husserl's later development: the life world; Gestalt psychology.
Chapter Four: Heidegger and Sartre: the question of being.
Heidegger; Sartre; The ultimate objection to Sartre. Chapter
Five: The changing vision of science. What is happening to
modern science?; Modern psychology; Maurice Merleau-Ponty;
A note on Shaw's Lamarckism. Chapter Six: The analysis of
man. "What is most important for man in the twentieth century
is that his creed should recognise the possibility of evolution"; a
note on the problem of human sexuality. Chapter Seven: New
directions. The new existentialism; The limitation of language;
Wittgenstein; Wells and "intellectual evolution." Appendix I:
The mescalin experience. Wilson describes his experiences with

the drug, and draws some conclusions. Appendix II: The rope trick. Bill Hopkins' *The Divine and the Decay* "should be regarded as a cornerstone of the literature of evolutionary existentialism." Appendix III: Culture in the Soviet Union. Wilson amends comments made in the preface of *The Age of Defeat.*

SECONDARY SOURCES AND REVIEWS:

1. Bendau, p. 40-41.
2. Bergström, Chapter 1, Part 2.
3. Black, C. *Books & Bookmen* 12 (Mar., 1967): 44.
4. *British Book News* no. 296 (Apr., 1965): 252.
5. Capouya, Emile. *Saturday Review of Literature* 48 (Mar. 20, 1965): 28.
6. *Choice* 2 (Sept, 1965): 398.
7. *Christian Century* 82 (Mar. 24, 1965): 369.
8. Cohen, Marshall. *New Statesman* 69 (Jan. 15, 1965): 80.
9. Flew, A. *Spectator* 212 (Jan. 29, 1965): 140.
10. Kirsch, Robert. "Wilson's Odyssey Filled with Ideas— Mostly Not His," in *Los Angeles Times* (Mar. 28, 1965): .
11. Lebowitz, Martin. "Back Seat Driver," in *Book Week* (May 9, 1965): 10.
12. Newman, Charles. "Unachieved Ambition," in *Chicago Tribune* (Apr. 4, 1965): .
13. Nott, Kathleen. *Observer* (Jan. 17, 1965): .
14. *Observer* (Nov. 6, 1966): 22.
15. Raymond, John. *Sunday Times* (Jan. 17, 1965): .
16. "Study of Mental Emancipation Limited by Author's Horizons," in *Chattanooga Times* (May 2, 1965): .
17. *Times Literary Supplement* (Jan. 28, 1965): 71.
18. Warwick, R. C. *Yorkshire Post* (Jan. 21, 1965): .
19. Weigel, p. 57-64.

A15. **Eagle and Earwig.** London: John Baker, 1965, 278 p, cloth. [criticism]

b. as: *Shinjidai no Bungaku.* Tokyo: Fukumura Shuppan, 1976, 238 p., cloth (?). Translated by Yasuo Nakamura. [Japanese]

Dedication: "For John Baker, whose enthusiasm and encouragement are unique in my experience of publishers." No introductory quotation, index, or bibliography.

ANALYTICAL TABLE OF CONTENTS:

Eleven: The work of Ayn Rand. "Miss Rand is a writer of extraordinary perception—probably of genius." Wilson also expresses reservations, however, of her political views; a personal note concerns the curious response Wilson received when he tried corresponding with Rand. Chapter Twelve: Henry Williamson. His Jekyll and Hyde personality; The Willie Maddison novels; *The Sun in the Sands*; Williamson's view of Hitler; The Philip Maddison novels.

PART THREE: The Writer and Society. Chapter Thirteen: The writer and publicity. Wilson outlines what happened to him and his fellow "Angry Young Men" when they were caught up in the publicity machine of the British press in the mid-1950s. Chapter Fourteen: The success problem. More about the publicity machine; the psychology of fame; "We are living...in one of the most culturally treacherous ages that has ever beset Western civilisation." Chapter Fifteen: Personal. Wilson outlines some of the influences on his own writing, in particular T. S. Eliot. Wilson also explains what he would like to do in modern literature. Written in 1958, this essay mentions Wilson's still-unfinished novel, *Lulu*.

COMMENTS: A collection of essays, many of which had been previously published in various literary journals or reviews. In some cases, as in the essays on Lindsay and Shaw, the pieces were rewritten, expanded, or otherwise adapted into later, more detailed assessments of those authors.

SECONDARY SOURCES AND REVIEWS:

1. Bendau, p. 40.
2. *Modern Fiction Studies* 12 (1966): 507.
3. *New Statesman* 70 (Dec. 3, 1965): 896.
4. Shrapnel, N. *Manchester Guardian* 93 (Dec. 9, 1965): 10.
5. *Times Literary Supplement* (1965): 939.
6. Weigel, p. 110-112.
7. Whittington-Egan, Richard. "Literary Criticism," in *Books & Bookmen* 11 (Jan., 1966): 32.

A16. **Chords and Discords: Purely Personal Opinions on** Music. New York: Crown Publishers, 1966, 215 p., cloth. [music]

b. as: *Colin Wilson on Music*. London: Pan Books, 1967, 237 p., paper.
c. as: *Colin Wilson Ongaku o Kataru*. Tokyo: Fuzanbo, n.d., 388 p., cloth (?). Translated by Kono Tetsu. [Japanese]

Identical to *Brandy of the Damned* (A11), with an additional chapter added.

ANALYTICAL TABLE OF CONTENTS:
Identical to the 1964 edition, with a new chapter added: Chapter Ten: American music. Edward MacDowell; Charles T. Griffes; Charles Ives; Aaron Copland; Carl Ruggles; John J. Becker; Roger Sessions; Elliott Carter *et al.*

SECONDARY SOURCES AND REVIEWS (see also A11):

1. *Booklist* 63 (Oct. 1, 1966): 150.
2. Finn, Robert. "Novelist Scratches Musical Surface," in *Cleveland Plain Dealer* (July 10, 1966): .
3. Haskins, John. "Self-Made Musicology," in *Kansas City Star* (July 3, 1966): .
4. McLellan, Joseph. "Critics Sound-Off in Sharps and Flats," in *Boston Pilot* (Oct. 15, 1966): .
5. Miller, P. L. *Library Journal* 91 (Oct. 1, 1966): 4667.
6. Potts, Dory. "Stravinsky, T. S. Eliot: Their Work Parallelled," in *St. Louis Globe-Democrat* (Aug. 14, 1966): .
7. Raymond, John. "Recent Paperbacks," *in Punch* 252 (Feb. 8, 1967): 209.
8. Sargent, W. *New Yorker* 43 (June 3, 1967): 110.

A17. **The Glass Cage.** London: Arthur Barker, 1966, 261 p., cloth. [novel]

b. as: *The Glass Cage: An Unconventional Detective Story.* New York: Random House, 1967, 209 p., cloth.
c. London: Pan Books, 1968, 283 p., paper.
d. as: *Le Cage de Verre.* Paris: Éd. Planète, 1969, 291 p., cloth (?). Translated by Marc Savona. [French]
e. New York: Bantam Books, 1973, 249 p., paper.
f. as: *La Jaula de Cristal.* Barcelona: Luis de Caralt, 1973, 301 p., cloth. Translated by Carmen de Azpiazu. [Spanish]
g. London: Village Press, 1974?, 209 p., paper. [with sub-title]
h. as: *A Gaiola de Vidro.* Rio de Janeiro: F. Alves, 1976, 275 p., cloth (?). Translated by Cesar Tozzi. [Portuguese]
i. as: *Glass Noori.* Tokyo: Shinchosha, n.d., 252 p., cloth (?). Translated by Yasuo Nakamura. [Japanese]

Dedication: "For Jonathan and Sue Guinness and to the memory of John Cowper Powys." No introductory quotation.

COMMENTS: The hero of this "unconventional detective story" is Damon Reade, a Blakean scholar-turned-detective who tracks down a murderer who leaves quotations from the poet near his victims. Kit Butler, hero of Wilson's later book, *Black Room*, makes an appearance as a secondary character. Wilson sees the book as "...an attempt to create a clearer contrast between the psychology of the criminal and the mystic" (*Craft of the Novel*, p. 236).

SECONDARY SOURCES AND REVIEWS:

1. Bendau, p. 42-43.
2. Bergström, p. 54-57, 72-78, 100-105.
3. *Booklist* 64 (Sept. 15, 1967): 110.
4. Cromie, A. *Books Today* 4 (May 14, 1967): 14.
5. Dempsey, Michael. "The End of Optimism," in *Illustrated London News* 249 (Sept. 24, 1966): 30-31.
6. Dillard, p. 10-11.
7. Grant, M. K. *Library Journal* 92 (June 1, 1967): 2180.
8. Grella, George. "Jack the Ripper, Blake, and Existentialism Too," in *Kansas City Star* (June 11, 1967): .
9. Harris, L. *Punch* 251 (Oct. 5, 1966): 528.
10. Kass, Carole. "Mystery by Wilson—Pointedly Intellectual," in *Richmond Times-Dispatch* (Aug. 6, 1967): .
11. *Publishers Weekly* 191 (Apr. 10, 1967): 75.
12. *Times Literary Supplement* (Nov. 3, 1966): 1008.
13. Towle, Lawrence. "Brutal Murders," in *Hartford Courant* (July 16, 1967): .
14. Tredell, Chapter 6.
15. Wardle, Irving. *Observer* (Sept. 18, 1966): 27.
16. *Washington Post Book World* 7 (Sept. 23, 1973): 13.
17. Weigel, p. 87-90.

A18. **Introduction to the New Existentialism.** London: Hutchinson & Co., 1966, 188 p., cloth. [philosophy]

b. Boston: Houghton Mifflin Co., 1967, 188 p., cloth (published simultaneously in trade paperback).
c. as: *The New Existentialism.* London: Wildwood House, 1980, 188 p., paper. Includes a new preface by Wilson.
d. Salem, NH: Salem House, 1983, 188 p., paper.
e. as: *Jitsuzon Shugi o Koete.* Tokyo: Fukumura Shuppan, n.d., 238 p., cloth (?). Translated by Yasuo Nakamura and Masaaki Nakamura. [Japanese]

f.   as: "Everyday Consciousness Is a Liar (*The New Existential-ism*)," in *The Essential Colin Wilson*. London: Harrap, 1985, cloth, p. 102-107. A reprint of a section from this volume, collected into a volume consisting largely of excerpts from Colin Wilson books.

Dedication: "For Maurice Cranston." No introductory quota-tion. Includes index and bibliographical footnotes.

ANALYTICAL TABLE OF CONTENTS:
PART ONE: The Crisis in Modern Thought. Introduc-tory: My own approach to the problem. Chapter One: The old existentialism. The destruction of meaning; Kierkegaard; Karl Jaspers; Martin Heidegger; Sartre; Camus; Why existen-tialism fails. Chapter Two: What is phenomenology? Why phenomenology became necessary; God the confidence trickster; Husserl's solution; The detective and the suspects; Intentional-ity; The basic concept of phenomenology; Crabbe's *Lover's Journey*. Chapter Three: The meaning of Husserl's revolution. The aim of phenomenology; How phenomenology is applied; Transactionism; Whitehead's revolution. Chapter Four: The new picture of the universe. The need to know; Existential psychology; The case of "Maria"; Peak experiences in psy-chotherapy; Alcoholics cured by mescalin and LSD.
PART TWO: The New Existentialism. Chapter One: The man in the fog. The advent of a new optimism; William James' analogy of the man in a boat; Why the old existentialism is a failure; Problem of man's contingency; The intentionality of consciousness; Practical disciplines—"maintaining the balance of objectivity." Chapter Two: The extension of consciousness. William James' "...increasing ranges of distant facts"; Dangers of extending consciousness: "the pit of insecurity"; The problem of boredom. Chapter Three: Inside the dark room. Sensory deprivation experiments; Man's need for distraction; His alien-ation from a sense of purpose; The "forgetfullness of existence"; The "indifference threshold"; The old woman in the vinegar bottle; The need to evolve; The "romantic" problem; The failure of mysticism; The need for purpose. Chapter Four: Languages and values. The nature of language; Koestler's experience; René Daumal's experience; Hugo von Hofmannsthal's Chandos letter; Failure of language to describe mystical states; A note on Maurice Merleau-Ponty. Chapter Five: Everyday conscious-ness is a liar. Insights; Nijinsky's "I am God"; Man the blink-ered horse; Values; Moods; The analysis of language. Chapter Six: The power of the spectre. The idea of the "mind para-sites"; Man does not yet exist; Habit breaking: Poe's "Imp of

the Perverse"; Sanity and insanity; Critique of Sartre's pessimism.

COMMENTS: Probably Wilson's most important work to date, *Introduction* provides a very clear and concise exposition of the ideas put forward in the six Outsider Cycle books. In the newly-penned introduction to the 1980 edition, Wilson states: "If I have contributed anything to existentialism—or, for that matter, to twentieth-century thought in general, here it is. I am willing to stand or fall by it."

SECONDARY SOURCES AND REVIEWS:

1. Bendau, p. 41-42.
2. Bergström, Chapter 1, Part 2.
3. *British Book News* no. 311 (July, 1966): 484-485.
4. Cacaturimus. *Minnesota Review* 7 (1967): 181-183.
5. *Choice* 4 (Oct., 1967): 854.
6. *Denver Quarterly* 2 (Summer, 1967): 179-180.
7. Edwards, C. W. *Christian Century* 84 (Apr. 5, 1967): 439.
8. Freyer, Grattan. *Irish Times* (June 4, 1966): .
9. Hansen, Carl. "Scientific Philosophy," in *Rocky Mountain News* (May 14, 1967): .
10. Kaufmann, Walter. *New York Times Book Review* (July 30, 1967): 6.
11. *Kirkus Reviews* 35 (Jan. 15, 1967): 104.
12. McEachran, Frank. *Scotsman* (Apr. 16, 1966): .
13. Perkins, R. L. *Library Journal* 92 (May 15, 1967): 1938.
14. Ricks, Christopher. *New Statesman* 71 (May 13, 1966): 695.
15. Schulz, Howard. *Richmond Times-Dispatch* (May 28, 1967): .
16. *Times Literary Supplement* (Jan. 26, 1967): 72.
17. Weigel, p. 131-133.
18. Whittington-Egan, Richard. *Books & Bookmen* 11 (June, 1966): 38.

A19. **Sex and the Intelligent Teenager.** London: Arrow Books, 1966, 192 p., paper. [psychology]

b. New York: Pyramid Books, 1968, 160 p., paper.
c. as: *Sexmoral og Teenagerkultur.* København: Stig Vendelkaer, n.d., 175 p., paper (?). Translated by Mogens Toft. [Danish]

d. as: *Sei to Chisel.* Tokyo: Futami Shobo, n.d., 262 p., cloth
    (?). Translated by Sakikibma Kozo. [Japanese]
e. as: *Sex en de Intelligente T(w)iener.* Amsterdam: Contact,
    n.d., 176 p., cloth (?). Translated by Jean A. Schalekamp.
    [Dutch]

No dedication, introductory quotation, or index.

ANALYTICAL TABLE OF CONTENTS:
Introduction. The "adult conspiracy against the teenager";
Our personalities are imitated from others; Wolf children; The
sexual revolution: where is it leading?; The teenager caught
between two types of dishonesty. Chapter One: The physical
side of sex. Roberta Cowell and "change of sex"; Origin of life;
Chromosomes; Woman's reproductive system; Male and female
sex organs; Hormones; Monkey glands; The "castrati"; W. B.
Yeats and the effect of "monkey glands." Chapter Two: History of sex. Primitive man was promiscuous; Eskimoes; Leisure
and sex; Breeding the race; Greeks, Hebrews, and Romans;
Christian revolution; Decline of the west?; Sexual morals in
modern Japan, Sweden, America; What is the next step?
Chapter Three: The problem of sexual perversion. Sexual at-
traction based on the "forbidden": hence perversion; Homosexuality and transvesticism; autoeroticism and fetishism; Sadism
and the Marquis de Sade; The "moonlight murderer" of *Texar-
kana*; Jack the Ripper; Lack of early affection the cause of
anti-social behavior and mental instability; Marilyn Monroe and
Lucia Joyce. Chapter Four: The male urge to conquest. Ca-
sual and aggressive nature to the male sexual impulse; Barbusse's Inferno; The gap between desire and its satisfaction;
Human sexuality is visual; A Pagan's Hosanna; Robert Irwin;
The Peoria murderer; Mezzrow and drugs; The great lovers:
Casanova, Frank Harris; The "desire for greatness"; Byron,
Henry Miller, Wells, and Shaw. Chapter Five: The paradoxes
of the sexual impulse. The "mental side of sex"; Maupassant's
story "The Unknown"; Bill Hopkins' *Divine and the Decay*; The
rape of Tamar; The two halves of man; sex and civilization; An
autobiographical digression; "Outsider" and "Insider"; The
"Outsider" and the paradoxes of the sexual impulse; Nietzsche
and his "vision on the hilltop"; The murder case of Jan and
Ada. Chapter Six: The great pornography battle. History of
pornography in the twentieth century; *Lady Chatterley's Lover*;
The *Ulysses* case; Faulkner's *Sanctuary*; *No Orchids for Miss
Blandish*; The James Bond novels; Nabokov's *Lolita*; Henry
Miller's *Tropic of Cancer*; *Fanny Hill*; *The Naked Lunch*;
Candy; The sensible attitude to pornography. Chapter Seven:

Sex and the future. The mechanism of the sex drive; What is "normal" sex?; D. H. Lawrence's views of sex; How Lawrence came to hold them; Even Lawrence tended to "perversion"; The parable of the blind man and the elephant; The "naive school"; Sex: illusion or greatest of all human drives?; The meaning of existence; The evolutionary theory of sex; The reaction against Freud; The new freedom; Juvenile deliquency; What is freedom?

COMMENTS: This simplification of the ideas expressed in *Origins of the Sexual Impulse* was issued only in paperback, and went quickly out-of-print. It is now among the most difficult of Wilson's books to obtain, in any condition.

SECONDARY SOURCES AND REVIEWS:

1. Bendau, p. 41. "One of Wilson's least significant works, it is sufficient to mention here [only] that it was published."
2. Ford, M. *Books & Bookmen* 11 (May, 1966): 37.
3. Hall, Ruth. *Sunday Times* (Apr. 3, 1966): .
4. Ricks, Christopher. *New Statesman* 71 (May 13, 1966): 695.
4. Weigel, p. 126-127.

A20. **The Mind Parasites.** London: Arthur Barker, 1967, 222 p., cloth. [novel]

b. Sauk City, WI: Arkham House, 1967, xxi, 222 p., cloth.
c. New York: Bantam Books, 1968, 196 p., paper.
d. London: Panther Books, 1969, 188 p., paper.
e. Oakland, CA: Oneiric Press, 1972, 222 p, paper. Reprinted in 1977 and 1981.
f. as: *I Parasitti della Mente.* Roma: Fanucci, 1977, p., cloth (?). [Italian]
g. as: *Les Parasites de l'Esprit.* Paris: Editions Planète, n.d., 224 p., cloth (?). Translated by Marie Decorme. [French]
h. as: *Seishin Kiseitai.* Tokyo: Hayakawa Shobo, n.d., 273 p., cloth (?). Translated by Ogura Takashi. [Japanese]
i. as: "Discovery of the Vampires (*The Mind Parasites*)," in *The Essential Colin Wilson.* London: Harrap, 1985, cloth, p. 200-207. A reprint of a section from this volume, collected into a volume consisting largely of excerpts from Colin Wilson books.

Dedication: "For August Derleth, who suggested it." Introductory quotation from Bertrand Russell's letter to Constance Malleson quoted in *My Philosophical Development*, p. 261.

COMMENTS: Wilson first wrote of "mind parasites" in his book, *Introduction to the New Existentialism* (see A18). In this new novel in the Lovecraft tradition, Prof. Gilbert Austin tells a story in journal format of how mankind fought the mind parasites. Wilson later wrote in *Science Fiction As Existentialism* that the novel was his "attempt to state symbolically what I felt to be wrong with human beings." On page 57 of his introduction to *The Necronomicon* is reproduced an interesting letter to Wilson by Dr. Hinterstoisser, claiming that the mind parasites are "in all truth existent, influential, and even, under different guises, visible." He goes on to complain of severe headaches; in a short note following the letter Wilson mentions that Hinterstoisser died shortly after completing it.

SECONDARY SOURCES AND REVIEWS:

1. Bendau, p. 43-44.
2. Bergström, p. 79-88.
3. *British Book News* no. 321 (May, 1967): 403-404.
4. Corke, H. *Listener* 77 (Feb. 16, 1967): 237.
5. Davis, H. *Science Fiction Review* no. 35 (Fall, 1970): 38-39.
6. Dick, Kay. *Sunday Times* (Feb. 5, 1967): .
7. Dillard, p. 11-12.
8. Flavin, Ian. "On Cancer Invaders." *Books & Bookmen* 12 (May, 1967): 35-36.
9. Lowndes, Robert A. W. *Famous Science Fiction* 1 (Winter, 1967/68): 111-113.
10. *Minneapolis Tribune* (Aug. 6, 1967): .
11. Morgan, E. *New Statesman* 73 (Feb. 3, 1967): 156.
12. Nye, Robert. "Mr. Wilson's 19th Try," in *Manchester Guardian* (Feb. 3, 1967): 11.
13. Russ, Joanna. *The Magazine of Fantasy & Science Fiction* 34 (Jan., 1968): 38-39.
14. Starrett, Vincent. *Books Today* 4 (July 23, 1967): 13.
15. *Times Literary Supplement* (Mar. 23, 1967): 235.
16. Tredell, Chapter 7.
17. Weigel, p. 90-94.
18. Wharton, Will. "Year 2000 World Crisis: Parasites from Moon," in *St. Louis Globe-Democrat* (July 30, 1967): .
19. Young, B. A. *Punch* 252 (Mar. 1, 1967): 320.

A21. **Bernard Shaw: A Reassessment.** London: Hutchinson & Co., 1969, xiv, 306 p., cloth. [biography]

  b. New York: Atheneum, 1969, xiv, 306 p., cloth.
  c. London: Macmillan, 1981, xiv, 314 p., cloth [published simultaneously in trade paperback].
  d. as: *Bernard Shaw.* Tokyo: Shinchosha, n.d., 307 p., cloth (?). Translated by Yasuo Nakamura. [Japanese]

Dedication: "To S. Foster Damon and to Foster's godson, John Damon Wilson." No introductory quotation. Includes index and bibliographical footnotes.

ANALYTICAL TABLE OF CONTENTS:
   Introductory. Chapter One: Who is then the gentleman? Shaw's early life. Chapter Two: The long apprenticeship. Shaw in London; His search for a hero: Immaturity and The Irrational Knot. Chapter Three: The economic basis. Shaw's introduction to socialism; Why he was so deeply committed; The Unsocial Socialist. Chapter Four: The unfair critic. William Morris; Various romantic attachments; Shaw the music critic; William Archer and Henrik Ibsen; *Widower's Houses.* Chapter Five: Public Shaw. Shaw and the Fabians; *The Philanderer*; *Mrs. Warren's Profession*; *Arms and the Man*; Shaw the drama critic; marriage. Chapter Six: Beyond the gospel of efficiency. *Candida*; Shaw and W. B. Yeats; *The Devil's Disciple*; Shaw's theory of "higher evolutionary types"; *Caesar and Cleopatra.* Chapter Seven: World celebrity. *Man and Superman*; *John Bull's Other Island*; *Major Barbara.* Chapter Eight: Cul-de-Sac. *The Doctor's Dilemma*; Shaw and the critics; Shaw and H. G. Wells; Plays, 1906-13; Shaw and Mrs. Patrick Campbell; World War I. Chapter Nine: Glimpse into chaos. *Heartbreak House*; Preface to *Androcles and the Lion*; *Back to Methuselah*: Shaw and evolution; The "Shavian philosophy." Chapter Ten: Sparks from a bonfire. *St. Joan*; *The Black Girl in Search of God*; *Too True To Be Good*; The plays of Shaw's last years. Postscript: My own part in the matter. Autobiographical and philosophical essay linking Wilson with Shaw.

COMMENTS: The 1981 edition contains a new afterword suggesting that there is now a Shaw revival in process, and proposing a possible link between his work and that of Mrs. J. H. Riddell, particularly her George Geith of Fen Court.

SECONDARY SOURCES AND REVIEWS:

1. Adams, Phoebe. *Atlantic* 224 (Nov., 1969): 176.
2. Bendau, p. 44-45.
3. *Booklist* 66 (Jan. 15, 1970): 594.
4. *Books & Bookmen* 15 (Jan., 1970): 26.
5. *British Book News* (Jan., 1970): 59.
6. *Choice* 7 (Apr., 1970): 247.
7. Cushman, Keith. *Library Journal* 94 (Oct. 1, 1969): 3452.
8. Dennis, Nigel. *Sunday Telegraph* (Oct. 19, 1969): .
9. *Economist* 233 (Nov. 8, 1969): ix.
10. Fagin, Bryllion. "A Shy Hater of Obscurity," in *Baltimore Sun* (Nov. 23, 1969): .
11. *Kirkus Reviews* 37 (Sept. 1, 1969): 989.
12. Leary, D. J. *Saturday Review of Literature* 52 (Nov. 15, 1969): 52-53.
13. Menn, Thorpe. *Kansas City Star* (Nov. 9, 1969): .
14. *New Yorker* 45 (Nov. 29, 1969): 212.
15. *Observer* (Oct. 26, 1969): 34.
16. *Publishers Weekly* 196 (Oct. 6, 1969): 47.
17. *Punch* 257 (Nov. 19, 1969): 844.
18. *San Francisco Chronicle* (Feb. 1, 1970): .
19. *Times Educational Supplement* (July 24, 1981): 18.
20. *Times Literary Supplement* (Nov. 27, 1969): 1349. Follow-up letters appear on pages 1450 (1969), and 12 and 34 (1970).
21. Weigel, p. 118-120.
22. Weintraub, Stanley. *New York Times Book Review* (Nov. 9, 1969): Pt. 1, 18.
23. Whittemore, Reed. *New Republic* 161 (Nov. 22, 1969): 23.

A22. **A Casebook of Murder.** London: Leslie Frewin Publishers, 1969, 288 p., cloth. [sociology]

b. New York: Cowles Book Co., 1970, 288 p., cloth.
c. London: Mayflower Books, 1971, 253 p., paper.
d. as: *Sai-Ineui Cheolhag.* Seoul: Daeundang, 1978, 350 p., cloth (?). Translated by Hwang Dong Mun. [Korean]
e. as: *Satsujin no Tetsugaku.* Tokyo: Takeuchi Shoten, n.d., 311 p., cloth (?). Translated by Takagi Susumu. [Japanese]
f. as: *Satsujin no Tetsugaku.* Tokyo: Kadokawa Shoten, n.d., 432 p., cloth (?). Translated by Takagi Susumu. [Japanese]

Dedication: "For Francis Camps." No introductory quotation or index. Select bibliography.

ANALYTICAL TABLE OF CONTENTS:
Introduction. Robert Irwin; The artist and the criminal; Raymond Morris and the Cannock Chase murder; Kurten; Leopold and Loeb. Chapter One: The beginning. Sawney Bean; Gilles de Rais; Thomas Arden of Faversham; The murder of Christopher Marlowe; Sir Thomas Malory. Chapter Two: The age of gin. Gin and the rising crime rate; Dick Turpin; History of hanging; The Newgate Calendar; Catherine Hayes; Murder and smuggling; Criminals who survived hanging; Formation of police force. Chapter Three: Cannibals and rapists. The nineteenth century; Transportations to Australia; The increase in sex crimes; The red barn murder; Ellie Hanley, the "Colleen Bawn." Chapter Four: Into the age of violence. Joy murder; Burke and Hare; Lacenaire; Poisoners; Thomas Neill Cream; Jack the Ripper; The "outsider" as a murderer. Chapter Five: The age of detection. Photography and criminal investigation; Pierre Voirbo; Fingerprints and criminal identification; Human blood identification; Lizzie Borden; Miles Giffard. Chapter Six: Chamber of horrors. Harry Howard Holmes; Ed Gein, the Wisconsin necrophile; The Moors murder case; "Inadequate motive" murders; Lucian Staniak, the "Red Spider"; homosexual murders; "Perfect" murders.

SECONDARY SOURCES AND REVIEWS:

1. Adams, Phoebe. *Atlantic* 225 (May, 1970): 132.
2. *American Scholar* 40 (Autumn, 1971): 710.
3. Bendau, p. 45.
4. *Books & Bookmen* 15 (Feb., 1970): 33.
5. *Choice* 8 (Apr., 1971): 301.
6. "Colin Wilson's Murder Philosophy," in *Washington Star* (Mar. 29, 1970):   .
7. deFord, Miriam Allen. "The Changing Patterns of Murder," in *This World* (Apr. 12, 1970):   .
8. Derleth, August. *Capitol Times* (Apr. 2, 1970):   .
9. Hough, C. A. *Library Journal* 95 (May 15, 1970): 1857.
10. Hubin, Allen J. *New York Times Book Review* (June 14, 1970): 28.
11. Keowin, Don. "Homicidal History of Mankind with the Colin Wilson Flair," in *San Rafael Independent Journal* (Apr. 4, 1970):   .
12. *Kirkus Reviews* 38 (Mar. 1, 1970): 312.
13. *Publishers Weekly* 197 (Feb. 23, 1970): 155.
14. Weigel, p. 115-116.

A23.   **The Philosopher's Stone.** London: Arthur Barker, 1969, 315 p., cloth. [novel]

b.   as: *The Philosopher's Stone: A Novel.* New York: Crown Publishers, 1971, 315 p., cloth.

c.   New York: Warner Books, 1974, 318 p., paper. Includes subtitle, and an introduction by Joyce Carol Oates. Reprinted in 1977 and 1981.

d.   London, New York: Granada, Panther Books, 1974, 268 p., paper.

e.   Berkeley, CA: Wingbow Press, 1979, 268 p., paper. Includes subtitle.

f.   as: *Jenja no Ishi.* Tokyo: Tokyo-Sogensha, n.d., 470 p., cloth (?). Translated by Yasuo Nakamura. [Japanese]

g.   Los Angeles: J. P. Tarcher, 1989,   p., cloth (?).

Dedication: "For Jorge Luis Borges." No introductory quotation.

COMMENTS: Like *The Mind Parasites*, this is a novel in the Lovecraftian tradition. The first section, "The Quest of the Absolute," deals with the early life and development of Howard Lester, a character similar to Hugh Greene of *The World of Violence*, and, inevitably, to Wilson himself. Lester meets Sir Henry Littleway, and together they experiment with an alloy which has the ability to expand consciousness when placed in the brain and stimulated. Part Two, "Journey to the End of Night" (borrowing, perhaps, from Louis-Ferdinand Céline), charts the illuminating and terrifying results of their experiments. Confusion arose over the name of the hero when the dustjacket of the British editions mentioned a Howard Newman, while the blurb inside the hardcover commented on a Harry Lester. The reviewer for the *Times Literary Supplement*, in the course of dismissing the novel, made the error of using the wrong name, resulting in a stiff response from Wilson (*TLS*, 1969, p. 820), accusing him of not having read the book. For Wilson's comments on the writing of *The Philosopher's Stone*, see *Science Fiction As Existentialism*, pages 14-15.

SECONDARY SOURCES AND REVIEWS:

1.   Bendau, p. 46-47. "One of Wilson's best novels to date."
2.   Bergström, p. 122-139.
3.   Boyer, A. *Library Journal* 96 (July, 1971): 2350-2351.

4. Cole, Barry. "Traveller's Tales," in *Spectator* 222 (June 28, 1969): 857.
5. Fenton, James. "Fossil Remains," in *New Statesman* 77 (June 27, 1969): 916.
6. *Guardian Weekly* 101 (July 3, 1969): 15.
7. *Listener* 82 (July 3, 1969): 24.
7. Miller, P. Schuyler. *Analog* 87 (July, 1971): 165-166.
8. *New Statesman* 77 (June 27, 1969): 916.
9. Newton, J. *Son of WSFA Journal* no. 53 (April, 1972): 3.
10. *Observer* (June 29, 1969): 24.
11. Otto, Herbert A. "New Light on Human Potential," in *Saturday Review* 52 (Dec. 20, 1969): 14-17.
12. Pierce, John. *Renaissance* 3 (1971): 16-17.
13. *Publishers Weekly* 199 (Mar. 22, 1971): 47.
14. "Shazam!" in *Times Literary Supplement* (July 10, 1969): 745.
15. Sisco, E. *Kliatt Young Adult Paperback Book Guide* 8 (Sept., 1974): 87.
16. *Times* (June 28, 1969): 23.
17. Tredell, Chapter 7.
18. *Washington Post Book World* 8 (Apr. 7, 1974): 4.
19. Weigel, p. 94-98.
20. Wilgus, Neal. *Science Fiction & Fantasy Book Review* 1 (Nov., 1979): 145.
21. Wilgus, Neal. *Science Fiction Review* 9 (Feb., 1980): 42.
22. Wilson, Gahan. *The Magazine of Fantasy & Science Fiction* 53 (August, 1972): 23-24.

A24. **Poetry and Mysticism.** San Francisco: City Lights Books, 1969, 79 p., paper. [philosophy]

Dedication: "For Lawrence Ferlinghetti." No introductory quotation. For a complete description of this book, see the extended version (A28).

A25. **Voyage to a Beginning: A Preliminary Autobiography.** New York: Crown Publishers, 1969, 344 p., cloth. [autobiography]

b. London: Cecil & Amelia Woolf, 1969, xv, 191 p., cloth.
c. as: *Hottan Eno Tabi.* Tokyo: Takeuchi Shoten, n.d., 356 p., cloth (?). Translated by Tobita Shigeo. [Japanese]

Dedication: British edition: "For J. W. Sidford"; American edition: "For Millen Brand." No introductory quotation. Includes index, and four black-and-white photographs of the author.

ANALYTICAL TABLE OF CONTENTS (British edition):
Introduction, by Father Brocard Sewell. Chapter One: Aims and motives. The narrowness of consciousness; The "St. Neot's Margin." Chapter Two: The tub of Diogenes. Early childhood: spoiled by mother and grandparents; Told he was "born lucky"; Affection for his mother and younger brother; An extrovert and seeker after knowledge from an early age. Chapter Three: Stimuli. Early interest in science and science fiction; Feels contempt for most adults; Becomes aware of the power of sex at age thirteen. Chapter Four: Nihilism. Why are we alive?; Shaw's *Man and Superman*; Leaves school, becomes laboratory assistant at sixteen; First short story published in a Durham factory magazine; Contemplates suicide; Sacked, finds employment in a tax office; Finds three close friends, and becomes happier; in 1949 joins the RAF. Chapter Five: The Air Force and after. Becomes bored with military service; Discharged; Travels around England; Returns home to Leicester; More jobs and a girlfriend; Decides to travel abroad. Chapter Six: Paris, Strasbourg, and London. Travels on the continent; Returns home; More jobs and marriage; Moves to London; Begins novel; Meets Bill Hopkins; To Paris, selling magazine subscriptions; Back to Leicester; Meets Joy Stewart. Chapter Seven: London and *The Outsider*. Returns to London: more jobs; Decides to live outdoors and work on the novel in the British Museum during the day; Meets Angus Wilson and Stuart Holroyd; Decides to write *The Outsider*; Book accepted by Gollancz. Chapter Eight: The success problem. Success and its backlash; The "horsewhip" episode; Moves to Cornwall with Joy. Chapter Nine: After the deluge. The hostility of the press; Bill Hopkins and Stuart Holroyd also suffer. Chapter Ten: Starting again. Completes *Ritual in the Dark* and *Age of Defeat*; *Ritual* receives some fair reviews; New existentialism; The "robot"; The "St. Neot Margin"; Peak Experiences—Abraham Maslow; Phenomenological existentialism; America and Britain: their cultural lives contrasted; The brevity of life.

The American edition renames Chapter Six "Paris, Strasbourg, London (1950-51)," and adds the following Chapters: Chapter Seven: "Marriage and London." Chapter Eight: "Paris, Leicester, London Again." Chapter Thirteen: "Sex." Chapter Fourteen: "America." Chapter Fifteen: "Insights." The black-and-white photographs are omitted in this version.

COMMENTS: Wilson is not so much concerned here with the actual events of his life as with how they shaped his ideas. Also see Campion's biography, the autobiographical introduction to *Religion and the Rebel*, and Holroyd's *Contraries*. First issued in Britain in an edition of about 700 numbered copies, bound in buckram, blocked in real gold, with a gilt top. Published for the financial advantage of *The Aylesford Review* in Spring, 1963. Brocard Sewell's original introduction is printed in *The Aylesford Review* 4 (Autumn, 1962): 277-281.

SECONDARY SOURCES AND REVIEWS:

1. *Antioch Review* 29 (Summer, 1969): 264.
2. Bendau, p. 45.
3. *Booklist* 66 (Oct. 15, 1969): 250.
4. *Books & Bookmen* 15 (Jan., 1970): 26.
5. *British Book News* (Feb., 1970): 157-158.
6. Churchill, R. C. "The Wilson Age: The Outsider at 40," in *Birmingham Post* (Oct. 3, 1970): .
7. Duke, Maurice. "Angry? Author Colin Wilson Is No Longer Angry," in *Richmond Times-Dispatch* (July 6, 1969): .
8. Gross, R. A. *Newsweek* 74 (July 21, 1969): 103.
9. Houston, Gary. "The Fields of Thought: One Man's Haymaking," in *Christian Science Monitor* 61 (Sept. 4, 1969): 9.
10. Irving, Maggie. "Autobiography of a Candid Writer," in *Worcester Telegram* (Aug. 10, 1969): .
11. *Kirkus Reviews* 37 (Mar. 13, 1969): 366.
12. Kirsch, Robert. "Awe Over Arrogance," in *Los Angeles Times* (July 14, 1969): .
13. Lancour, Harold. *Library Journal* 94 (May 15, 1969): 1984.
14. *Listener* 82 (Nov. 20, 1969): 704.
15. Marshall, Arthur. *New Statesman* 78 (Oct. 24, 1969): 582.
16. *Observer* (Oct. 26, 1969): 34.
17. *Publishers Weekly* 195 (Mar. 17, 1969): 54.
18. *Punch* 257 (Nov. 19, 1969): 844.
19. *Times* (Dec. 20, 1969): 4.
20. *Times Literary Supplement* (Nov. 6, 1969): 1275.

A26. **The God of the Labyrinth.** London: Rupert Hart-Davis, 1970, 305 p., cloth. [novel]

b. as: *The Hedonists*. New York: A Signet Book, New American Library, 1971, 253 p., paper.
c. as: *De God van het Labyrint*. Amsterdam: Contact, 1972, 332 p., cloth (?). Translated by Jean A. Schalekamp. [Dutch]
d. London: Mayflower Books, 1971, 286 p., paper. Reprinted 1974.
e. St. Albans: Panther Books, 1977, 286 p., paper.
f. as: *El Dios del Laberinto*. Barcelona: Luis de Caralt, 1978, 302 p., cloth (?). Translated by Joaquín Adsuar Ortega. [Spanish]
g. Berkeley, CA: Wingbow Press, 1982, 305 p., paper.

Dedication: none. Introductory quotations taken from a poem by Robert Browning, and an extract from Rabelais, Books 2, Chapter 15.

COMMENTS: The third book in the Gerard Sorme trilogy "experiments with the conventions of the pornographic novel" (*The Craft of the Novel*, p. 239). The novel itself has a thirteen-page "note" at the end in which Wilson defends himself against accusations of writing pornography, and also gives his opinions on the censorship of literature, while providing one or two interesting insights into the writing of his earlier novels. About *God*, he writes: "The 'Sect of the Phoenix' is developed from a hint by Jorge Luis Borges [and so] may be said to be based on the mythologising of Borges." Wilson's fiction has always posed problems for the critics, and this book was no exception. Bendau dismisses it as: "...no more than a minor part of Wilson's canon," while Weigel says: "Wilson has gone far beyond D. H. Lawrence, for example, in glorifying sexuality...."

SECONDARY SOURCES AND REVIEWS:

1. Bendau, p. 49.
2. Bergström, p. 112-120.
3. Capitanchik, Maurice. *Spectator* 224 (June 27, 1970): 852.
4. Churchill, R. C. "The Wilson Age: The Outsider at 40," in *Birmingham Post* (Oct. 3, 1970): .
5. Jordan, Clive. "Dogbitten," in *New Statesman* 79 (June 26, 1970): 920.
6. *Observer* (June 21, 1970): 30.
7. *Sunday Times* (June 21, 1970): .
8. *Times Literary Supplement* (June 18, 1970): 653.
9. Tredell, Chapter 8.
10. Weigel, p. 101-104.

A27. **The Killer: A Novel.** London: New English Library, 1970, 221 p., cloth. [novel]

ab. London: New English Library, 1970, 221 p., paper.
b. as: *Lingard: A Novel.* New York: Crown Publishers, 1970, 286 p., cloth.
c. St. Albans: Panther Books, 1977, 221 p., paper.
d. New York: Pocket Books, paper. [no record]
e. as: *Satsujin-sha.* Tokyo: Hayakawa Shobo, n.d., 276 p., cloth (?). Translated by Nagai Jun. [Japanese]
f. as: *El Caso Lingard.* Barcelona: Luis de Caralt, n.d., 296 p., cloth (?). Translated by Ramón Margaief Llambrich. [Spanish]

No dedication or introductory quotations.

COMMENTS: In this novel Wilson, more than ever before, graphically exposes the connection between creative frustration and violence. Arthur Lingard (whence the American title) is the killer; the narrator is his psychiatrist. The book contains an explanatory introduction expounding the "right man" theory put forward by A. E. van Vogt.

SECONDARY SOURCES AND REVIEWS:

1. Bartek, Zenka. *Daily Telegraph* (June 18, 1970): .
2. Bendau, p. 47-48.
3. Bergström, p. 94-100.
4. Churchill, R. C. "The Wilson Age—The Outsider at 40," in *Birmingham Post* (Oct. 3, 1970): .
5. Duke, Maurice. "Colin Wilson Produces Shocker in Strange Tale of Psychopath," in *Richmond Times-Dispatch* (June 14, 1970):.
6. Hall, Joan J. "The Criminal Personality," in *Houston Post* (June 28, 1970): .
7. *Kirkus Reviews* 38 (Mar. 15, 1970): 348.
8. *Library Journal* 95 (June 1, 1970): 2183.
9. *Listener* 83 (May 21, 1970): 693.
10. Mahon, Derek. "Games and Cases," in *The Listener* 83 (May 21, 1970): 693.
11. Menn, Thorpe. *Kansas City Star* (June 14, 1970): .
12. *Observer* (Nov. 15, 1970): 27.
13. Price-Turner, W. *Yorkshire Post* (May 21, 1970): .
14. *Publishers Weekly* 197 (Mar. 30, 1970): 62.
15. *Publishers Weekly* 202 (Oct. 23, 1972): 47.

16. Symons, Julian. *Sunday Times* (May 24, 1970):   .
17. *Times* (June 6, 1970): 22.
18. "Tragic—in the Sense of Wrong Choices Made Freely," in *Rocky Mountain News* (May 7, 1970):   .
19. Tredell, Chapter 8.
20. Tube, Henry. "Thrills and Spills," in *Spectator* 224 (May 30, 1970): 718.
21. *Washington Post Book World* 4 (July 12, 1970): 6.
22. Weigel, p. 98-101.

A28. **Poetry & Mysticism.** London: Hutchinson & Co., 1970, 227 p., cloth. [philosophy]

b. San Francisco: City Lights Books, 1986, 227 p., paper.

An expanded version of A24. Dedication: "For Lawrence Ferlinghetti." Introductory quotation from William James' *The Energies of Man.*

ANALYTICAL TABLE OF CONTENTS:
PART ONE. Introductory. Origins of this book; The disease of civilisation; T. E. Hulme; Musil's *Man without Qualities*; Hemingway, Proust, Joyce, D. H. Lawrence: all unsuccessful attacks on the same problem. Chapter One: Absurd good news. Intensity consciousness; Chesterton's "absurd good news"; Yeats and Auden; Poetry's power to cause subconscious relaxation; T. S. Eliot; John Davidson; James Thomson; Wagner's concept of "wahn"; The pessimism of Schopenhauer and Buddhism; Positive aspects of Buddhism; Hinduism; Dostoyevsky's *Stravrogin and Kirilov*; "Short term" and "long term" self. Chapter Two: The robot. Mysticism as "bird's eye view"; The robot; Zen as method of escaping the robot; Ramakrishna; Phenomenology of the poetic experience; Joyce's *Portrait of the Artist as a Young Man*; The use of symbols to induce "suspension of disbelief." Chapter Three: The relationality of consciousness. Tendency of consciousness to congeal; Mono and duo-consciousness; Faculty X; Intentionality and relationality; Faust and the Easter bells; Homing instinct in animals; Jacob Boehme's mystical experience; Graham Greene; Intentionality of moods of depression; Crisis as the destroyer of pessimism; The evolution of animals and human beings; Promotion. Chapter Four: The automatic gearbox. "Revolving in sympathy"; The robot in Blake's *Spectre*; Boredom; Van Gogh; The concept of "worthwhileness"; Interest; Wilson's own attempts to solve the problem; The problem of death; Summary.

PART TWO. Introductory. Chapter One: Rupert Brooke. Chapter Two: W. B. Yeats. Chapter Three: A. L. Rowse. Chapter Four: Nikos Kazantzakis. Chapter Five: Postscript. Ultimate failure of Brooke, Yeats, Rowse, Kazantzakis; Art and science as "mind stretchers"; Human complexity produces boredom; Empty consciousness becomes negative; The concept of ambiguity; The sense of contingency, the "short-term self"; The "long-term self"; The basic problem: to destroy ambiguity and negation; Personal postscript; Evolution as the struggle to escape the trivial; Nausea; Habit neurosis; False fatigue; Consciousness: a leaky bucket; Bullying the false fatigue; The need to arrest the forward flow of perceptive consciousness; Conclusion.

COMMENTS: The earlier American edition did not contain either the introduction to Part One or the entire section comprising Part Two, nor did it split its text into chapters.

SECONDARY SOURCES AND REVIEWS:

1. Bendau, p. 46.
2. Churchill, R. C. "The Wilson Age—The Outsider at 40," in *Birmingham Post* (Oct. 3, 1970): .
3. Nye, Robert. *Scotsman* (Sept. 5, 1970): .
4. *New Statesman* 80 (Sept. 18, 1970): 338.
5. *Times Literary Supplement* (Feb. 5, 1971): 153.
6. Weigel, p. 122-124.

A29. **Strindberg.** London: Calder and Boyars, 1970, 77 p., cloth. [play]

b. as: *Strindberg: A Play in Two Scenes.* New York: Random House, 1972, 94 p., cloth.

No dedication or introductory quotation.

COMMENTS: Wilson's only published play was first performed as *Pictures in a Bath of Acid* on Sept. 15, 1971 at the Leeds Play house, directed by Bill Hays and starring Alfred Burke. In 1974 it was performed in New York as *Strindberg: A Psychological Portrait.* In 1975 it was produced as *Strindberg: A Fool's Decision.* Other plays by Wilson which have been performed (but not published) are: *The Metal Flower Blossom*, later incorporated into the novel, *Adrift in Soho*, produced at Southend-on-Sea, Autumn, 1960; *Viennese Interlude*, produced at Scarborough and London in the same year; and *Mysteries*, performed in Britain in the 1980s. The reviews cited below, except for Bendau and Weigel, are of the stage performances of *Pictures* in 1971.

SECONDARY SOURCES AND REVIEWS:

1. Bates, Merete. *Guardian* (Sept. 16, 1971): .
2. Bendau, p. 49.
3. *Kirkus Reviews* 40 (Mar. 1, 1972): 315.
4. *Library Journal* 97 (May 1, 1972): 1738.
5. O'Connor, Gary. *Financial Times* (Sept. 17, 1971): .
6. Pratt, Desmond. *Yorkshire Post* (Sept. 15, 1971): .
7. Shorter, Eric. *Daily Telegraph* (Sept. 16, 1971): .
8. Weigel, p. 120-122.

A30. **The Black Room: A Novel.** London: Weidenfeld & Nicolson, 1971, 348 p., cloth. [novel]

b. New York: Pyramid Books, 1975, 380 p., paper.
c. London: Sphere Books, 1977, 298 p., paper.
d. as: *Kuroi Heya.* Tokyo: Shincho-sha, n.d., 343 p., cloth (?). Translated by Yasuo Nakamura. [Japanese]
e. as: "Vision on the Eiger (*The Black Room*)," in *The Essential Colin Wilson.* London: Harrap, 1985, cloth, p. 208-212. A reprint of a section from this volume, collected into a volume consisting largely of excerpts from Colin Wilson books.

Dedication: "For Roger Staples." Introductory quotations: Part One: from Heidegger's *Kant and the Problem of Metaphysics*; Part Two: from E. T. A. Hoffmann—"Every man has an innate inclination to fly."

COMMENTS: A spy story concerned with the use of sensory deprivation techniques, in particular, a black, completely silent room. Kit Butler is the hero, a man better equipped than most for challenging the considerable psychological pressures involved. An earlier draft of part of the novel, "Margin of Darkness," appeared in *Minnesota Review* in 1966; at about the same time Wilson's book, *Introduction to the New Existentialism*, was published, with a chapter called "Inside the Dark Room," his first lengthy assessment of the subject.

SECONDARY SOURCES AND REVIEWS:

1. Bendau, p. 51-52.
2. Bergström, p. 139-143.
3. DeQuincey, Christian. "Towards a Superman," in *Irish Times* (Apr. 26, 1971): .
4. Eadie, Douglas. *Scotsman* (Mar. 13, 1971): .
5. Grant, Violet. *Daily Telegraph* (Mar. 11, 1971): .
6. *Guardian Weekly* 104 (Mar. 20, 1971): 18.
7. *Publishers Weekly* 208 (Oct. 6, 1975): 87.
8. Shrapnel, Norman. *Guardian* (Mar. 11, 1971): .
9. *Times* (Apr. 1, 1971): 11.
10. Tredell, Chapter 8.
11. Waugh, Auberon. *Spectator* 226 (Mar. 27, 1971): 426-427.
12. Weigel, p. 104-107.

A31. **The Occult.** London: Hodder & Stoughton, 1971, 601 p., cloth. [occult]

b. New York: Random House, 1971, 601 p., cloth.
c. New York: Random House, 1972?, 603 p., cloth. [book club edition].
d. St. Albans: Mayflower, 1973, 795 p., paper.
e. as: *The Occult: A History.* New York: Vintage Books, 1973, 601 p., paper.
f. as: *L'Occulte.* Paris: Albin Michel, 1973, 425 p., cloth (?). Translated by Robert Genin. [French]
g. as: *Lo Oculto: La Facultad X del Hombre.* Barcelona: Editorial Noguer, 1974, 476 p., cloth. Translated by Carmen Criado. [Spanish]
h. as: *L'Occulto.* Roma: Astrolabio, 1975, 623 p., cloth (?). Translated by Paolo Valli. [Italian]
i. as: *Den Hemmelighedsfulde Videnskab.* Viby: Strube, 1978, 372 p., cloth (?). Translated by Benjamin Saxe. [Danish]
j. London: Granada, 1979, 795 p., paper.
k. as: *Das Okkulte.* Berlin: Marz, 1982, p., cloth (?). [German]
l. as: *Okaruto.* Tokyo: Shinchosha, n.d., 2 v., cloth (?). Translated by Yasuo Nakamura. [Japanese]
m. as: *Het Occulte.* Deventer: Ankh-Hermes, n.d., 335 p., cloth (?). Translated by Margot Bakker. [Dutch]
n. as: *L'Occulte.* Lausanne: Ex Libris, n.d., 427 p., cloth (?). Translated by Robert Genin. [French]
o. as: "Magic—the Science of the Future (*The Occult*)," in *The Essential Colin Wilson.* London: Harrap, 1985, cloth, p. 108-

129. A reprint of a section from this volume, collected into a volume consisting largely of excerpts from Colin Wilson books.

Dedication: "For Robert Graves." No introductory quotation. Includes a large bibliography, bibliographical footnotes, and a thorough index. The cloth editions contain a set of black-and-white plates between pages 304-305.

ANALYTICAL TABLE OF CONTENTS:
Preface: Faculty X. Introduction. "Unseen forces"; The need for an occult revival; The attitude of science; Cybernetics: the intelligent universe; Wilson's change of attitude towards occultism. PART ONE: A Survey of the Subject. Chapter One: Magic—the science of the future. P. D. Ouspensky and "infinitely remote horizons"; Homing instinct; Dowsing; Synchronicity; Precognition; Telepathy; Evil eye; John Cowper Powys' spectre; Faculty X; Arnold Toynbee's experience. Chapter Two: The dark side of the moon. The dominant 5%; Robert Graves and *The White Goddess*; Man's "lunar powers"; Hypertension; *I Ching*; Taoism and Zen. Chapter Three: The poet as occultist. Louis Singer and paranormal phenomena; A. L. Rowse's telepathy; W. B. Yeats' theory of symbols; Yeats and *A Vision*; The tarot.

PART TWO: A History of Magic. Chapter One: The evolution of man. H. G. Wells and evolution; Life—accidental or purposive?; J. B. Rhine's PK tests; Peak experiences; Contemplative objectivity; Failure of psychedelic drugs; Use of sex; The superconscious. Chapter Two: The magic of primitive man. Shamanism; The dawn of magic; Man becomes a city-dweller; The rise of his sexual obsession; *The Epic of Gilgamesh*; Atlantis; Egyptian religion and magic. Chapter Three: Adepts and initiates. Thaumaturgy; "Positive consciousness"; Ancient Greece; The Essenes; Orphism and the worship of Dionysus; Pythagoras; Apollonius of Tyana; Dowsing. Chapter Four: The world of the Kabbalists. Gnosticism; *The Kabbalah*; Simon Magus; Early Christianity; Joseph of Copertino, the flying monk; Possessed nuns; Benvenuto Cellini; Dionysius the Areopagite; Albertus Magnus; Cornelius Agrippa; Paracelsus; Alchemy; Astrology; Nostradamus and his prediction of the French Revolution. Chapter Five: Adepts and imposters. John Dee; Emanuel Swedenborg; Anton Mesmer; Casanova; Cagliostro; The Count of Saint-Germain. Chapter Six: The nineteenth century—magic and romanticism. Saint-Martin; Eliphaz Levi; The Fox sisters; Madame Blavatsky and the Theosophical Society; W. B. Yeats, Mathers, and the Order of the Golden Dawn. Chapter Seven: The beast himself. Crowley's childhood; His sexual obsession; Magic; Marriage; The abbey of Theleme; His death. Chapter Eight: Two Russian mages. Gregory Rasputin; His thaumaturgic powers; Success at court; Enemies; His Murder; Georges Gurdjieff; His childhood; Travels; His basic ideas; "disciples," particularly P. D. Ouspensky and J. G. Bennett; Subud.

PART THREE: Man's Latent Powers. Chapter One: Witchcraft and lycanthropy. Origins of European witchcraft; Catharism; The spread of the witch-craze; Exorcism of nuns; Matthew Hopkins, the witch-finder general; Why the witchcraft craze died out; The rise of the novel; Valery Briussov's *The Fiery Angel*; Vampirism and lycanthropy: their sexual basis; The case of Sally Beauchamp; Cases of vampirism; The witchcraft revival. Chapter Two: The realm of the spirits. Daniel Dunglas Home; C. G. Jung and the unconscious; Aldous Huxley and J. B. Rhine; Founding of the Society for Psychical Research; Harry Price; Poltergeists; Spontaneous combustion; Ted Serios; Reincarnation; Arthur Guirdham; UFOs; The Tunguska explosion; Jack Schwarz. Chapter Three: Glimpses. The "vital force" and animal magnetism; Reichenbach's "odic force"; Wilhelm Reich; Precognition; J. B. Priestley; J. W. Dunne; Eternal recurrence; Experiences of mystical consciousness; The seventh degree of concentration; The pineal eye; Serotonin, the Faculty X hormone; Development of life on Earth; The need for challenge and crisis. "Man's future lies in the cultivation of Faculty X."

COMMENTS: Wilson's most important work since the Outsider Cycle. Faculty X, "the latent power that human beings possess to reach beyond the present," is the thread that links together this massive peregrination of the occult. Viewed simply as a reference source for its subject, it rates alongside some of the classics in the field. But *The Occult* goes further than merely presenting supernatural "evidence." Part Three, Chapter Three, "Glimpses," points the way to a new stage in the evolution of mankind, presented with Wilson's usual optimism and zeal.

SECONDARY SOURCES AND REVIEWS:

1. Adams, Phoebe. *Atlantic* 229 (Jan., 1972): 96.
2. Bendau, p. 52-53.
3. Bergström—mentioned throughout.
4. *Booklist* 68 (Feb. 15, 1972): 470.
5. *Books & Bookmen* 20 (Jan., 1975): 81.
6. Byatt, A. S. *Times* (Oct. 21, 1971): 12. [second review]

7. *Choice* 9 (Apr., 1972): 200.
8. Clare, John. "Colin Wilson Tackles 'Faculty X,' So Fateful for Man," in *Times* (Oct. 20, 1971): 4.
9. *Economist* 241 (Oct. 6, 1971): R22.
10. Galbreath, R. *American Society of Psychical Research Journal* 69 (Jan., 1975): 84-91.
11. *Guardian Weekly* 105 (Dec. 16, 1971): 22.
12. *Kirkus Reviews* 39 (Sept. 1, 1971): 1005.
13. *Life* 71 (Dec. 31, 1971): 25.
14. Lima, Robert. *Saturday Review of Literature* 55 (Jan. 15, 1972): 48.
15. Needleman, Jacob. *Commonweal* 96 (Apr. 21, 1973): 173.
16. Oates, Joyce Carol. *American Poetry Review* 2 (Jan./Feb., 1973): 8-9.
17. *Observer* (Oct. 17, 1971): 33.
18. *Publishers Weekly* 200 (Sept. 27, 1971): 64.
19. *Publishers Weekly* 203 (Jan. 8, 1973): 66.
20. Rees, Gorownwy. "Gurus Galore." *Encounter* 39 (Aug., 1972): 56-58.
21. *Spectator* 227 (Nov. 6, 1971): 654.
22. Stanford, Derek. *Scotsman* (Oct. 9, 1971): . .
23. *Times Literary Supplement* (Nov. 26, 1971): 1471.
24. Walton, Alan Hull. "Wilson's Occult." *Books & Bookmen* 17 (Dec., 1971): 50-51.
25. Weigel, p. 124-126.
26. West, R. H. *Review of Politics* 37 (Oct., 1975): 547-556.

A32. **L'Amour: The Ways of Love.** New York: Crown Publishers, 1972, unpaged, cloth. [sex manual]

No dedication or introductory quotation. The book measures 21 x 26 cm.

COMMENTS: Wilson's text has been matched with 70 too-tastefully posed color photographs by Piero Rinaldi, of a nude couple supposedly making love. According to the backcover blurb, this is "a photographic celebration of love—a joyful, abandoned tribute to the physical union between the sexes." The text is unmistakably Wilson's, with quotations from Blake, Yeats, Lawrence, Brooke, Whitman, Kazantzakis, and Shaw, and with references to Powys, Hemingway, Lindsay, etc. The message is there—"...man possesses powers that he does not yet understand"—but somehow text and illustrations do not quite fuse together successfully. Both Bendau and Weigel tactfully ignore the book's existence.

A33. **New Pathways in Psychology: Maslow and the Post-Freudian Revolution.** London: Victor Gollancz, 1972, 288 p., cloth. [psychology and biography]

b. New York: Taplinger Publishing Co., 1972, 288 p., cloth.
c. New York: A Mentor Book, New American Library, 1974, 268 p., paper.
d. London: Victor Gollancz, 1979, 288 p., paper.
e. as: *Nuevos Derroteros en Psicología: Maslow y la Revolución Postfreudiana.* México: Editorial Diana, 1979, 325 p., cloth (?). [Spanish]
f. as: *Shiko Taiken.* Tokyo: Kawade Shobo Shinsha, 1979, 332 p., cloth (?). Translated by Yura Kimiyoshi and Yomoda Goki. [Japanese]
g. as: *Van Frend Naar Maslow.* Rotterdam: Lemniscaat, n.d., 287 p., cloth (?). Translated by W. van Broekhoven. [Dutch]
h. as: *Nya Fragestailningar Inom Psykologin.* Staffanstorp: Cavefords, n.d., 317 p., cloth (?). Translated by Estrid Fenggren. [Swedish]
i. as: "Personal Notes on Maslow (*New Pathways in Psychology*)," in *The Essential Colin Wilson.* London: Harrap, 1985, cloth, p. 62-83. A reprint of a section from this volume, collected into a volume consisting largely of excerpts from Colin Wilson books.

Dedication: "For Bertha Maslow." No introductory quotation. Includes a selected bibliography and an excellent 12-page index.

ANALYTICAL TABLE OF CONTENTS:
Introductory: Personal notes on Maslow. "Peak experience"; "The robot"; "The St. Neot Margin"; Psychology of the self-image.
PART ONE. Chapter One: The age of machinery. Descartes; Thomas Hobbes; David Hume and free will; James and John Stuart Mill; Hermann Lotze. Chapter Two: Towards a psychology of the will. Franz Brentano and intentionality; Edmund Husserl; The transcendental ego; William James and pragmatism; "How can I become more awake?"; A summary of James' ideas. Chapter Three: Freud and after. Sigmund Freud; The sexual theory; Alfred Adler; Carl G. Jung; Jung's quarrel with Freud; Archetypes; Introvert and extrovert; Otto Rank; Gestalt psychology.

PART TWO. Chapter Four: Maslow: a biographical sketch. Chapter Five: Higher ceilings for human nature. Early work; The study of healthy people; Sexuality and dominance; The "Hierarchy of Needs"; Self actualization; Peak experiences; "Eupsychian Management"—theory "Z"; Summary of Maslow's achievement.

PART THREE. Chapter Six: Where now? Viktor Frankl; Ludwig Binswanger; Georges Gurdjieff; Roberto Assagioli; Rollo May and R. D. Laing; Existential psychology; "[Man's] mental being must be understood as something essentially dynamic, forward flowing..."; William Glasser's "reality therapy"; Attitude and mental health; Dominant 5%; A. E. van Vogt's "right man"; A general phenomenology of mental health; Boredom; Neurosis and schizophrenia; "The central need, at the moment, is to develop a psychology of man's higher consciousness..."; "Preparedness"; The web of consciousness; "Human consciousness operates at too low a pressure for efficiency"; Self image and peak experiences; Intentionality.

COMMENTS: A very readable book on a difficult subject. Wilson and Maslow became acquainted in 1959 after the latter had read *The Stature of Man*. They remained friends until Maslow's death in June of 1970. The biographical chapter was made possible by Maslow supplying Wilson with several taped interviews. Quotations in the book are often transcribed verbatim from these tapes.

SECONDARY SOURCES AND REVIEWS:

1. Bendau, p. 53-55.
2. *Books & Bookmen* 17 (July, 1972): 50.
3. *British Book News* (July, 1972): 551.
4. *Choice* 10 (May, 1973): 537.
5. Dennis, Nigel. "Emphasise the Positive," in *Sunday Telegraph* (May 14, 1972): .
6. Gordon, James S. *New York Times Book Review* (Jan. 28, 1973): 2-3.
7. Kalisch, B. J. *Library Journal* 97 (Nov. 15, 1972): 3720.
8. *London Magazine* 12 (1972): 145.
9. *Observer* (May 7, 1972): 37.
10. *Publishers Weekly* 202 (July 10, 1972): 43.
11. Ryecroft, Charles. "Still Outside," in *Spectator* 228 (May 27, 1972): 818-819. A letter responding to this review appeared in the June 17, 1972 issue, p. 948.
12. Storr, Anthony. *Sunday Times* (May 14, 1972): 39.
13. Weigel, p. 133-135.

A34. **Order of Assassins: The Psychology of Murder.** London: Rupert Hart-Davis, 1972, 242 p., cloth. [sociology]

b. as: *La Filosofia degli Assassini.* Milano: Longanesi, 1974, 320 p., cloth (?). Translated by Sem Schlumper. [Italian]
c. St. Albans: Panther Books, 1975, 266 p., paper.
d. as: *Los Asesinos: Historia y Psicología del Homicidio.* Barcelona: Luis de Caralt, 1976, 278 p., cloth (?). Translated by Lena J. Poole. [Spanish]
e. as: *Etre Assassin.* Paris: A. Moreau, 1977, 369 p., cloth (?). Translated by Claudie Herrens. [French]
f. as: *Junsui Satsujin Sha No Sekai.* Tokyo: Shinchosha, n.d., 273 p., cloth (?). Translated by Yasuo Nakamura. [Japanese]

Dedication: "For Andrew Crawshaw." No introductory quotation or index. Includes a bibliography and bibliographical notes.

ANALYTICAL TABLE OF CONTENTS:
Introduction: Assassination, "murder committed for its own sake." Chapter One: Creatures of nightmare. The order of assassins of Persia, the first murderers for political gain; Assassination as a political weapon; The thugs of India, descendants of the assassins; Thug methods and ceremonies; Origin of sadism; Dualism; Kurten; Jack the Ripper; Examples of assassination. Chapter Two: The philosophy of the will. The difference between assassination and murder; Nietzsche's insight; The dominant 5%; Sexual dominance; Sadism as defiant self-assertion; Wilson's "self image" psychology; Lindsay's *Arcturus* and sexual dominance; Evertsz, the Dominican assassin; De Sade. Chapter Three: Pornography and the law of diminishing returns. Victorian pornography; *The Pearl*; *My Secret Life*; Apollinaire; *The Story of O*; The law of frustration; Increased sadism in pornography; The desire to disgust. Chapter Four: "Magical" thinking. Sartre and his theories of emotions as magic; Sex crime and motiveless murder; Jack the Ripper; Christie; Ed Gein; Evolutionary blockage. Chapter Five: The right man. Self-esteem and self-assertion murders; The "zodiac" murders; van Vogt's "violent man" theory; Compulsive need to be in the right; The changing patterns of murder; The Krays and Richardsons; Raymond Morris and Norman Collins. Chapter Six: Murder and romanticism. Change from economic murders to sexual murders during second half of the twentieth century; Vandalism; Lovecraft; Beauty starvation; Boredom as a

motive for murder; The Moors murder case. Chapter Seven: The Dostoyevskian synthesis. The need for adventure; Dostoyevsky and the need for violence; Displacement activity; Stavrogin in The Possessed; Svidrigailov in Crime and Punishment; Charles Manson; The Beat generation. Chapter Eight: The passive fallacy. Boredom; Freud's theory of the death instinct; Gorky; Gide and Sartre; The age of defeat; The new pessimism. Chapter Nine: The way forward. Maslow's industrial psychology; Crime due to "faulty blocking"; Peak experiences; Faculty X. Appendix: The new Ripper theory. Stowell's theory of the Duke of Clarence as the Ripper; arguments against, and more likely candidates.

COMMENTS: Order completes Wilson's murder trilogy, which began with *The Encyclopedia of Murder* (A6), and was followed by *The Casebook of Murder* (A22). The first was intended to be a basic reference book on the subject, the second a sociological study, and this volume a psychology of murder. Never published in the United States.

SECONDARY SOURCES AND REVIEWS:

1. Bendau, p. 53-54.
2. *British Book News* (Jan., 1973): 27.
3. Conford, Philip. *Spectator* 229 (Oct. 7, 1972): 546.
4. *Observer* (Oct. 22, 1972): 36.
5. *Times* (Oct. 19, 1972): 10.
6. *Times Literary Supplement* (Dec. 8, 1972): 1507.
7. Weigel, p. 116-117.

A35. **Strange Powers.** London: Latimer New Directions, 1973, 130 p., cloth. [occult]

b. New York: Random House, 1975, 146 p., cloth.
c. New York: Vintage Books, 1976, 163 p., paper.
d. London: Abacus, 1975, 126 p., paper.
db. London: Abacus, 1977, 160 p., paper.
e. as: *Sannin No Chonoryoku-sha No Hanashi.* Tokyo: Shinchosha, n.d., 200 p., cloth (?). Translated by Yasuo Nakamura. [Japanese]

Dedication: "To the memory of Tom Lethbridge" (see the last paragraph of the introduction). No introductory quotation, index, or bibliography.

ANALYTICAL TABLE OF CONTENTS:
Introduction. The end of scientific determinism; The occult revival; Faculty X. Chapter One: Robert Leftwich. A sales manager who developed powers of thought transference, astral projection, ESP, dowsing, etc.; Believes anyone can develop such powers. Chapter Two: Mrs. Eunice Beattie. A retired nurse and devoted family-woman who has powers of automatic writing; Also able to make inner voyages without the aid of drugs. Chapter Three: Dr. Arthur Guirdham. The incredible relationship between Dr. Guirdham and the Cathars, a thirteenth-century French religious sect—if true, Guirdham's case establishes reincarnation as a fact.

COMMENTS: Wilson explains in the introduction that he came across these three people after writing *The Occult*, and thought them important enough to warrant a slim volume to themselves. "...[They seemed] to confirm my supposition that unusual powers may be a kind of by-product of complete 'normality'..." Serialized in *Gnostica* magazine during 1974.

SECONDARY SOURCES AND REVIEWS:

1. Bagby, J. S. *Library Journal* 101 (Mar. 15, 1976): 823.
2. Bendau, p. 56.
3. *Booklist* 74 (July 15, 1978): 1761.
4. *Books & Bookmen* 19 (Mar., 1974): 78.
5. Dennis, Nigel. *Sunday Telegraph* (Jan. 29, 1974):   .
6. *Kirkus Reviews* 42 (Dec. 1, 1974): 1294.
7. Leader, Mary. "Faculty X—3 Case Studies," in Milwaukee Journal (Mar. 30, 1975):   .
8. Macari, Joy. *School Library Journal* 22 (Apr., 1976): 98.
9. *Observer* (Feb. 24, 1974): 33.
10. *Publishers Weekly* 207 (Jan. 6, 1975): 54.
11. Richardson, Boris. "Spirit Guides." *New Statesman* 87 (Feb. 15, 1974): 228.
12. *Times Educational Supplement* (Feb. 1, 1974): 25.
13. *Times Literary Supplement* (Apr. 26, 1974): 456.

A36. **Tree by Tolkien.** London: Covent Garden Press, INCA Books, 1973, 20 p., paper. [literary criticism]

   b. Santa Barbara, CA: Capra Press, 1974, 47 p., paper.
   c. London: Village Press, 1974, 30 p., paper.

No dedication, introductory quotation, or index.

ANALYTICAL TABLE OF CONTENTS:
Introduction. Wilson attempts to write to Tolkien; Encounters Tolkien's solicitor; Interview refused; Reasons for Tolkien's popularity in the Sixties. Tree by Tolkien. W. H. Auden and *The Lord of the Rings*; The Tolkien "club"; Wilson and *The Lord of the Rings*; Edmund Wilson's attack on Tolkien; Possible influences: Chesterton, Yeats; *Smith of Wootton Major* considered; Belloc's *Path to Rome*; Farnol's *The Broad Highway* compared; Tolkien's early work; Tolkien and T. S. Eliot's *The Waste Land*; *Leaf by Niggle* considered; The artist and society; *The Hobbit* and *The Lord of the Rings* considered. "Purely as an imaginary travel book, *The Lord of the Rings* is a very remarkable work." Tolkien's appeal explained; a final analysis: "...it lacks that final cutting edge of moral perception and seriousness. It is a fine book but it does not belong in the first rank."

COMMENTS: The 1974 editions contain a new introduction by Wilson. See also the small section on Tolkien in *The Strength to Dream*.

SECONDARY SOURCES AND REVIEWS:

1. Bendau, p. 55.

A37. **A Book of Booze.** London: Victor Gollancz, 1974, 207 p., cloth. [wine]

b. as: *Waga Sake No Sanka*. Tokyo: Tokuma Shoten, n.d., 326 p., cloth (?). Translated by Tamura Ryuichi. [Japanese]

Dedication: "For Paul Griffiths." No introductory quotation. Includes a two-page bibliography, and a nine-page index.

ANALYTICAL TABLE OF CONTENTS:
Introduction: The poetry of wine. Wilson and wine; Writers and alcoholism: Scott Fitzgerald, Hemingway, and Joyce; Personality change under wine; Heightened consciousness. Chapter One: On the antiquity of wine. How was wine invented?; A history from the earliest times to "The Age of Connoisseurs." Chapter Two: France: The world's vineyard. Burgundy; Bordeaux; Champagne. Chapter Three: Germany, Italy, Spain, and Portugal. Chapter Four: Beer and spirits. Mead, beer, whisky, brandy, and other spirits; What is proof?

Chapter Five: In praise of pubs. The English pub, with particular reference to Cornwall; Argument for and against teetotalism; Abraham Maslow on alcoholism; Wine and human evolution.

COMMENTS: A very personal book, but full of information and fascinating anecdotes.

SECONDARY SOURCES AND REVIEWS:

1. *Hibernia* [Dublin] (Jan. 10, 1975): .
2. Huntley, Walter. *Liverpool Daily Post* (Nov. 9, 1974): .
3. *Observer* (Dec. 22, 1974): 22.
4. *Times* (Nov. 28, 1974): 7.

A38.　**Hermann Hesse.** London: Village Press, 1974, 43 p., paper. [literary criticism]

No dedication, introductory quotation, or index; a Hesse bibliography is included, however. See also *Hesse—Reich—Borges* (A39).

ANALYTICAL TABLE OF CONTENTS:
　　The Hesse revival; Wilson and Hesse; Early biographical details; *Peter Camenzind* and Gottfried Keller's *Green Heinrich*; Hesse's marriage; *The Prodigy*; *Gertrude*; *Rosshalde*; and *Knulp*; Philosophy of the open road; Hesse and World War I; *Journey to the East*; Hesse and Gurdjieff contrasted; *Demian*; *Siddartha*; *Steppenwolf*; *Narziss and Goldmund*; Hesse and sex; *The Glass Bead Game*; Hesse and Thomas Mann compared and contrasted; An advocation of existential criticism; Hesse's failure.

COMMENTS: Wilson seems to have been at least partially responsible for the modern Hesse revival: his *Outsider* contained the first lengthy assessment of the German author published in English. Readers should refer to this book for a more detailed discussion of Hesse's later novels, particularly *Steppenwolf*. A fuller explanation of "existential criticism" can be found in *Eagle and Earwig*, Chapter Two, and in *The Strength to Dream*, Chapter Seven.

SECONDARY SOURCES AND REVIEWS:

1. Bendau, p. 55-56.

A39. **Hesse—Reich—Borges: Three Essays.** Philadelphia: Leaves of Grass Press, 1974, 78 p., paper. [literary criticism]

No dedication, introductory quotation, index, or bibliography. Published in England as three separate monographs (see A38, A40, and A44).

COMMENTS: This edition contains an autobiographical introduction concerning Wilson's discovery of Hesse's works, via a remarkable man named Alfred Reynolds. For the full story, see Wilson's essay, "On the Bridge: A Memoir of the Fifties," printed in *Encounter*, Vol. 14.

SECONDARY SOURCES AND REVIEWS:

1. Bendau, p. 55-56.

A40. **Jorge Luis Borges.** London: Village Press, 1974, 12 p., paper. [literary criticism]

No dedication, introductory quotation, index, or bibliography. Collected in *Hesse—Reich—Borges* (A39). Published in an odd size, 30 x 14 cm.

ANALYTICAL TABLE OF CONTENTS: Short biography; Initial impressions of *Labyrinths*; Borges' way of seeing the world; Criticism of his work; "Borges is not a great writer because he is not a mature writer..."; Classed with Nabokov; J. C. Powys and Charles Fort.

SECONDARY SOURCES AND REVIEWS:

1. Bendau, p. 56.

A41. **Ken Russell: A Director in Search of a Hero.** London: Intergroup Publishing, 1974, 71 p., paper. [film criticism and biography]

No dedication, introductory quotation, or index. Contains filmography, plus numerous photographs and stills.

ANALYTICAL TABLE OF CONTENTS: "He is the most controversial film director in the world at the moment—perhaps the most controversial there has ever been." The general reaction to Russell's films; Wilson and *The Boyfriend*; Impressions of *The Music Lovers* and *The Devils*; The theme of Russell's work; The search for a hero; Wilson interviews Russell for Westward Television; Short biography; The Monitor films; *Savage Messiah*; Plans for future films.

COMMENTS: Later reprinted in *The Sunday Times*.

A42. **The Return of the Lloigor.** London: Village Press, 1974, 60 p., paper. [story]

b. as: *Roiga No Fukkatsu.* Tokyo: Hayakawa Shobo, 1977, 167 p., cloth (?). Translated by Dan Seiji. [Japanese]

No dedication or introductory quotation.

COMMENTS: This book is a revised edition of a story which first appeared in the anthology, *Tales of the Cthulhu Mythos*, edited by August Derleth, and published by Arkham House as a tribute to H. P. Lovecraft's imaginative genius. Paul Dunbar Lang, in the course of his investigations into a medieval manuscript, discovers curious references to the *Necronomicon*, an ancient magical sourcebook mentioned in Lovecraft's stories. His further investigations lead him to a remote spot in Wales, where he learns more about the Cthulhu Mythos than he ever wanted to know. See also the shorter version (B11).

A43. **The Schoolgirl Murder Case.** London: Hart-Davis, MacGibbon, 1974, 200 p., cloth. [novel]

b. New York: Crown Publishers, 1974, 211 p., cloth.
c. London: Thriller Book Club, 1975, 200 p., cloth.
d. St. Albans: Panther Books, 1976, 205 p., paper.
e. Toronto, New York: Bantam Books, 1976, 243 p., paper.
f. as: *El Caso de la Colegiala Asesinada.* Barcelona: Editorial Noguer, 1976, 245 p., cloth. Translated by Enrique de Obregon. [Spanish]
g. as: *Meisje Vermoord.* Aartselarr, Belgium and Utrecht: A. W. Bruna, 1978, 223 p., cloth (?). Translated by Peter van Dijk. [Dutch]
h. as: *Sukura Garu Satsujin Jiken.* Tokyo: Shinchosha, 1978, 224 p., cloth (?). Translated by Takami Hiroshi. [Japanese]
i. Chicago: Academy Chicago, 1982, 205 p., paper.

j.　as:　*Alles für die Kundschaft*.　München:　Goldmann, n.d., 152 p., cloth (?).　Translated by Wulf Berger.　[German]

Dedication:　"For Don Rumbelow."　No introductory quotation.

COMMENTS:　Something new from Wilson:　a more-or-less straightforward whodunit, the first of a dozen such books originally planned by the author (just one more has appeared, however, *The Janus Murder Case* [A68], and no more will be written).　The detective here is Chief Inspector Saltfleet, who is facing the usual baffling mystery.　Judged purely on the basis of the rules governing the police procedure novel, it works very well indeed.　But this is definitely not the usual Colin Wilson novel.　As Tredell writes:　"...the novel has a kind of anonymity:　it might be by anyone."　Wilson does leave a few clues to his identity lying around, particularly at the end, when Saltfleet is asked:　"...it's a lousy world.　Don't you agree?"　The Chief Inspector replies:　"Well no.　That's what puzzles me, I suppose.　I don't think so."

SECONDARY SOURCES AND REVIEWS:

1. *AB Bookman's Weekly* 54 (Dec. 9, 1974):　2499.
2. Adams, Phoebe.　*Atlantic* 234 (July, 1974):　100.
3. Bendau, p. 57.
4. Bergström, p. 88-89.
5. "Callendar, Newgate."　*New York Times Book Review* (July 21, 1974):　18.
6. Datchery, Dick.　*Critic* 33 (Oct., 1974):　92.
7. Grant, Violet.　*Daily Telegraph* (July 25, 1974):　.
8. *Kirkus Reviews* 42 (Apr. 15, 1974):　450.
9. *New Yorker* 50 (Sept. 16, 1974):　18.
10. *Observer* (June 2, 1974):　32.
11. *Publishers Weekly* 205 (Apr. 29, 1974):　42.
12. *Publishers Weekly* 222 (Aug. 20, 1982):　70.
13. *Punch* 266 (May 29, 1974):　922.
14. *Sunday Times*. (May 5, 1976):　38.
15. *Times* (Apr. 3, 1976):　11.
16. *Times Literary Supplement* (June 14, 1974):　629.
17. Tredell, p. 139-140.
18. Veit, H. C.　*Library Journal* 99 (July, 1974):　1852.
19. *Washington Post Book World* 8 (June 16, 1974):　4.
20. Weigel, p. 107-108.

A44. **Wilhelm Reich.** London: Village Press, 1974, 11 p., paper. [biography]

No dedication, introductory quotation, index, or bibliography. Collected in *Hesse—Reich—Borges* (A39).

ANALYTICAL TABLE OF CONTENTS:
The Reich revival; Some early biographical notes; Meeting with Freud; Puritanical response to his *Function of the Orgasm*; Reich and *Peer Gynt*; Joins the Austrian Socialist Party; Quarrel with Freud; Illness; *The Mass Psychology of Fascism*; Expelled from Communist Party; *Character Analysis*; Settles in America; Orgone energy; *Listen, Little Man!*; Problems with the authorities; Reich's standing today; *Adamenko*; Reichenbach and the "odic force"; Reich's achievements summarized.

COMMENTS: First published as an article in *Books & Bookmen*, this pamphlet formed the bare outline for Wilson's later book, *The Quest for Wilhelm Reich*.

SECONDARY SOURCES AND REVIEWS:

1. Bendau, p. 55-56.

A45. **The Craft of the Novel.** London: Victor Gollancz, 1975, 256 p., cloth. [literary criticism]

b. as: *Shosetsu No Tameni.* Tokyo: Kinokuniya Shoten, 1977, 350 p., cloth (?). Translated by Susuki Kenzo. [Japanese]
c. Bath, Avon: Ashgrove Press, 1986, 256 p., paper.
d. Salem, NH: Salem House, 1986, 256 p., paper.

Dedication: "For Roald Dahl, that splendid craftsman." No introductory quotation. Includes a lengthy bibliography, and a nine-page index compiled by H. E. Crowe.

ANALYTICAL TABLE OF CONTENTS:
Chapter One: The craft of creation. Wilson's experiences teaching "creative writing"; Shaw's search for a hero; Self image. Chapter Two: The mind-moulders. Richardson's *Pamela* and its impact; Rousseau's *Julie*; Goethe's *Sorrows of Young Werther*; Schiller's *Robbers*; A new dimension in human freedom. Chapter Three: Decline and fall. From romanticism to realism; Balzac's *Comédie Humaine*; Flaubert's *Madame Bovary*; Zola and Maupassant; The problem of freedom; The rise and

fall of the Russian novel. Chapter Four: As for living... The novel as substitute for experience; The novel as a form of "thought experiment"; The narrowness of everyday consciousness; The need for a "wider" view; Saki's *Unbearable Bassington*; The decline of D. H. Lawrence. Chapter Five: The formula for success. The build-up and release of tension; Meredith's *Egoist*; Jane Austen's *Persuasion*; Sartre's *Roads to Freedom*; Low flyers and high flyers; Hofmannsthal's *The Difficult Man*; Connell's *The Chinese Room*. Chapter Six: The varieties of wish-fulfillment. Jeffery Farnol's *Broad Highway*; James Thurber's *Secret Life of Walter Mitty*; Romain Gary's *Roots of Heaven*; The "hierarchy of needs"; Arnold Bennett; H. G. Wells; Daphne du Maurier's *Rebecca*; Kinsley Amis' *Lucky Jim* and John Braine's *Room at the Top*. Chapter Seven: Experiments. James Joyce, with particular reference to *Ulysses*; Robert Musil's *Man without Qualities*; John Dos Passos' *Manhattan Transfer*; Ernest Hemingway. Chapter Eight: Ideas. A. E. van Vogt's "right man" theory; The importance of exploring the implications of a situation; The need for wider consciousness; John Cowper Powys' *Glastonbury Romance*. "The novelist's task is a spiritual one: to free himself from narrowness, to achieve 'wide angle' vision, and to convey this to his readers." Chapter Nine: Structure and technique. The technique of contrast; The "cymbal effect"; The objective correlative; Henry James; The rise and decline of the novel. Chapter Ten: Limits. Problems of "photographic realism"; James Joyce; Violence; William Faulkner; The failure of violence; The novel as a balance of forces; Samuel Beckett. Chapter Eleven: Fantasy and new directions. Serious novels and bestsellers; The fantasy revival; Tolkien's *Lord of the Rings*; Mervyn Peake's *Titus Trilogy*; The work of David Lindsay. Chapter Twelve: Conclusion. Wilson's own novels; The novel and human evolution.

COMMENTS: An examination of novels and novelists from the viewpoint of teaching creative writing. Typically positive, readable, and entertaining, although it has been criticized, mainly by Mike Bygrave, for concentrating overmuch on literary criticism, and not enough on the practical side of creative writing.

SECONDARY SOURCES AND REVIEWS:

1. *Books & Bookmen* (Feb., 1976): 43.
2. *British Book News* (Jan., 1976): 57.
3. Bygrave, Mike. *Times Education Supplement* (Dec. 12, 1975): 22.

4. De'ath, Wilfred. *Hampstead & Highgate Express* (Oct. 10, 1975): .
5. Hughes, David. *New Fiction Magazine* no. 4 (July, 1975): 1.
6. *Sunday Times* (Oct. 12, 1975): 38.
7. *Times Literary Supplement* (Dec. 12, 1975): 22.

A46. **Mysterious Powers.** London: Aldus Books/Jupiter Books, 1975, 142 p., cloth. Bound with *Spirits and Spirit Worlds*, by Roy Stemman (which is separately paginated). [occult]

b. New York: Danbury Press, 1975, 142 p., cloth.
c. as: *They Had Strange Powers.* Garden City, NY: Doubleday & Co., 1975, 142 p., cloth.
d. as: *Seres con Poderes Ocultos.* Barcelona: Editorial Noguer, 1976, 144 p., cloth. Translated by Martha Pessarradona. [Spanish]
e. as: *Facolto Paranormali.* Milano: RM, 1976, 142 p., cloth (?). Translated by Maria Rosa Parigi. [Italian]
f. as: *Kyoi No Chonoryukusha Tachi.* Tokyo: Gailushu Kenkyusha, 1976, 142 p., cloth (?). Translated by Kimura Ichiro. [Japanese]

No dedication, introductory quotations, index, or bibliography.

ANALYTICAL TABLE OF CONTENTS:
Chapter One: Wild talents. Strangely gifted people: Geller and others. Chapter Two: The will to power. The urge for mastery and the development of psychic powers through the ages. Chapter Three: Wonderworkers. An East-West study. Chapter Four: The magicians. Mesmer; Cabalism; Agrippa; Paracelsus; etc. Chapter Five: Magic at work. Development of ritual magic. Chapter Six: The great magical revival. Golden Dawn; Crowley; etc. Chapter Seven: Three modern magicians. Rasputin; Gurdjieff; Dion Fortune. Chapter Eight: They live among us. Psychic phenomena today: Leftwich, Geller, etc.

COMMENTS: Another profusely and colorfully illustrated spin-off from Wilson's book, *The Occult.* See also *Mysteries of the Mind* (A53).

SECONDARY SOURCES AND REVIEWS:

1. Bagby, Jeanne S. *Library Journal* 101 (Mar. 15, 1976): 823.
2. Bendau, p. 56-57.
3. *Booklist* 74 (July 15, 1978): 1761-1762.
4. *British Book News* (Mar., 1976): 168.
5. Macari, Joy. *School Library Journal* 22 (Apr. 1976): 98.

A47. **The Unexplained.** Lake Oswego, OR: Lost Pleiade Press, 1975, 65 p., cloth. [occult]

No dedication, introductory quotation, index, or bibliography.

ANALYTICAL TABLE OF CONTENTS:
Chapter One: Mysteries of the mind. "Thought pressure"; Uri Geller. Chapter Two: Voyage to inner space. Our habitual "speed reading" of life; Slowing down: the "vision of increasing ranges of distant fact." Chapter Three: Unknown faculties.   Plant sensitivity; Homing instinct in animals; Dowsing; Prophecy; Faculty X. Chapter Four: Spirits, ghosts, and demons. The astral body; The "aura" or life-field; T. C. Lethbridge's ghost theory; Poltergeists. Chapter Five: Some conclusions. The development of "Faculty X."

COMMENTS: A drastically abridged version of *The Occult*, edited down by Robert Durand and Roberta Dyer.

SECONDARY SOURCES AND REVIEWS:

1. Bendau, p. 56.

A48. **Enigmas and Mysteries.** London: Aldus Books, 1976, 144 p., cloth. [occult]

b. New York: Danbury Press, 1976, 144 p., cloth.
c. Garden City, NY: Doubleday & Co., 1976, 144 p., cloth.
d. as: *Realtà Inesplicabili.* Milano: RM, 1977, 142 p., cloth (?). Translated by Irene Z. Bertolotti. [Italian]
e. as: *Shinpi To Kaiki.* Tokyo: Gakushu Kenkyusha, 1977, 143 p., cloth (?). Translated by Yasuda Yohei. [Japanese]

No dedication, introductory quotation, index, or bibliography.

ANALYTICAL TABLE OF CONTENTS:
Chapter One: Disturbing contacts. Some peculiar, unexplained happenings. Chapter Two: Strange disappearances. People who have vanished without a trace. Chapter Three: Devil's graveyards. Areas of the ocean where disasters often occur. Chapter Four: The road to the fifth dimension. Techniques of dowsing. Chapter Five: Uninvited visitors. Monsters and UFOs. Chapter Six: Jinxes and curses. Objects and disasters. Chapter Seven: Secrets of the ancients. Ancient wisdom now misunderstood. Chapter Eight: Creatures from other worlds. Strange beings.

COMMENTS: Still another offshoot from *The Occult*, illustrated throughout with black-and-white and color drawings and photo graphs.

SECONDARY SOURCES AND REVIEWS:

1. *Booklist* 74 (July 15, 1978): 1761-1762.

A49. **The Geller Phenomenon.** London: Aldus Books, 1976, 144 p., cloth. [occult study and biography]

b. New York: Danbury Press, 1976, 143 p., cloth.
c. as: *Rätsel von Geller*. Frankfurt: Lehmann, 1979, 92 p., cloth (?). Translated by Hans Theis. [German]

No dedication, introductory quotation, index, or bibliography. Illustrated throughout with black-and-white and color drawings and photographs.

ANALYTICAL TABLE OF CONTENTS:
Chapter One: The making of a mystic. Geller's early years. Chapter Two: The debunking. After international acclaim, accusations of fraud. Chapter Three: The scientists investigate. Laboratory experiments aimed towards a definition and explanation of Geller's powers. Chapter Four: Monsters from the subconscious. Examination of poltergeist activity similar to Geller's. Chapter Five: Getting to know Geller. Wilson meets Geller. Chapter Six: What does this all mean? "There are vast areas within the brain about which we know nothing."

SECONDARY SOURCES AND REVIEWS:

1. Holroyd, Stuart. "Curiouser and Curiouser," in *Books &
   Bookmen* 22 (July, 1977): 56.

A50. **The Space Vampires.** London: Hart-Davis, MacGibbon, 1976,
214 p., cloth. [novel]

b. New York: Random House, 1976, 214 p., cloth.
c. New York: Pocket Books, 1977, 220 p., paper.
d. London: Granada, Panther Books, 1977, 214 p., paper.
e. as: *Los Vampiros del Espacio.* Barcelona: Editorial Noguer,
   1977, 246 p., cloth. [Spanish]
f. as: *Uchu Banpaia.* Tokyo: Shinchosha, 1977, 412 p., cloth (?).
   Translated by Yasuo Nakamura. [Japanese]
g. as: *Les Vampires de l'Espace.* Paris: Albin Michel, 1978, 279
   p., cloth (?). [French]
h. as: *De Ruimtevampiers.* Haarlem: Gottmer, 1978, 200 p., cloth
   (?). Translated by Dolf Koning. [Dutch]
i. as: *Rymdens Demoner.* Stockholm: Bukad, 1978, 200 p., cloth
   (?). Translated by Ann Bjorkem. [Swedish]
j. as: *The Space Vampires, Filmed As Life Force.* London:
   Granada, 1985, 214 p., paper.
k. as: *Lifeforce.* New York: Warner Books, 1985, 220 p., paper.

Dedication: "For June O'Shea, my criminological adviser." No
introductory quotation.

COMMENTS: Captain Olof Carlsen, master of the spaceship
Hermes, discovers a derelict spacecraft floating near the aster-
oids. Upon investigating the interior of the craft, he and his
crew find a number of apparently lifeless, humanoid creatures,
and return with them to Earth. The aliens soon prove to be
very much alive, feeding on the life-force of their human victims, much as the conventional vampire draws blood from his
mesmerized prey. The rest of the novel concerns mankind's
efforts to stop this alien menace from sweeping the planet.
Concerning *Vampires* the critics differed widely. Bendau
writes: "[It] remains one of Wilson's most successful creations,
philosophical without being dull, a thoroughly entertaining fiction in every respect." Tredell, however, dismisses it as having
"...an anonymous quality: some of it might be a transcription
of an episode *of Star Trek.*" For Wilson's own comments, see
Science Fiction As Existentialism, p. 15-16. The book was
made into a movie in 1985 under the title *Lifeforce*, the first

of Wilson's novels to be filmed; the production received generally unfavorable notices.

SECONDARY SOURCES AND REVIEWS:

1. Bendau, p. 57-59.
2. Bergström, p. 88-89.
3. Geis, Richard E. *Science Fiction Review* no. 17 (May, 1976): 46.
4. Geis, Richard E. *Science Fiction Review* no. 21 (May, 1977): 52.
5. Hauptman, R. *Best Sellers* 36 (June, 1976): 75.
6. Justice, Keith L. *SF Booklog* no. 10 (July/Aug., 1976): 5.
7. *Kirkus Reviews* 44 (Jan. 15, 1976): 97.
8. Leiber, Fritz. *Fantastic Stories* 26 (June, 1977): 115.
9. MacPherson, W. *Science Fiction Review Monthly* no. 15 (May, 1976): 20.
10. Miller, D. *Booklist* 72 (June 1, 1976): 1394.
11. Napier, S. *Science Fiction Review* 14 (Nov., 1985): 39.
12. *Observer* (Dec. 5, 1976): 30.
13. *Publishers Weekly* 209 (Feb. 9, 1976): 96.
14. *Publishers Weekly* 211 (Jan. 31, 1977): 74.
15. Rottensteiner, Franz. *Quarber Merkur* no. 47 (Dec., 1977): 67-68 [German].
16. Ruebel, J. *Library Journal* 101 (May 1, 1976): 1146.
17. Smyser, Craig. *Houston Chronicle* (Apr. 4, 1976): .
18. *Times* (Nov. 11, 1976): 14.
19. Tredell, p. 140.
20. *Wall Street Journal* 187 (June 17, 1976): 14.
21. Weschcke, Carl L. *Gnostica* no. 41 (Feb./Mar., 1977): 90.

SELECTED REVIEWS OF THE FILM *LIFEFORCE*:

1. Johnstone, Iain. *Sunday Times* (Oct. 6, 1985): 38.
2. Petley, Julian. *Monthly Film Bulletin* 52 (Oct., 1985): 311-312.
3. Robinson, David. *Times* (Oct. 4, 1985): .

A51. **Colin Wilson's Men of Mystery.** London: W. H. Allen, 1977, 206 p., cloth. [occult anthology]

  ab. London: A Star Book, W. H. Allen, 1977, 206 p., paper.
  b. as: *Dark Dimensions: A Celebration of the Occult.* New York: Everest House, 1977, 236 p., cloth.

No dedication, introductory quotation, or index. Includes bibliography.

ANALYTICAL TABLE OF CONTENTS:
Introduction, by Colin Wilson. Chapter One: Rasputin, by Colin Wilson. Chapter Two: Gurdjieff, by Colin Wilson. Chapter Three: Helena Petrovna Blavatsky, by Christmas Humphreys. Chapter Four: Nikola Tesla, by Kit Pedler. Chapter Five: Aleister Crowley, Rest in ?, by Oliver Marlow Wilkinson. Chapter Six: Hellfire Dashwood, by Pat Silver and Jesse Lasky, Jr. Chapter Seven: Uri Geller, by Pat Silver and Jesse Lasky, Jr. Chapter Eight: Franz Anton Mesmer, by Peter Tompkins. Chapter Nine: Nostradamus, by Pat Silver and Jesse Lasky, Jr.

COMMENTS: Wilson's contributions are restatements of his earlier work. The book was planned originally as a television series intended to provide "an introduction to some of the puzzling psychic phenomena that have baffled and intrigued people from ancient to modern times." The series never materialized.

SECONDARY SOURCES AND REVIEWS:

1. *Choice* 16 (Mar., 1979): 62.
3. Gjettum, Pamela. *Library Journal* 103 (Sept. 1, 1978): 1644-1645.
4. Holroyd, Stuart. "Explorers of the Occult," in *Books & Bookmen* 23 (Feb., 1978): 50.
5. *Kirkus Reviews* 46 (July 1, 1978): 742.
6. *Publishers Weekly* 214 (July 3, 1978): 54.
7. Rowe, Dorothy. "Hazardous Environments," in *New Scientist* 77 (Jan. 26, 1978): 231-232.

A52. **Mysteries: An Investigation into the Occult, the Paranormal, and the Supernatural.** London: Hodder and Stoughton, 1978, 667 p., cloth. [occult]

b. New York: G. P. Putnam's Sons, 1978, 667 p., cloth. [no subtitle]
bb. New York: A Paragon Book, G. P. Putnam's Sons, 1980, 688 p., paper. [no subtitle]
c. London, New York: Granada, Panther Books, 1980, 667 p., paper.
d. as: "The Ladder of Selves (*Mysteries*)," in *The Essential Colin Wilson*. London: Harrap, 1985, cloth, p. 130-149. A reprint

of a section from this volume, collected into a volume consisting largely of excerpts from Colin Wilson books.

Dedication: "For Eddie Campbell, with affection." No introductory quotation. Includes index, extensive bibliography, and bibliographical notes.

ANALYTICAL TABLE OF CONTENTS:
Introduction: The ladder of selves. Wilson and "panic attacks"; The "schoolmistress effect"; Gurdjieff's power to transfer energy; The ladder of selves and paranormal phenomena; "All is well" feeling; Attempt at a comprehensive theory of the occult.
PART ONE. Chapter One: Ghosts, ghouls, and pendulums. Tom Lethbridge and dowsing; How to use the pendulum; Ghouls; Lethbridge's "field" theory of ghosts and ghouls; Sir Oliver Lodge's "tape recording" theory; Electrical theory of the paranormal; The pendulum and the afterlife; Summary of Lethbridge's work. Chapter Two: Giants and witches. Lethbridge and the Wandlebury Camp giant; Margaret Murray; Silbury Hill: Michael Dames' theory; The "old religion" in Cornwall; Are the stone megaliths storage batteries? Chapter Three: The path of the dragon. Lethbridge and Erich von Däniken; The latter's inaccuracies; Stonehenge; Robert Temple's Sirius Mystery; Alfred Watkins and ley lines; Guy Underwood; John Michell; The earth as a living being; Poltergeists and ley lines; More about Stonehenge: the theories of Alexander Thom and Gerald Hawkins. Chapter Four: The timeless zone. Dreams of the future; Lethbridge and J. W. Dunne; Levels of sleep; Rapid eye movements; Robert Monroe's out-of-body experiences and precognitive dreams; Can electrical fields aid telepathy?; W. E. Boyd and Peter Maddock.
PART TWO. Chapter One: The curious history of human stupidity. Van Vogt's "right man" theory; Science versus occultism and theology; Persecution of Giordano Bruno, Galileo, etc.; The evolution controversy: Cuvier, Lamarck, Darwin, etc.; Charles Fort and his ideas. Chapter Two: How many me's are there? Dual personality; Jung's first case; His poltergeist experiences; Multiple personality: Mary Reynolds, Doris Fischer, etc.; Wilder Penfield's discovery of "memory playback"; Pierre Janet and the nine levels of consciousness; The inhibition of personality. Chapter Three: In search of Faculty X. Levitation; The control of psi-power; Magic; Importance of will and imagination; Visualization; What is imagination?; Bruno on man's godlike powers; Modern pessimism; Consciousness is intentional. Chapter Four: The rediscovery of magic. Jung and

the collective unconscious; John Layard; Jung's technique of "active imagination"; Symbolism; The phases of the moon and their corresponding character types; H. P. Blavatsky and "multiple personality"; Completing the "partial mind." Chapter Five: Descent into the unconscious. Hypnosis; The mind's internal barriers; Techniques of "dream study"; Borderland between sleeping and waking; Swedenborg and dreams; Alexis Didier; George Russell and Aeons. Chapter Six: Revelations. Mysticism and reality; Drugs as a means of contacting the unconscious; The evolution of ideas; Retrocognition of the past: Miss Moberly and Miss Jourdain at Versailles; Jane O'Neill in Fotheringhay Church; How does perception work? Chapter Seven: Worlds beyond. Lucid dreams; Out-of-body experiences; "Odic force"; Psychometry; Kirlian photography; Acupuncture; The Kabbala as a psychological system. Chapter Eight: Ancient mysteries. Alchemy; Mary Ann South's Suggestive Inquiry; Jung and alchemy; The mandala symbol; The philosopher's stone as a search for integration. Chapter Nine: The great secret. Israel Regardie and Albert Riedel; The "vital essence" of minerals; Armand Barbault; Thomas Vaughan; Gurdjieff on alchemy; The transcendence of the personal; Matthew Manning and Uri Geller; The secret of the alchemists. Chapter Ten: Powers of evil? Has evil an objective existence?; Unlucky ships, jinxed cars, aircraft, etc.; Ghosts and poltergeists; Frustrated adolescents and poltergeist phenomena; Connection with ley lines; Powers of the mind: Thomas Castellan, Franz Walter, Crowley, Rasputin, Gurdjieff; Our hidden powers.

PART THREE. Chapter One: Evolution. Man: the god who has forgotten his own identity; What is wrong with Darwinism; Stan Gooch's theory of evolution; Charlotte Bach's sexual theory; The sleeping areas of the brain; The "robot"; The need for inner freedom; The Outsider as an evolutionary force. Chapter Two: Messages from space and time. Ted Owens, the PK man; Space intelligences; UFO sightings; Men in black; Andrija Puharich and Uri Geller; Phyllis Schlemmer and Tommy Wadkins; UFO contacts; Theories concerning UFO sightings; Spiritualism. Chapter Three: The mechanisms of enlightenment. The structure of the ladder of selves; Moving up and down the ladder; Mystical experiences; The right and left hemispheres of the brain; Raynor C. Johnson; The great reservoir of energy; Rodney Collins' *The Theory of Celestial Influence*; Karl Ernst Krafft and Michel Gauquelin; Gustav Fechner; Control of the robot: alertness. Chapter Four: Other dimensions. The fifth dimension: human freedom?; Charles Fort's investigations; Arthur Young's *Reflexive Universe*; Science and the paranormal; Death and dying; The problem of time; The trick of inducing "inner expansion"; The importance of "focusing"; The concept of the "feedback point"; The need for more consciousness; The "recycling" of evolutionary energy. Appendix: Electromagnetic induction of psi states, by Peter Maddock.

COMMENTS: A sequel to *The Occult* which attempts "to place the world of the 'unseen' in a scientific framework," and to point a way towards "a new stage in the history of the planet earth." Wilson begins with an account of the author's experiences when he came close to a nervous breakdown; his subsequent self-examination led to the discovery of a higher self which could take control in an internal emergency. But should we be able to call upon these higher selves at will, and if so, how? Wilson's answer, as always, is positive and encouraging. A refreshing antidote to the popular school of thought which sees no future for the human race.

SECONDARY SOURCES AND REVIEWS:

1. Benson-Gyles, Dick. "It's All in the Mind," in *Western Morning News* (Oct. 13, 1978): 7.
2. Bird, C. *Washington Post Book World* 12 (Dec. 24, 1978): E3.
3. *Choice* 16 (May, 1979): 372.
4. Dingwall, J. *British Book News* (Jan. 1, 1979): 20.
5. Hudnall, Clayton. *Best Sellers* 38 (Mar., 1979): 403.
6. *Illustrated London News* 266 (Oct., 1978): 121.
7. *Kirkus Reviews* 46 (Dec. 1, 1978): 1348.
8. Martin, Vernon. *Library Journal* 104 (Feb. 1, 1979): 410.
9. McNeil, Helen. "A Severed Head." *New Statesman* 96 (Dec. 22-29, 1978): 885.
10. Merchant, Norris. *Christian Century* 96 (July 4-11, 1979): 712-713.
11. *National Review* 31 (Nov. 9, 1979): 1448.
14. Pedlar, Kit. *New Scientist* 79 (Sept. 28, 1978): 956-957.
15. *Publishers Weekly* 214 (Nov. 6, 1978): 67.
16. *Publishers Weekly* 217 (Mar. 7, 1980): 88.
17. *Times* (Sept. 28, 1978): 8.
18. Walton, Alan Hull. "Colin Wilson's Magnum Opus." *Books & Bookmen* 24 (Mar., 1979): 41-43.
19. *Writer's Review* (Feb./Mar., 1979): 4.

A53. **Mysteries of the Mind,** by Colin Wilson and Stuart Holroyd. London: Aldus Books, 1978, 256 p., cloth. [occult]

No dedication or introductory quotation.

COMMENTS: Originally published as *Mysterious Powers*, by Colin Wilson, and *Minds without Boundaries*, by Stuart Holroyd. The text remains the same; however, some illustrations have been altered or moved.

A54. **Science Fiction As Existentialism.** Hayes, Middlesex: Bran's Head Books, 1978, 16 p., paper. [literary criticism]

b. as: "Science Fiction and Existentialism: A Personal View," in *Existentially Speaking: Essays on the Philosophy of Literature*, by Colin Wilson. San Bernardino, CA: The Borgo Press, 1989, cloth, p. 17-32. Published simultaneously in trade paperback. Slightly revised for this edition.

ANALYTICAL TABLE OF CONTENTS:
Wilson's rediscovery of science fiction in the 1960s; The development of the genre; The connection with existentialism. "The importance of S.F. lies in its attempt at objectivity—to convey an exciting and life-enhancing sense of the mystery of the universe..." H. G. Wells; Wilson's *The Mind Parasites* and *The Philosopher's Stone*; The subconscious inspiration for *The Space Vampires*. "...the real aim of S.F....is to serve as a catalyst in the evolution of a new human consciousness."

COMMENTS: The pamphlet was published as part of the Bran's Head Library of SF Criticism series, and provides interesting insights into Wilson's own thoughts on the writing of his three SF novels. No dedication or introductory quotation. See also: A93.

SECONDARY SOURCES AND REVIEWS:

1. Strick, Philip. "Metafictions from the Physical Sciences," in *Futures* 10 (Dec., 1978): 525-526.

A55. **The Haunted Man: The Strange Genius of David Lindsay.** The Milford Series: Popular Writers of Today, Vol. 20. San Bernardino, CA: The Borgo Press, 1979, 63 p., cloth. [literary criticism]

ab. San Bernardino, CA: The Borgo Press, 1979, 63 p., paper.

No dedication, introductory quotation, or index. Includes a brief bibliography of Lindsay's works.

ANALYTICAL TABLE OF CONTENTS:
Wilson's first impressions of Lindsay's work; *A Voyage to Arcturus*; Lindsay's basic idea of "another reality" or "two worlds"; The meaning of *Arcturus*; *The Haunted Woman*; Influenced by George MacDonald; *Sphinx*; *Devil's Tor*; Shaw's message and Lindsay's compared and contrasted; Lindsay's lack of an evolutionary vision; His pessimism; Are his "two worlds" really irreconcilable, or two intentional states of consciousness?; Brief biography.

COMMENTS: An expanded version of an essay that was first published in *Eagle and Earwig*, then revised as "Lindsay As Novelist and Mystic" for inclusion in *The Strange Genius of David Lindsay*. Wilson also writes at some length about Lindsay in *The Craft of the Novel*.

SECONDARY SOURCES AND REVIEWS:

1. *Choice* 16 (Dec., 1979): 1311.
2. *SFRA Newsletter* no. 76 (Nov., 1979): 2.
3. Weinstein, L. *Science Fiction Review* 10 (Summer, 1981): 51.
4. Wilgus, Neal. *Science Fiction Review* 9 (Feb., 1980): 37-38.
5. Wolfe, Gary K. *Science Fiction & Fantasy Book Review* 1 (Nov., 1979): 145.

A56. **The Book of Time**, edited by John Grant; Colin Wilson, Consultant Editor. Newton Abbot, Devon: Westbridge Books, 1980, 320 p, cloth. [science]

b. North Pomfret, VT: David & Charles, 1980, 320 p., cloth.

ANALYTICAL TABLE OF CONTENTS:
Chapter One: The history of time, by Roy Porter. Chapter Two: The moving earth in space, by Richard Knox. Chapter Three: From sundial to atomic clock, by Chris Morgan. Chapter Four: Bodytime, by E. W. J. Phipps. Chapter Five: Mutable time, by Iain Nicolson. Chapter Six: Measuring time past, by Brian John. Chapter Seven: Time in disarray, by Colin Wilson (see C239).

COMMENTS: Contains a three-page index, and selected bibliographies for each author. Numerous black-and-white illustrations help to break up the sometimes difficult text.

SECONDARY SOURCES AND REVIEWS:

1. Ghose, R. N. *Science Books & Films* 17 (Sept./Oct., 1981): 14-15.
2. Langford, David. *Vector* no. 98 (June, 1980): 25-26.
3. *Times Educational Supplement* (Sept. 12, 1980): 25.

A57. **Frankenstein's Castle—The Double Brain, Door to Wisdom.** Sevenoaks, Kent: Ashgrove Press, 1980, 128 p., paper. [psychology]

ab. Sevenoaks, Kent: Ashgrove Press, 1981, 128 p., cloth.
b. as: "The 'Other Mode' (*Frankenstein's Castle*)," in *The Essential Colin Wilson*. London: Harrap, 1985, cloth, p. 150-153. A reprint of a section from this volume, collected into a volume consisting largely of excerpts from Colin Wilson books.

Dedication: "For Tony Britton, with affection." No introductory quotation or index. Includes bibliographical footnotes.

ANALYTICAL TABLE OF CONTENTS:
Chapter One: The "other mode." Flashes of the "other mode" of consciousness; Roger W. Sperry's experiments; Maslow and "peak experiences"; The robot and the "doors of perception." Chapter Two: The riddle of the two selves. Man has two separate minds; Poltergeists and the right brain; The right brain controls our energy supply; Getting the right balance between the two halves; Split and multiple personality cases; Most human beings are only half awake; Stan Gooch and his "seat of the unconscious" theory. Chapter Three: More mysteries. Personality transference cases; "Levels" of personality; Is the left brain a villain?; Is the right brain a hero?; Faculty X; The left brain and the robot; How can we break through to a new evolutionary level? Chapter Four: Frankenstein's castle. Psychedelic drugs; The pineal gland; Dr. Julian Jaynes' theory of the "bicameral mind"; Left brain consciousness; Stress and its release; Biofeedback; Mystical experiences. "...this other mode of consciousness is not in any way remote from everyday consciousness." Chapter Five: The powers of the right. Thomson J. Hudson's *The Law of Psychic Phenomena*; The "objective" and "subjective" minds; The powers of the subjective mind.

Chapter Six: Clues. The importance of optimism; Raskolnikov and his "narrow ledge"; The "St. Neot Margin"; Further experiences of widening consciousness; Panic attacks; The instinct-robot alliance. Chapter Seven: Discoveries. Howard Miller and hypnosis; The "unit of pure thought"; Left-brain ego: controller of consciousness?; The hidden powers of the right—our "rightful resources"; The control of energy; The triple alliance of instinct, robot, and consciousness; Consciousness, the sleeping partner; Peak experiences—can we induce them at will?

COMMENTS: Intended more as a reaffirmation of Wilson's philosophy in light of recent discoveries about the split-brain than as a textbook of split-brain psychology. Anyone who has read Wilson's previous work will understand what a revelation these discoveries were to a writer whose life "has been dominated by a single obsession: a search for what I call 'the other mode' of consciousness." Thus, this little book is a kind of compendium of analogies, experiences (both personal and nonpersonal), quotations, examples, all of which have occurred in Wilson's previous books back to his first work, and can now be called upon in even greater confidence.

SECONDARY SOURCES AND REVIEWS:

1. Greenwell, Tom. "Shared Experience," in *Yorkshire Post* (Mar. 26, 1981): .

A58. **Starseekers.** London: Hodder and Stoughton, 1980, 271 p., cloth. [cosmology]

b. Garden City, NY: Doubleday & Co., 1980, 271 p., cloth.
c. St. Albans: Granada, 1982, 331 p., paper.

No dedication or introductory quotation. Includes index, bibliography, and bibliographical notes, plus numerous color and black-and-white illustrations and photographs.

ANALYTICAL TABLE OF CONTENTS:
PART ONE: Ancient Cosmology. Chapter One: The great stone observatories. Poe's *Eureka!*; Split-brain theory; Stonehenge speculations; Planetary influence on human beings; Dowsing; Ley lines; Primitive man's awareness of the earth forces. Chapter Two: The pyramid mystery. Early world maps; Determination of the size of the earth; The well at

Syrene; Inside the Great Pyramid; Evidence suggesting it was used as an observatory; The importance of the "Earth Mother" in primitive religion; The Dogon and Sirius; Intuitive knowledge: synchronicity; Primitive man and the right half of the brain. Chapter Three: The age of abstraction. Pythagoras and the dawn of the "left brain" man; Greek ideas about the universe; Aristarchus; The Dark Ages: man loses contact with the gods; Ptolemy; The Arabic influence; The invention of the printing press.

PART TWO: The Era of Discovery. Chapter Four: The harmony of the world. Nicolaus Copernicus; Tycho Brahe; Johannes Kepler. Chapter Five: The lawgivers. Galileo; William Gilbert; Isaac Newton. Chapter Six: The explorers. Giovanni Domenico Cassini; Jean Richer and Ole Roemer; Edmund Halley; James Bradley; Sir William Herschel; Pierre Simon de Laplace; Friedrich Wilhelm Bessel; Robert Wilhelm Bunsen; Gustav Kirchhoff; Wilhelm Conrad Roentgen and others.

PART THREE: The Exploding Universe. Chapter Seven: A voyage around the planets. The earth's atmosphere; The moon; Mercury, the sun, Venus, Mars, the asteroid belt, Jupiter, Saturn, Uranus, Neptune, Pluto. Chapter Eight: The world turned inside out. Roentgen and X-rays; Planck and the quantum theory; Einstein and relativity; The expanding universe. Chapter Nine: In the beginning. Supernovas, quasars, pulsars, black holes; theories on the origins of the universe; How did life begin?; Could our current ideas about the universe be mistaken? Postscript: "A true grasp of the mystery of the universe will involve a true grasp of the mystery of ourselves."

COMMENTS: The rather lavish "coffee-table" appearance of this book lends it a somewhat misleading aura of superficiality. The general thesis is well defined: Wilson draws a fine line between science and speculative cosmology, in a level-headed approach that provides careful consideration of both points-of-view. The 1982 paperback edition has considerably fewer illustrations, greatly aiding the continuity of the text.

SECONDARY SOURCES AND REVIEWS:

1, Acheson, L. K. Jr. *Science Books & Films* 17 (Sept., 1981): 14.
2. *Choice* 18 (July, 1981): 1565.
3. Cribbin, Dr. John. "It's a Real-Life Mystery Tour," in *Evening News* (Oct. 13, 1980): .
4. Crick, Philip. *Literary Review* no. 31 (Dec. 18, 1980): 19.

5. Ehresmann, J. M. *Booklist* 77 (May 15, 1981): 1233.
6. Gaskell, Jane. "Colin Has a Way with the Stars," in *Daily Mail* (Oct. 20, 1980): .
7. Greenwell, Tom. "Shared Experience," in *Yorkshire Post* (Mar. 26, 1981): .
8. Henbest, Nigel. *New Scientist* 88 (Nov., 1980): 383.
9. Hughes, David W. "Tuning into Astronomy," in *Nature* 288 (Nov. 6, 1980): 35-36.
10. Langley, Andrew. "Cosmo Wilson Guides the Ley Reader," in *Bath and West Evening Chronicle* (Oct. 25, 1980): .
11. *San Francisco Review of Books* 7 (Sept., 1982): 28.
12. Smith, J. P. *Library Journal* 106 (Apr. 15, 1981): 892.
13. Stuewe, Paul. *Quill & Quire* 47 (July, 1981): 66.

A59. **The War Against Sleep: The Philosophy of Gurdjieff.** Wellingborough, Northants.: Aquarian Press, 1980, 95 p., cloth (published simultaneously in trade paperback). [biography]

Dedication: "For Cyril Tilburn, whose help was invaluable." No introductory quotation. Includes index and bibliography.

ANALYTICAL TABLE OF CONTENTS:
Introductory Note. Chapter One: The magician. First impressions of Gurdjieff by his pupils; His ability to transfer energy; J. G. Bennett's experience at Fontainbleau. Chapter Two: The early years. Early interest in the paranormal; Friendship with Sarkis Pogossian; Search for the Sarmoung Brotherhood; Becomes "professional hypnotist"; His eventual decision not to use his powers for self-gratification. Chapter Three: Moscow and St. Petersburg. Sets up Institute for Harmonious Development of Man in Moscow; *Glimpses of Truth*—an anonymous record of a meeting with Gurdjieff; Gurdjieff's cosmology: the universe as a living organism; The law of octaves; Meets P. D. Ouspensky; The concept of "sleeping man"; The importance of attention. Chapter Four: The deluge and after. The importance of self-remembrance and super-effort; Gurdjieff and Ouspensky part company, Gurdjieff moving to Constantinople, Ouspensky to London. Chapter Five: The awakening of courage. "Personality" and "essence"; Gurdjieff moves to France and rents Château de Prieuré; Adverse publicity; Gurdjieff stresses the importance of effort; Visit to America. Chapter Six: New directions. Gurdjieff hurt in a car accident; Decides to write *Beelzebub's Tales to His Grandson*; Reactions to the book; Sheds disciples; World War II and after; Another car accident; His death. Chapter

Seven: Gurdjieff versus Ouspensky? Their different approaches to the work; Ouspensky far too rigid; Gurdjieff more successful, but still not capable of fulfilling himself; Wilson's criticism of Gurdjieff's system: he failed to see the importance of meaning, relaxation, and the "bird's-eye view."

COMMENTS: Wilson explains in his introduction that the book is bound to contain a fair amount of repetition, but points out that in the course of repeating himself he has discovered "...an entirely new set of meanings and implications in Gurdjieff." This is an experience typical to anyone who has studied Gurdjieff's system, and explains why repetition is stressed as being fundamental to the art of learning. *War* is an expansion of Wilson's essays in *The Occult*, *Mysteries*, *The Outsider*, and *Men of Mystery*, and provides a good basic introduction to the study of Gurdjieff's work. See also the revised 1986 edition, *G. I. Gurdjieff: The War Against Sleep* (A76).

A60. **Anti-Sartre, with an Essay on Camus.** San Bernardino, CA: The Borgo Press, 1981, 63 p., cloth. [literary criticism]

ab. San Bernardino, CA: The Borgo Press, 1981, 63 p., paper.

No dedication, introductory quotation, or index.

ANALYTICAL TABLE OF CONTENTS:
Part One: Anti-Sartre. Sartre's mescalin experience; Nausea: Roquentin and contingency; Sartre's philosophy of pessimism: a critique; Husserl, Sartre, and the "transcendental ego"; Roquentin's "peak experiences"; Sartre's politics; The nature of freedom; Split-brain psychology: evidence for a "dual ego"; Sartre's apparent ignorance of "right-brain ego"; The "Robot." "Reading Sartre's novels and plays, it is obvious that most of his characters suffer from 'too much robot,' as well as 'too much left-brain ego'..." Part Two: Sartre Obituary. Brief biography and assessment written for the *London Evening News*, April 16, 1980. Part Three: An Essay on Albert Camus. Wilson's thoughts on Camus' death; Brief biographical details; His success; Sartre and Camus; Camus' decline; Assessment of his achievements; Wilson's meeting with Camus. "Camus' achievement, while considerable, was nonetheless overrated."

COMMENTS: "Anti-Sartre" first appeared in *The Literary Review*, and represents Wilson's full-scale attack on Sartre's philosophy of pessimism, a consolidation of doubts first expressed in *Introduction to the New Existentialism*. The Camus essay is interesting mostly for Wilson's account of their meeting in Paris in 1957. Camus agreed to write an introduction to the French edition of *Religion and the Rebel*, but died before making a start.

SECONDARY SOURCES AND REVIEWS:

1. *Choice* 20 (Sept., 1982): 93.

A61. **The Directory of Possibilities,** edited by Colin Wilson and John Grant. Exeter, Devon: Webb and Bower, 1981, 255 p., cloth. [occult anthology]

b. New York: Rutledge Press, 1981, 255 p., cloth.
c. New York: State Mutual Books, 1981, 272 p., cloth.
d. Toronto: John Wiley & Sons, 1981, 255 p., paper.
e. London: Corgi Books, 1982, 303 p., paper.

No dedication. Introductory quotations from Sir Isaac Newton and J. D. Bernal. Includes index and bibliography.

ANALYTICAL TABLE OF CONTENTS:
About the Contributors: short paragraphs about Paul Begg, Daniel Farson, John Grant, Robert Holdstock, Stuart Holroyd, David Langford, A. T. Lawton, Brian Marriner, Iain Nicolson, J. B. Pick, Robert Turner, Michael Wenyon, and Wilson. Introduction: The New Science, by Colin Wilson. Part One: Mythology and the ancient world. Wilson writes the introductory essay to this section, plus the following entries: Ancient Astronauts, Ancient Man, Arthur, Atlantis, *Book of the Dead*, Fertility Religion; Glastonbury, Gog and Magog, Ley Lines, Megalithic Monuments, Pyramids, Rennes-le-Château (Mystery of). Part Two: The Occult and the Miraculous. Wilson contributes the introductory essay, plus the following: Alchemy, Doppelgängers, Ghosts, Healing, Jinxes and Curses, Possession, Primitive magic, Pyramid Power, Witchcraft. Part Three: Strange Creatures and Unusual Events. Wilson writes the introductory essay to this section. Part Four: Time in Disarray. Wilson pens the introductory essay, plus: Astrology, Clairvoyance, Precognition, Seers and Prophets, Time, Time Slip. Part Five: Inner Space: Mind and Body. Wilson writes the introduction, plus: Acquired Characteristics, Acupuncture, Aura, Automatic Writing, Biofeedback, Dianetics, Dowsing, Dreams and Visions, ESP, Gurdjieff (Georgi Ivanovitch), Homeopathy,

Hypnosis, Jung, Jungianism, Kirlian Photography, Levitation, Life After Death, Mediums, Multiple Personality; Out-of-Body Experiences, Peak Experience, Pineal Eye, Plant Communication, Poltergeists, Reich (Wilhelm), Reincarnation, Revelations (Mystical), Rosicrucians, Spiritualism, Steiner (Rudolph), Stigmata, Tantrism, Transcendental Meditation, Yoga, Zen. Part Six: Outer Space: The Universe at Large. Wilson contributes the introduction, plus: Flat Earth, Relativity, UFOs. Part Seven: The World of Tomorrow. Wilson writes the introduction, plus: Utopia.

COMMENTS: A fascinating and useful book, although the decision to divide the book into independently alphabetized sections was unfortunate: one straightforward sequence would have made the work much easier to use. Also, the meaning of the asterisk—used profusely throughout the text to signify a cross-reference—should have been stated clearly at the beginning, and not buried midway through John Grant's introduction. However, the comprehensive index does make up for some of the book's shortcomings. Wilson's contribution to the work is prodigious: over sixty entries and eight introductory essays.

SECONDARY SOURCES AND REVIEWS:

1. *Choice* 19 (Dec., 1981): 495.

A62.   **Poltergeist! A Study in Destructive Haunting.** Sevenoaks, Kent: New English Library, 1981, 382 p., cloth. [occult]

  ab. Sevenoaks, Kent: New English Library, 1982, 382 p., paper.
  b. New York: G. P. Putnam's Sons, 1982, 384 p., cloth.
  bb. New York: Perigee Books, 1983, 382 p., paper.

Dedication: "For Guy Playfair." No introductory quotation. Includes bibliography and index.

ANALYTICAL TABLE OF CONTENTS:
    Prefatory note. Chapter One: Professor Lombroso investigates. Sir Oliver Lodge; Psychometry; Lethbridge and ghosts; Jung's "exteriorization" theory; Psychokinesis; Uri Geller; Split brain; Dowsing. Chapter Two: Possession is nine points of the law. Table rapping; The Fox sisters; Aldous Huxley's *Devils of Loudon*; Multiple personality; Reincarnation; The "ladder of selves." Chapter Three: Cases ancient and modern. Watkins

and ley lines; Are poltergeists juvenile delinquents?; Are they electrical in nature? Chapter Four: The black monk of Pontefract. A "classic" case. Chapter Five: Fairies, elementals, and dead monks. The Cottingley fairies, an admitted fake; E. T. Stringer's "Telluric force"; Houses with negative vibrations; Findhorn; Frederick Bligh Bond and the Glastonbury scripts. Chapter Six: The black magic connection. Modern theories of the poltergeist; Guy Playfair; Black magic and witchcraft. Chapter Seven: Ghost hunters and ghost seers. Mesmerism; Poltergeist phenomena caused by a medium; Daniel Dunglas Home; Harry Price; Nandor Fodor. Chapter Eight: Speculations and conclusions.

COMMENTS: An absorbing survey of the subject; particularly interesting is the chapter on the "Black Monk of Pontefract." Wilson comes to the conclusion that poltergeists do exist, and presents some interesting theories why.

SECONDARY SOURCES AND REVIEWS:

1. B., S. E. *Booklist* 78 (Apr. 1, 1982): 1012 [second review].
2. Beidler, J. *Best Sellers* 42 (June, 1982): 107.
3. Byer, J. H. *Library Journal* 107 (Apr. 1, 1982): 736.
4. Ehresmann, J. M. *Booklist* 78 (Apr. 1, 1982): 989.
5. Grosvenor, Peter. "There Are More Spirits in This Pub Than Meet the Eye," in *Daily Express* (Nov. 24, 1981): .
6. *Kirkus Reviews* 50 (Jan. 1, 1982): 62.
7. *Kliatt Young Adult Paperback Book Guide* 18 (Winter, 1984): 85.
8. *Los Angeles Times Book Review* (May 9, 1982): 11.
9. Newman, Fred. "Things That Go Bump in the Night," in *Book Choice* no. 13 (Jan, 1982): .
10. *Publishers Weekly* 221 (Jan. 15, 1982): 91.
11. *Sunday Times* (Mar. 7, 1982): 40.

A63. **The Quest for Wilhelm Reich.** St. Albans: Granada, 1981, xiv, 306 p., cloth. [biography]

ab. St. Albans: Granada, 1982, 306 p., paper.
b. Garden City, NY: Anchor Press/Doubleday, 1981, xv, 272 p., cloth.
c. as: *A la Búsqueda de Wilhelm Reich.* Barcelona: Editorial Argos Vergara, 1981, 272 p., cloth. [Spanish]

No dedication or introductory quotation. Includes index and bibliography, the latter divided into three parts: Works by Reich, Journals, Works About Reich.

ANALYTICAL TABLE OF CONTENTS:
Prefatory note. Acknowledgements. Introduction: Reich and criticism; van Vogt's "right man" theory applied to Reich; Anticipators of Reich's orgone energy: Mesmer, Reichenbach, Harold Burr; Wilson meets Robert Ollendorff, Constance Rooth-Tracey, and Ilse Reich; A. S. Neill on Reich; Reich's mistakes; Critique of Freud's sexual theory. Chapter One: The European scene at the time of Reich's birth; Reich's childhood; Death of mother and father; Student years; Sexology: Krafft-Ebing, Hirschfeld, Forel, Bloch, and Ellis; Reich and Freud. Chapter Two: History of psychoanalysis; Hypnosis; Charcot; The power of the unconscious mind; The importance of the "feedback mechanism"; Freud's failure to recognize this; The sexual theory; A reexamination of the classic cases: Little Hans, the Wolf Man; Freud's bitterness about dissenting disciples; Viktor Tausk. Chapter Three: Reich on Freud; Reich's Peer Gynt paper; Reich and sexual theory; The orgasm theory; Freud's rejection of Reich; Reich's breakdown. Chapter Four: Was Reich's life work based on a fallacy?; Split-brain research; The "ego" as the left hemisphere, the "id" as the right; The mechanism of neurosis. Chapter Five: Reich joins the Communist Party; Freud abandons the sexual theory; Character Analysis published; Reich moves to Berlin, and attempts to combine sexual reform and communism; The Mass Psychology of Fascism published; Breakdown of his marriage; Suppression of German communists after Reichstag fire; Reich escapes to Vienna. Chapter Six: Quarrel with Freud, who refuses to publish Character Analysis; Reich moves to Copenhagen, then Malmo; Publishes What Is Class Consciousness?; Expelled from Sweden and the Psychoanalytic Association; The Oslo period; Muscular armour. Chapter Seven: Arrives in U.S.; Orgone box; Cure for cancer?; Reich and Einstein; Spontaneous creation of matter; Publishes Listen, Little Man!; Emotional plague; The FDA investigates. Chapter Eight: The Oranur experiment; Radiation; The cloudbuster; Weather control; The Murder of Christ published; Reich and UFOs; The FDA's complaint; Reich appears in court; His arrest, trial, and imprisonment; His death in prison; The Reich revival. Postscript: Was Reich a martyr?; His scientific methods; Was Reich's character conducive to the production of exteriorization phenomena?; His loyalty to Freud; Pierre Janet's psychology of tension; Creative tension; Reich as a visionary: Cosmic Superimposition.

COMMENTS: A balanced and seemingly fair account of the varied work of a remarkable man, who Wilson finds "so hard to like." The reasons for his dislike of Reich's character led Reich's executor to refuse permission to quote at any length from his books. Hence this assessment lacks Reich's own voice. Nevertheless, Reich's work is carefully and thoughtfully considered throughout. Even his later work—so often dismissed—is treated seriously.

SECONDARY SOURCES AND REVIEWS:

1. Abrams, William. *Library Journal* 106 (Jan. 15, 1981): 154.
2. Brosnahan, J. *Booklist* 77 (Feb. 15, 1981): 780.
3. *Choice* 18 (May, 1981): 1344.
4. *Economist* 278 (Feb. 28, 1981): 89.
5. Grosskurth, Phyllis. "The Man with the Orgone Box," in *Observer* (Feb. 22, 1981): 32.
6. *Kirkus Reviews* 48 (Dec. 1, 1980): 1565.
7. *National Review* 34 (June 25, 1982): 782.
8. *Publishers Weekly* 218 (Nov. 21, 1980): 52.
9. Storr, Anthony. "Reich: Have Box, Will Travel," in *Sunday Times* (Mar. 8, 1981): 43. Storr's assessment is curious, in that he describes the book as "silly," but gives no real indication that he has actually read it, being content to provide his thoughts about Reich, and little else.
10. Stuewe, Paul. *Quill & Quire* 47 (May, 1981): 35.

A64. **Witches.** Limpsfield, Surrey: Dragon's World/Paper Tiger, 1981, 158 p., cloth. [occult]

ab. Limpsfield: Dragon's World, 1982, 158 p., paper.
b. New York: A. & W. Visuals, 1982, 158 p., cloth.
c. New York: Crescent Books, 1988, 157 p., cloth.

No dedication or introductory quotation. Includes index.

ANALYTICAL TABLE OF CONTENTS:
Introduction. Montague Summers; Uri Geller; Psychic powers; H. G. Wells; African and South American witchcraft; The Cathars; Margaret Murray: the "old religion." Chapter One: Primitive sorcery. The moon; Stonehenge. Chapter Two: The coming of the witches. Chapter Three: The left-hand path. Magicians and magic. Chapter Four: The earliest

witches. Chapter Five: The devil. Invention of Christian theologians; Early Christian church. Chapter Six: Erichto the witch. Most famous witch of classical times. Chapter Seven: Merlin and Morgan le Fay. King Arthur; Who was Merlin? Chapter Eight: The destruction of the Templars. Knights Templar: among the first victims of the witchcraft craze. Chapter Nine: The first witch trial. Chapter Ten: Jehanne de Brigue. First secular witch trial; Torture. Chapter Eleven: The Malleus Maleficarum. Famous book on witchcraft. Chapter Twelve: Magic and magicians. Dowsing; Psychometry; Kabbalah. Chapter Thirteen: Werewolves. Chapter Fourteen: Dame Alice Kyteler. Irish witch. Chapter Fifteen: The Chelmsford witch trials. Chapter Sixteen: Witchcraft in Germany; Very widespread witch trials; Many of the witchfinders were sexual sadists. Chapter Seventeen: Gilles de Rais. Sadist, dabbled in alchemy. Chapter Eighteen: Mother Shipton. Her prophecies. Chapter Nineteen: Isobel Gowdie. Chapter Twenty: Witches' salve. Enabling them to fly on broomsticks. Chapter Twenty-One: Possession. Inhabited by a demon; Poltergeists; Multiple personality. Chapter Twenty-Two: The Louvier nuns. The sexual and religious emotions at the root of witchcraft. Chapter Twenty-Three: Matthew Hopkins: the rise and fall of the Witchfinder General. Chapter Twenty-Four: The witches of Salem. The result of hysteria. Chapter Twenty-Five: The Chambre Ardente affair. An international "poisons ring." Chapter Twenty-Six: The birth of spiritualism. Fox sisters; Poltergeists. Chapter Twenty-Seven: Madame Blavatsky. Founder of the Theosophical Society. Chapter Twenty-Eight: The Golden Dawn. Chapter Twenty-Nine: Aleister Crowley. Chapter Thirty: Gerald Gardner and the modern witchcraft revival. Chapter Thirty-One: The death of Jayne Mansfield. Church of Satan. Chapter Thirty-Two: Brazilian magic and witchcraft. Witch doctors; Spiritualism. Chapter Thirty-Three: Afterword. White witches.

COMMENTS: Copiously illustrated by Una Woodruff, this large-format picture book seems designed for the teenage market. Though original and colorful, the illustrations are overpowering, and not wholly suited to the text. Wilson's writing is interesting and informative, as usual.

A65.   **Access to Inner Worlds: The Story of Brad Absetz.** London: Rider, 1983, 143 p., cloth (published simultaneously in trade paperback). [philosophy and biography]

Dedication: "For Brad Absetz and Jurij Moskvitin." No introductory quotation, index, or bibliography.

ANALYTICAL TABLE OF CONTENTS:

COMMENTS: Wilson has been accused in the past of heralding a new dawn in man's evolution, but not providing any practical clues as to how this can be achieved. This brief but extremely important work lays that criticism to rest; it should be considered as a pendant to the Outsider cycle. One of Wilson's most important works to date, it ends on a characteristically optimistic note: "...in our generation...a new direction of evolution has suddenly opened up in front of us."

SECONDARY SOURCES AND REVIEWS:

1. *Light* (Summer, 1983): 80-81.

A66. **Encyclopaedia of Modern Murder, 1962-82**, by Colin Wilson and Donald Seaman. London: Arthur Barker, 1983, xx, 267 p., cloth. [crime]

   b. New York: G.P. Putnam's Sons, 1984, 304 p., cloth. [published simultaneously in trade paperback]
   bb. New York: Perigee Books, 1986, 304 p., paper.
   c. London & Sydney: Pan Books, 1986, 384 p., paper.
   d. as: *The Encyclopedia of Modern Murder*. New York: Arlington House, 1988, xx, 279 p., cloth.

No dedication, introductory quotation. Includes classified index and select bibliography, plus name index.

ANALYTICAL TABLE OF CONTENTS:
   Acknowledgements. "The age of Murder," an introductory essay by Wilson. An A-Z listing of modern murderers, terrorist organizations, and victims.

COMMENTS: Wilson here updates his (and Pat Pitman's) *Encyclopaedia of Murder* (see A6), this time with the aid of his friend and nearby neighbor, Donald Seaman, an ex-Daily Express crime reporter-turned-thriller writer. The original volume, long since out-of-print, has since been hastily reprinted by Pan Books to complement this new book, which follows the same successful format. The text is interspersed with black-and-white photographs.

SECONDARY SOURCES AND REVIEWS:

1. *American Reference Books Annual* 17 (1986): 213.
2. B., M. A. *Booklist* 81 (May 1, 1985): 1223.

3. *Observer* (June 1, 1986): 22.
4. Preston, Gregor A. *Library Journal* 110 (May 15, 1985): 76.

A67. **A Criminal History of Mankind.** London, New York: Granada, 1984, xviii, 702 p., cloth. [crime]

b. New York: G. P. Putnam's Sons, 1984, xviii, 702 p., cloth.
bb. New York: Perigee Books, 1985, xviii, 702 p., paper.
c. London, New York: Panther, 1985, xviii, 702 p., paper.
d. as: "Human Evolution (*A Criminal History of Mankind*)," in *The Essential Colin Wilson.* London: Harrap, 1985, cloth, p. 173-174. A reprint of a section from this volume, collected into a volume consisting largely of excerpts from Colin Wilson books.
e. as: "A Report on the Violent Man (*A Criminal History of Mankind*)," in *The Essential Colin Wilson.* London: Harrap, 1985, cloth, p. 175-199. A reprint of a section from this volume, collected into a volume consisting largely of excerpts from Colin Wilson books.

No dedication or introductory quotation. Includes 27-page index, and a disappointingly brief bibliography.

ANALYTICAL TABLE OF CONTENTS: Introduction: Crime as an integral part of history. PART ONE: The Psychology of Human Violence. Chapter One: Hidden patterns of violence. Changing types of crime; "Motiveless murder" Maslow's "Hierarchy of needs"; "Self esteem" crime; Dominance behavior; Moors murder case; Hypnosis; The Sala case: Dr. Sigvard Thurneman; Suicide. Chapter Two: A report on the violent man. Peking man; The city as the origin of crime; Overcrowding; Tension and illness; Stress resistance; The "Right man"; Human dominance. Chapter Three: The psychology of self-destruction. Jack Henry Abbott; Carl Panzram; The paradox of human self-destruction; Dan MacDougald's experiments in rehabilitating "hard core psychopaths"; Alcoholism; The "ego" and the "robot"; Defiance of authority. Chapter Four: How man evolved. Sadism; Criminality and sex; Is war as old as humanity?; The foundation of the cities; The theories of Louis Mumford, Elaine Morgan, Robert Ardrey, Oscar Maerth, and Louis Leakey; Primitive violence; The invention of long-distance weapons; Early art and writing; The Earth's magnetic field. Chapter Five: The disadvantages of consciousness. Crime and the sense of identity; Julian Jaynes' "bicameral mind"; The left and right brains; The coming of cruelty; The Assyrians and torture; Spartans; Alexander the Great; Boredom; Anti-authoritarianism; De Sade; Slowing down the left brain.

PART TWO: A Criminal Outline of History. Chapter One: Pirates and adventurers. Lawlessness of ancient man; Crime in 17th- and 18th-century England; Execution of children; Wreckers; Piracy; Minos; The Greek tyrants; The development of individualism and imagination; The golden age of Athens. Chapter Two: No mean city. Foundation of Rome; Its rise to power; The wars against Carthage; Revolt of Spartacus; Rise of Pompey and Julius Caesar; Augustus, Tiberius, Caligula, and Claudius; Queen Boudica. Chapter Three: From Nero to Constantine. Nero; Rise of Christianity; Jesus; St. Paul; Constantine and the triumph of Christianity. Chapter Four: End of the Roman Empire. Christian squabbles; Christian attitude to sex; The rest of Europe and Asia in Roman times; Attila the Hun; Reasons for the downfall of the empire. Chapter Five: Europe in chaos. The World scene, 500 B.C.- 500 A.D; Arnold Toynbee's theory of challenge and response; Mahomet; Rise of the Arabs; Europe in the Dark Ages; Law of "expansion" in history; Charlemagne; The Vikings; The Crusades. Chapter Six: Assassins and conquerors. Marco Polo's travels; Hasan bin Sabah and the Assassins; New inventions which revolutionized the world; Genghis Khan, Kubla Khan: the rise and fall of the Mongol empire. Chapter Seven: Travellers and adventurers. Prester John; The power of the Papacy; Black Death; The Medici family; Exploration of Africa and the New World; The invention of printing and its importance. Chapter Eight: The church over-triumphant. The Borgia family; Martin Luther; Henry VIII of England; Charles V, Holy Roman Emperor; Duke of Alva and the Netherlands; Massacre of the Huguenots. Chapter Nine: History changes its rules. Astronomical discoveries; Witchcraft craze; Philip II of Spain; Vlad the Impaler; Ivan the Terrible; Gilles de Rais; Gin; 18th-century crime wave; Punishments; Catherine Hayes case. Chapter Ten: From individualism to rebellion. Daniel Defoe; Importance of the novel; Samuel Richardson; Industrial revolution; French revolution; Napoleon; Critique of Marxism. Chapter Eleven: A century of crime. 18th-century crime; Henry Fielding and the Bow Street Runners; Newgate Calendar; Murder in the red barn; Burke and Hare; Lacenaire; Some American murder cases; H. H. Holmes.

PART THREE: The Age of Mass Murder. Chapter One: The rise of sex crime. Realism in the 18th-century attitude to sex; Victorian prudery; Pornography; Sex murders of the late 19th century; Jack the Ripper; Rape; Cases of Theodore Durrant and Leo Frank. Chapter Two: Revolt. Anarchism; The Irish problem; The characters of Tsar Nicholas II and Kaiser Wilhelm II; Assassination of Archduke Franz Ferdinand; World War I; Russian revolution. Chapter Three: The Mafia. Origins of Mafia in Sicily; New Orleans; Prohibition; Rise of Al Capone and Lucky Luciano; The Syndicate; Murder Inc.; Gangsterism in Britain; The Richardson gang; Rise and fall of the Kray twins. Chapter Four: Political gangsterism. Russia under the Bolshevists; Stalin; Rise of Hitler; His capacity for self-delusion; His mistakes. Chapter Five: The crime explosion. Crime after World War II; Sex crime and self-assertion; The "self-justified" killer; Albert DeSalvo, the Boston Strangler; Charles Manson; Baader-Meinhof gang; Crime in the 1970s; The Yorkshire Ripper. Chapter Six: The sense of reality. Breakdown of social prohibitions; Need for "objectivity"; Two modes of perception; Husserl and the intentionality of consciousness; The consciousness explosion; Crime and personal evolution; "Leakage" of vital energy; Maslow and "peak experiences"; "Clenching" consciousness; The criminal as a "collective nightmare."

COMMENTS: A work of epic proportions covering a vast field. For me, Parts One and Three were the most interesting, dealing with the psychology of human violence and modern crime. Part Two reads like an attempt at an outline history of the World, and as such tends to get bogged down in a mass of names, dates, events, places, etc. But the critique of Marxism contained in Chapter 10 of this Part is particularily interesting and controversial, politics being a subject that Wilson has hitherto generally avoided: "...*Das Kapital* is full of promises that could never be fulfilled because they are based on a false view of human nature." And: "Marx's demonstration of the inevitable downfall of capitalism is based on a fallacy that is little more than a schoolboy howler."

SECONDARY SOURCES AND REVIEWS:

I have struggled to find any serious, lengthy reviews. This is a great pity, because *Criminal History* is a book that should not have been overlooked. Taylor's piece is little more than a joke: his ignorance of Wilson's work is obvious when he says that his "...historical generalisations are largely vacuous..."

1. Fromm, Roger W. *Library Journal* 109 (August, 1984): 1447.
2. *History Today* 34 (July, 1984): 60.

3. *History Today* 35 (July, 1985): 64.
4. Kaminer, Wendy. *New York Times Book Review* (July 29, 1984): 21.
5. Kushner, Harvey. *Annals of the American Academy of Political and Social Sciences* 481 (Sept., 1985): 195.
6. *Los Angeles Times Book Review* (Sept. 9, 1984): 8.
7. *Publishers Weekly* 225 (May 4, 1984): 44.
8. Reynolds, Stanley. "Vile Bodies," in *Punch* 286 (Apr. 4, 1984): 50-51.
9. Taylor, Laurie. "The Dark Side." *New Society* 67 (Mar. 29, 1984): 488-489.
10. *Time Out* (Mar. 29, 1984): 18-19.
11. *Washington Post Book World* 14 (June 24, 1984): 7.
12. Welch, Colin. "Peasants and Bankers." *The Spectator* 252 (Apr. 7, 1984): 22.

A68. **The Janus Murder Case.** London: Granada, 1984, 235 p., cloth. [novel]

ab. London: Granada, 1985, 240 p., paper.

Dedication: "For Jackie—with affection." No introductory quotation.

COMMENTS: Thoroughly entertaining and highly unconventional whodunit featuring Inspector Gregory Saltfleet, who previously starred in *The Schoolgirl Murder Case* (see A43). Although officially on leave, he can't resist getting his teeth into the case of a murdered Polish sailor; but it gradually becomes apparent that the murderer is no ordinary villain. Although not by any means an important novel in Wilson's canon, it still ties in with his interests in split-brain psychology and multiple personality. Indeed, the novel has, by way of an appendix, an essay on the latter. And the unmistakable message still manages to appear when the psychologist Dr. Roberto Moro, whom Saltfleet meets in the course of his investigations, says to one of his patients: "...And just as every baby is a fully grown adult in embryo, so he's also a complete human being in embryo. But this is the really interesting thing. Because, you see, no human being on earth has ever become a complete human being...We all stop growing before we reach that stage."

SECONDARY SOURCES AND REVIEWS:

1. *Leicester Mercury* (Aug. 18, 1984): 8.

2. *Times* (Sept. 20, 1984): 11.

A69. **Lord of the Underworld: Jung and the Twentieth Century.**
Wellingborough, Northants.: The Aquarian Press, 1984, 160
p., cloth. [biography]

ab. as: *C. G. Jung: Lord of the Underworld.* Wellingborough,
Northants.: The Aquarian Press, 1988, 160 p., paper.
b. as: *C. G. Jung: Lord of the Underworld.* San Bernardino, CA:
The Borgo Press, 1988, 160 p., cloth.
c. as: "Active Imagination (*The Lord of the Underworld*)," in *The
Essential Colin Wilson.* London: Harrap, 1985, cloth, p. 164-
172. A reprint of a section from this volume, collected into a
volume consisting largely of excerpts from Colin Wilson
books.

No dedication or introductory quotation. Includes index.

ANALYTICAL TABLE OF CONTENTS:
Introduction: Jung's "near death" experience; *The I Ching*;
His interest in the occult; The "sage of Küsnacht"; The struggle
between his logical and intuitive "selves." Chapter One: A dual
personality.   Early life; Early semi-mystical experiences; University; His "Number One" and "Number Two" personalities;
Thomson Jay Hudson's The Law of Psychic Phenomena; Jung
"discovers" spiritualism; His cousin Helene Preiswerk develops
mediumistic powers; Jung reads Krafft-Ebing's Textbook of
psychiatry. Chapter Two: How to become a scientist. Eugen
Bleuler and the Burghölz mental hospital; Jung introduces word
association tests; Dream analysis; Studies under Pierre Janet;
Marries Emma Rauschenbach; Reads Freud's *Interpretation of
Dreams*; Writes to Freud; They meet; Why was Freud so ob-
sessed with his sexual theory?; Jung develops his own alternative. Chapter Three: How to lose friends and alienate people.
The "poltergeist" in Freud's bookcase; Jung's dream of the
house with basements; Studies ancient mythology; Formulates
his theory of the "collective unconscious"; Antonia Wolff becomes his mistress; He writes *Symbols of Transformation*; The
decay of his relationship with Freud. Chapter Four: Lord of
the underworld. Jung experiences a series of dreams and hal-
lucinations; "Active imagination": Philemon; Jung the "Outsider";
Split-brain psychology; The essential differences between Jung
and Freud; He writes *Seven Sermons to the Dead*; Man is a religious as well as a sexual animal; The importance of the Mandala symbol. Chapter Five: The invisible writing. Jung's trip

to Africa in 1920; Jung and the *I Ching*; He writes *Psychological Types*; Extraversion and introversion; He builds a home at Bollingen; The "sheer feebleness of the human mind"; Richard Wilhelm's translation of *The Secret of the Golden Flower* triggers an interest in alchemy; Sets about interpretation of the alchemical symbols; Critique of Jung's conclusions about alchemy. Chapter Six: The sage of Küsnacht. Reservations about Jung's character; Synchronicity; Jung's attempts to "play down" his interest in the occult and religion; Jung and UFOs; Publishes *Aion and Answer to Job*; His important concept of "individuation"; His death. Chapter Seven: Doubts and reservations. Critique of Jung's idea of archetypes; The lowering of the mind threshold: the relation between lack of motivation and neurosis; Viktor Frankl's "law of reverse effort"; "Individuation" and the "positive unconscious"; Jung's failure to place sufficient emphasis on conscious effort. Appendix: Active imagination.

COMMENTS: A very personal assessment of Jung which inevitably sheds as much light on Wilson as it does on Jung. Particularly interesting are the last two chapters, in which Wilson states his doubts and reservations about aspects of Jung's work, while still highlighting what he considers to be the psychiatrist's major achievements.

SECONDARY SOURCES AND REVIEWS:

1. "Books Plus," in *Economist* 292 (July 14, 1984): 85-86.

A70. **The Psychic Detectives: The Story of Psychometry and Paranormal Crime Detection.** London: Pan Books, 1984, 288 p., paper. [occult and crime]

b. San Francisco: Mercury House, 1985, xxii, 242 p., cloth.
c. New York: Berkley Books, 1987, xxiv, 263 p., paper.

Dedication: "For Andrija Puharich." No introductory quotation. Includes an index and an excellent bibliography.

ANALYTICAL TABLE OF CONTENTS:
Introduction: On the difficulties facing a writer who attempts a serious assessment of psychical phenomena; the importance of remaining "...open minded and good humoured..." Chapter One: Telescope into the past. Joy Aken's disappearance; Nelson Palmer discovers the body; Joseph Rodes

Buchanan's work; Baron Reichenbach's "odic force"; Caspar Hauser; The Fox sisters and the rise of spiritualism. Chapter Two: The unknown guest. The work of William Denton; Maurice Maeterlinck's *The Unknown Guest*; Split-brain research; Thomson Jay Hudson's *Law of Psychic Phenomena*; Carl Jung and "active imagination." Chapter Three: White crows and black sheep. The Society for Psychical Research; Henry Sidgwick and Frederick Myers; William James and the medium Leonore Piper; Dr. Richard Hodgson and the American S.P.R.; Eleanor Sidgwick's research; Sceptics and frauds; Ada Goodrich Freer; The "cross correspondences" of Sidgwick, Myers, and Edmund Gurney. Chapter Four: The Akasic records. Madame Blavatsky and the rise of the Theosophical Society; The Akasic records; Atlantis and Lemuria; Rudolf Steiner; The astral body; Knowledge of previous lives?; Joe Keeton and "regression"; Barney Camfield and "psycho-expansion" "Waking dreams" and "half dream states". Chapter Five: Spirits high and low. Pascal Forthuny; Eugène Osty and Madame Morel; The work of Dr. Gustav Pagenstecher and Maria de Zierold; Poltergeist phenomena. Professor George Henslow and "Olwen," the Welsh medium; Max Freedom Long's *The Secret Science Behind Miracles*; Dowsing: why it works. Chapter Six: The mind link. Maximilien Langoner; Animal telepathy; Freud and telepathy; The work of Dr. J. Hettinger; Murder of Maria Marten; "Dream telepathy"; Estelle Roberts and the murder of Mona Tinsley; Tom Lethbridge and psychometry. Chapter Seven: Psychic archaeology. Stefan Ossowiecki and psychic archaeology; Frederick Bligh Bond and Glastonbury; Edgar Cayce; Norman Emerson and George McMullen; Geoffrey Goodman and Aron Abrahamsen; David E. Jones's *Visions of Time*. Chapter Eight: The art of psychic detection. Peter Hurkos; Gerard Croiset; Robert Cracknell and the Genette Tate case; Cracknell and the Yorkshire Ripper; Suzanne Padfield; The brainscale of Dr. Oscar Brunler. Postscript: "...ordinary consciousness is a rather low-grade product..." Why scientists reject psychical research; Gustav Geley's *From the Unconscious to the Conscious*.

COMMENTS: A fascinating book with a rather misleading title: it is, in fact, a serious and well structured history of psychometry, of which the detection of crime is merely a much publicized aspect. In an interesting introduction Wilson outlines the frustrations experienced by writers who attempt serious, well-researched books on psychical phenomena. He attacks Erich von Däniken, Lyall Watson, and a journalist called John Macklin for "...unscientific reporting...." In his postscript he discusses the reasons why scientists reject psychical research.

SECONDARY SOURCES AND REVIEWS:

1. *Library Journal* 111 (June 1, 1986): 128.
2. *New Age* 2 (June, 1986): 68.
3. *San Francisco Review of Books* 11 (June (?) 15, 1986): 7.
4. *School Library Journal* 33 (Nov., 1986): 116.
5. Thaw, George. *Daily Mirror* (Mar. 8, 1984): 20.
6. Thomas, Suzanne. *Woman Magazine* (Jan. 7, 1984): 46-47.
   A lengthy interview article.

A71. **Afterlife: An Investigation of the Evidence of Life After Death.** London: Harrap, 1985, 269 p., cloth. [occult]

  b. Garden City, NY: A Dolphin Book, Doubleday & Co., 1987, 269 p., cloth. Also published in paper.
  c. London: Grafton, 1987, 301 p., paper.

Dedication: "For Simon Scott with affection and gratitude." Includes a five-page analytical list of contents, a four-page select bibliography, and an excellent index.

ANALYTICAL TABLE OF CONTENTS:
   Chapter One: Voices in the head. Adam Crabtree's patients; Split-brain research; Two types of voices: "Higher order" and "Lower order"; Swedenborg; Brad Absetz; Rev. Bertrand's near-death experience. Chapter Two: The world of the clairvoyant. Rosalind Heywood; Experiences of Sir Auckland Geddes and Sir Alexander Ogston; Rudolf Steiner's fourfold vision of man. Chapter Three: Invasion of the spirit people. Catherine Crowe's *Night Side of Nature*; The Fox sisters; Daniel Dunglas Home. Chapter Four: Psychical research comes of age. Founding of the Society for Psychical Research; Hoaxers and cheats; Some convincing cases; Professor James Hyslop hits out at sceptics. Chapter Five: Rediscovering a masterpiece. Frederick Myers' *Human Personality and Its Survival of Bodily Death*; Multiple personality; Leonore Piper; Myers and "cross correspondences"; Geraldine Cummins' *Swan on a Black Sea*. Chapter Six: Dr. Steiner and the problem of reincarnation. Rudolf Steiner; Madame Blavatsky; Mary Lurancy Vennum/Mary Roff case; The Pollock twins; Shanti Devi; Jasbir Lal Jat; Regression: Joe Keeton and Kitty Jay; Arthur Guirdham and the Cathars. Chapter Seven: Decline and rebirth. Sir Oliver Lodge and "Raymond"; Near-death experiences; Raymond Moody's *Life After Life*. Postscript: Wilson's encounter

with a medium. The problem of personality; The problem of human beings; Imagination; Force "T" and Force "C"; "Faculty X"; The "absurd" powers of the human mind.

COMMENTS: Wilson sums up the evidence for survival after death, concluding: "It is not my purpose to try to convince anyone of the reality of life after death: only to draw attention to the impressive inner consistency of the evidence, and to point out that, in the light of that evidence, no one need feel ashamed of accepting the notion that human personality survives bodily death." Most of the evidence he brings together has been gleaned from earlier books. The "Postscript" is by far the most important section of the book: it is here that Wilson applies his personal philosophy to the subject.

SECONDARY SOURCES AND REVIEWS:

1. *British Book News* (Feb., 1986): 85.
2. Taylor, John. "Beyond This Mortal Coil." *Weekend Australian* (May 3, 1986):   .
3. Warwick, R. C. "Anybody there?" *Yorkshire Post* (Dec. 12, 1985):   .

A72. **The Bicameral Critic**, by Colin Wilson, edited and introduced by Howard F. Dossor. Bath: Ashgrove Press, 1985, 271 p., paper. [philosophy]

b. Salem, NH: Salem House, 1985, 271 p., cloth.

No dedication or introductory quotation. Two pages of notes and references, no index.

ANALYTICAL TABLE OF CONTENTS:
Introduction: "Colin Wilson: The Case for Optimism," by Howard F. Dossor (see I63). Chapter One: Civilisation and individual fulfilment (1973) (first published in *Philosophy Forum* [see C82]). Chapter Two: Existential psychology: a novelist's approach (1967) (first published in a symposium entitled *Challenges of Humanistic Psychology* [see C54]). Chapter Three: Love as an adventure in mutual freedom (1972) (first published in a symposium entitled *Love Today, a New Exploration* [see C77]). Chapter Four: Spinoza—the outsider (1977) (first published in a symposium entitled *Speculum Spinozanum* [see C227]). Chapter Five: "Dual value response"—a new key to Nietzsche (1972) (first published in *Malahat Review* [see

C78]). Chapter Six: An integrity born of hope: notes on Christopher Isherwood (1976) (first published in *Twentieth Century Literature* [see C210]). Chapter Seven: Some notes on Graves's prose (1962) (first published in *Shenandoah* [see C32]). Chapter Eight: Valeri Briussov and *The Fiery Angel* (1975) (first published as a foreword to Briussov's book [see D17]). Chapter Nine: Daniel Defoe and *Moll Flanders* (1965) (first published as an introduction to Defoe's novel [see D3]). Chapter Ten: A personal response to *Wuthering Heights* (1976) (first published as part of the symposium *The Art of Emily Brontë* [see C212]). Chapter Eleven: George Bernard Shaw: a personal view (1979) (first published as part of the symposium *The Genius of Shaw* [see C232]). Chapter Twelve: Ronald Duncan: a self-revealing poet (1975) (first published as part of the symposium *A Tribute to Ronald Duncan...* [see C195]). Chapter Thirteen: Crimes of freedom and their cure (1964) (first published in *Twentieth Century* [see C48]). Chapter Fourteen: Introduction to *The Dark Gods* (1980) [see D34]. Chapter Fifteen: Writer in residence (1969) (first published in *Encounter* [see C57]). Chapter Sixteen: A memoir of the Fifties (1960) (first published in *Encounter* [see C17]).

COMMENTS: An important volume of essays, all previously published, but made freely available in book form for the first time. The essays have been carefully and skillfully selected to reveal the tremendous breadth of Wilson's interests, and the philosophical thread linking all of these seemingly diverse subjects together. Further volumes by the same editor—a senior administrator at the University of La Trobe, Melbourne, and a lifetime collector and admirer of Wilson's work—are planned.

SECONDARY SOURCES AND REVIEWS:

1. *The Armchair Detective* 19 (Fall, 1986): 427.

A73. **The Essential Colin Wilson.** London: Harrap, 1985, 248 p., cloth. [philosophy]

  b. Berkeley, CA: Celestial Arts, 1986, 273 p., paper.
  c. London: Grafton, 1987, 336 p., paper.

A book of philosophical essays, mostly collected from previously published works. No dedication, bibliography, or index.

ANALYTICAL TABLE OF CONTENTS:

Schumacher lecture: the triviality of everyday consciousness; Objective consciousness; "Reasons for delight" and "forgetfulness"; "Three-dimensional consciousness."

COMMENTS: This book is aptly titled, being essential reading for any student wishing to understand Wilson's work. Writers are notoriously bad when it comes to looking at their own work objectively, but Wilson is the exception. Typically, the book has been almost totally ignored by the press. All the pieces save two were previously published in book form. "The Laurel and Hardy Theory of Consciousness" has since been reprinted in pamphlet form in the U.S. (see A77). The Schumacher lecture and its postscript are particularly important, the latter including some very important insights into the nature of "depression" and its relief.

SECONDARY SOURCES AND REVIEWS:

1. Rosewall, John. *Cornish Scene* 1 (Dec., 1985/Jan., 1986): 14-15: "This is a fine volume, underlining the brilliance, the originality of the author..."

A74. **The Personality Surgeon.** Sevenoaks, Kent: New English Library, 1985, 339 p., cloth. [novel]

ab. Sevenoaks, Kent: New English Library, 1987, 339 p., paper.
b. as: *The Personality Surgeon: A Novel.* San Francisco: Mercury House, 1986, 322 p., cloth.

Dedication: "For Karen Arthur who suggested it."

COMMENTS: Wilson's most substantial novel since *The God of the Labyrinth* (1970) marks his very definite return to fiction writing as a means of conveying ideas. It also introduces a new kind of Wilson hero—hinted at in the previous two Inspector Saltfleet novels—Charlie Peruzzi: amiable, rounded, middle class, altogether lacking "edge," and rather too bland, a far cry from Gerard Sorme. Yet he still manages to "invent" a revolutionary form of psychotherapy using a video camera and a digital paintbox. The novel progresses rapidly, taking the reader along with it: the last chapter, in which Wilson introduces himself as the author, is an interesting ploy, an attempt to give the novel authenticity. Near the end, an account of a brutal murder case offsets the rest of the novel and reminds the reader of the Wilson of old. However, in the final analysis, as with all of Wilson's major fiction, it's the ideas that count. The thesis of the book is a fascinating and logical extension of psychological ideas expressed in his recent nonfiction, in particular the "self-image concept," as explained in greater detail in the compact disc recording, *The Essential Colin Wilson* (see F8).

SECONDARY SOURCES AND REVIEWS:

1. *British Book News* (June, 1987): 370.
2. *Kirkus Reviews* 54 (June 1, 1986): 821.
3. *Leicester Mercury* (April 17, 1986):   .
4. *Library Journal* 111 (Sept. 1, 1987): 217.
5. Nicholson, John. *Times* (Mar. 20, 1986):   .
6. *Publishers Weekly* 229 (June 13, 1986): 69.
7. *Quill & Quire* 52 (Aug., 1986): 50.
8. Rosewall, John. *Cornish Scene* 1 (April/May, 1986): 10.

A75. **Rudolf Steiner: The Man and His Vision: An Introduction to the Life and Ideas of the Founder of Anthroposophy.** Wellingborough, Northants: The Aquarian Press, 1985, 176 p., paper. [biography]

b. as: *Rudolf Steiner*. Milano: Longanesi, 1986, 180 p., paper (?). Translated by Leone Diena. [Italian]

No dedication or introductory quotation, but the book does include a three-page bibliography and a two-page index.

ANALYTICAL TABLE OF CONTENTS:
    Chapter One: The door to the inner universe. Wilson's initial difficulty in reading Steiner; His philosophical standing; The essence of his philosophy. Chapter Two: Childhood of a visionary. His early interest in geometry; His anti-scientific-materialism; His introduction to Goethe; The development of his "soul life." Chapter Three: The Goethe scholar. Meets Felix Koguzki and Maria delle Grazie; Steiner's anti-pessimism; His introduction to theosophy. Chapter Four: The long apprenticeship. Marriage to Anna Eunicke; Communication with the dead. Chapter Five: Rebirth. *The Philosophy of Freedom*; Moments of spiritual perception; *Friedrich Nietzsche, Fighter for Freedom*; Steiner and Nietzsche; *Goethe's Weltanschauung*; His W.E.A. lectures in Berlin; Meets Marie von Sivers. Chapter Six: Occultist and guru. Steiner and Christianity; His cosmology; Was he a genuine seer?; His spiritual perceptions of the

King Arthur legends challenged. Chapter Seven: The building of the temple. Publishes *Theosophy*; His disapproval of spiritualism; Meets Edouard Schuré; Presents his mystery drama *Sacred Drama of Eleusis*; Steiner and Rosicrucianism; Publishes *Occult Science—an Outline*; His mystery plays. Steiner and Kafka; The break with the Theosophical Society; Krishnamurti; Founds the Anthroposophical Society; The building of the Goetheanum. Chapter Eight: Disaster. *The Threefold Commonwealth*; Opposition mounts in Germany, but he gains a reputation as an educationalist; Goetheanum burns down; His influential agricultural and medical ideas; *Esoteric Reflections on Karmic Relationships*; His death. Chapter Nine: Postscript. Steiner's achievement.

COMMENTS: Readable introduction to the philosophy of a difficult writer, one whom Wilson describes as "...one of the greatest men of the 20th century." One of a series of short introductory books to famous "occult" thinkers. See also *Lord of the Underworld* (A69) and *G. I. Gurdjieff: the War Against Sleep* (A76). A volume on Aleister Crowley appeared in 1987 (A82).

SECONDARY SOURCES AND REVIEWS:

1. *British Book News* (Nov., 1985): 650.

A76. **G. I. Gurdjieff: The War Against Sleep.** Wellingborough, Northants.: The Aquarian Press, 1986, 127 p., paper. [biography]

b. San Bernardino, CA.: The Borgo Press, 1986, 127 p., cloth.

COMMENTS: Reprint of *The War Against Sleep* (see A59) with the addition of a new chapter: Chapter 4: Ouspensky in search of miracles. Gurdjieff's deliberate attempts to inconvenience pupils; Man's four bodies; The "fourth way"; Man's seven "centers"; Reservations about some of Gurdjieff's ideas; His central thesis: man's powers are greater than he realises; Gurdjieff communicates with Ouspensky telepathically; Gurdjieff's experience of "the opening of inner consciousness."

A77. **The Laurel & Hardy Theory of Consciousness.** Mill Valley, CA: Robert Briggs Associates, 1986, 15 p., paper. Broadside Editions Series. [psychology]

COMMENTS: A straightforward reprint of a piece that forms Chapter Ten of *The Essential Colin Wilson* (see 73).

A78. **Scandal!: An Encyclopaedia,** edited by Colin Wilson and Donald Seaman. London: Weidenfeld & Nicolson, 1986, vii, 392 p., cloth. [biography]

b. New York: Stein & Day, 1986, vii, 392 p., cloth. No subtitle.
c. as: *An Encyclopedia of Scandal.* London: Grafton, 1987, 480 p., paper.

No dedication or introductory quotation.

ANALYTICAL TABLE OF CONTENTS:
Introduction by Wilson. An A-Z listing of fifty-two famous scandals. Bibliography. Eight-page index.

COMMENTS: An entertaining collection of scandals interspersed with 32 pages of black-and-white photographs. Seaman's years as a reporter on the *Daily Express* have obviously helped greatly with his contributions, and Wilson's interests are well represented. In a short introduction Wilson explains why he decided to help compile the book: "The great scandals afford the same opportunity to study the curious complexities of human nature as the famous criminal cases."

SECONDARY SOURCES AND REVIEWS:

1. C., I. *Booklist* 83 (Jan. 1, 1987): 681.
2. "Coming Clean with Scandal." *Leicester Mercury* (April 17, 1986):   .
3. *Contemporary Review* 249 (Aug., 1986): 111.
4. Davies, Clive. "Social Advantages of the Scandal." *Yorkshire Post* (Mar. 11, 1986):   .
5. *Publishers Weekly* 229 (June 6, 1986): 64.
6. *Spectator* 257 (Aug. 30, 1986): 25.

A79. **An Essay on the 'New' Existentialism.** Nottingham: Paupers' Press, 1986, 16 p., paper. [philosophy]

b. San Bernardino, CA: The Borgo Press, 1988, 16 p., cloth.

ANALYTICAL TABLE OF CONTENTS:
Sartre and contingency; Simone de Beauvoir; Sartre's basic
fallacy; "Low pressure" consciousness; Camus and "absurdity";
The sense of "unknown modes of being"; Which is true: vision
or nausea? "Life failure"; Husserl and the intentionality of
consciousness; The "transcendental ego" as the archer who fires
consciousness; Moods of intensity; Wilson meets Camus—they
disagree; *The Age of Defeat*—Wilson's attack on pessimism in
modern literature; Abraham Maslow writes to him; "Peak experiences"; Negative attitude—negative feedback; "Romanticism
Mark Three"; Our minds are hypnotised by triviality; Inducing
"peak experiences."

COMMENTS: An important new essay outlining the philosophical ideas expressed in the Outsider Cycle. A refreshingly
lucid, succinct, and bold attack on pessimism in general, and
on Sartre's ideas in particular. Wilson is positive in his attempt
to liberate existentialism from the cul-de-sac of contingency,
by a return to "...true Husserlian foundations...," pointing the
way toward a new stage in the evolution of mankind. Includes
a short Foreword by Colin Stanley, and a selected bibliography.

SECONDARY SOURCES AND REVIEWS:

1. Rosewall, John. *Cornish Scene* 2 (March/April, 1987): 28.
2. Wallis, Peter. "Consciousness and Existence." *Lodestar* no.
    5 (Spring, 1987): 21-22.

A80. **The Book of Great Mysteries,** edited by Colin Wilson and Dr.
Christopher Evans. London: Robinson Publishing, 1986, 493
p., paper. [occult]

No dedication or introductory quote. Includes five-page index,
and 32 pages of black-and-white illustrations grouped between
pages 246-247.

COMMENTS: Reprints of various articles from the "Great
Mysteries" series published by Aldus Books between 1975-79.
There are contributions from Daniel Farson, Angus Hall, Stuart
Holroyd, Francis King, Jeremy Kingston, David Lambert, Neil
Powell, Frank Smythe, Roy Stemman, and Wilson himself, but
no indication of who has written what. A detailed comparison
with the original multi-volume set would be necessary to un-
ravel the mystery of this mysterious volume!

A81. **Marx Refuted: The Verdict of History**, edited by Ronald Duncan and Colin Wilson. Bath: Ashgrove Press, 1987, 284 p., cloth. Published simultaneously in trade paperback. [political science]

No dedication or introductory quote, but includes a good six-page index.

COMMENTS: An interesting book of political essays conceived by Ronald Duncan prior to his death in 1982. Contributors include: Karl Popper, Arthur Koestler, Friedrich von Hayek, A. L. Rowse, Alexander Solzhenitsyn, Milton Friedman, and Margaret Thatcher. Wilson's contribution is considerable, including an introductory note about the book's extraordinary history (apparently Robert Maxwell's Pergamon Press offered to publish it on two separate occasions, but changed its mind both times), plus essays on Popper, Koestler, von Hayek, and Thatcher; and a lengthy piece on Marx himself called "The Darwin of Sociology," and an Afterword.
    The book was eventually published under the auspices of the literary foundation established after Duncan's death.

A82. **Aleister Crowley: The Nature of the Beast.** Wellingborough, Northants.: Aquarian Press, 1987, 174 p., paper. [biography]

b. San Bernardino, CA: The Borgo Press, 1989, 174 p., cloth.

Includes a bibliography and an adequate index.

ANALYTICAL TABLE OF CONTENTS:
    Chapter One: Does Magic Work? How Wilson came across Crowley's work; Wilson's conversion from scepticism in the face of evidence for witchcraft, poltergeists, etc.; The importance of mental preparation in magic. Chapter Two: The Reluctant Christian. Crowley's early life; His rebellion against strict Christian upbringing; Crowley and sex; His poetry; His magical "awakening"; Mountaineering; His relationship with Herbert Pollitt; Crowley becomes a member of the Order of the Golden Dawn. Chapter Three: Raising Hell. Samuel Liddell Mathers; Crowley experiments with Abra-Melin magic; Rents Boleskine House; Joins unsuccessful expedition to climb Chogo-Ri. Chapter Four: The Chosen of the Gods. Crowley and Mr. and Mrs. "Horos"; Marries Rose Kelly; "Receives" *The Book of the Law*; Disastrously unsuccessful assault on Kanchenjunga;

Travels through China. Chapter Five: The Master and the Gurus. Meets Captain John Fuller, who becomes a disciple; Forms his own magical order—"Argenteum Astrum"; Victor Benjamin Neuburg becomes another disciple; Launches *Equinox*, a bulky, twice-yearly periodical; Publishes the secret rituals of the Golden Dawn; His reputation deteriorates. Chapter Six: The Magic Wand. Sex Magic. Chapter Seven: The Abbey of Do-What-You-Will. Sets up the Abbey of Thelema on Sicily; Writes *Diary of a Drug Fiend*; Attacks on Crowley in the popular press proliferate. Chapter Eight: Paradise Lost. More bad publicity; Meets Karl Germer; Completes *Magick in Theory and Practice*; Unsuccessfully Sues Constable & Co.; His death. Epilogue: The three facets of Crowley's make-up: his sexuality, dislike of authority, and romantic mysticism.

COMMENTS: Dubbed by the media of his day "the wickedest man in the world," Crowley was a fascinating and complex character who explored both sexual and black magic. Wilson examines his life, from his thrill-seeking expeditions and extensive writings on philosophy, religion, and yoga, to his sexual magic rites and rituals, his synthesis of magical traditions, oriental esoteric techniques, and his Law of Thelema. Another book in this excellent series of introductions to the lives and works of famous and important occult personalities.

SECONDARY SOURCES AND REVIEWS:

1. *Books* (October, 1987): 26.
2. Smith, Grub. *Literary Review* no. 112 (October, 1987): 60.

A83. **The Encyclopedia of Unsolved Mysteries**, by Colin Wilson, with Damon Wilson. London: Harrap, 1987, 318 p., cloth. [occult]

b. Chicago: Contemporary Books, 1988, 318 p., cloth.
c. London: Blandford, 1989, 318 p., paper.

Includes a ten-page index, maps, diagrams, line drawings, and thirty pages of black-and-white illustrations.

COMMENTS: An A-Z sequence of forty-two famous mysteries, including the Devil's footprints, Loch Ness monster, Jack the Ripper, etc. The book also contains important pieces on alchemy, reincarnation, and other related subjects. Damon Wilson is Colin's son.

SECONDARY SOURCES AND REVIEWS:

1. *British Book News* (Apr., 1987): 211.
2. Smith, Godfrey. *Sunday Times* (June 5, 1988): A13.

A84. **Jack the Ripper: Summing Up and Verdict,** by Colin Wilson and Robin Odell, edited by J. H. H. Gaute. London, New York: Bantam Press, 1987, xii, 318 p., cloth.

b. London: Corgi Books, 1988, xii, 382 p., paper.

Includes an impressive bibliography by Alexander Kelly, an index, and eight pages of black-and-white illustrations between pages 148-149.

COMMENTS: Probably the most authoritative of the many books released to "celebrate" the 100 years of speculation about the identity of the most infamous murderer of modern times. Wilson contributes "A Psychological Portrait of Jack the Ripper," a chapter entitled "Royal Jack," a summing-up and an appendix on "The Ripper's Disciples." He also shares responsibility with Odell for a number of other chapters.
Preface by J. H. H. Gaute; Foreword by Richard Whittington-Egan.

SECONDARY SOURCES AND REVIEWS:

1. *Books* (Oct., 1987): 8.
2. Coady, Matthew. "A Better Class of Suspect." *Guardian* (Oct. 16, 1987): 13.
3. *Guardian Weekly* 137 (Nov. 15, 1987): 28.
4. *Illustrated London News* 275 (Dec., 1987): 73.
5. *Listener* 118 (Dec. 17, 1987): 54.
6. *New Statesman* 114 (Nov. 13, 1987): 28.
7. Pile, Stephen. "Ripper Yarns That Are Ripping Us Off." *Sunday Times* (Dec. 6, 1987): 15.
8. *Punch* 293 (Oct. 21, 1987): 58.
9. *Spectator* 259 (Dec. 19, 1987): 77.
10. Thomas, Sean. "Hunt the Kidney." *Literary Review* no. 115 (Jan., 1988): 34-35.
11. *Times Literary Supplement* (Dec. 25, 1987): 1427.

A85.   **The Musician As 'Outsider.'**   Nottingham: Paupers' Press, 1987, 35 p., paper. [music/philosophy]

b.   San Bernardino, CA: The Borgo Press, 1989, 35 p., cloth.

COMMENTS: In this, his first substantial essay on music since *Brandy of the Damned* (see A11), Wilson extends his examination of the dilemma that destroyed so many of the great romantic artists, turning the spotlight on Liszt, Berlioz, Schumann, Brahms, and, in particular, Beethoven, whom he describes as "...one of the first of the great Outsider-Artists—perhaps the greatest of them all."

Essential reading for students of modern philosophy and music. Includes the two-page checklist, "Colin Wilson on Music," compiled by Colin Stanley.

SECONDARY SOURCES AND REVIEWS:

1.   Wallis, Peter. *Lodestar* no. 7 (Winter, 1987/88): 21

A86.   **Spider World: The Tower.**   London: Grafton, 1987, 398 p., cloth. Published simultaneously in trade paperback. The Spider World Trilogy, Volume 1. [novel]

ab.   London: Grafton, 1988, 496 p., paper.
ba.   as: *Spider World: The Desert*. New York: Ace Books, Sept. 1988, 163 p., paper. Comprises the first third of the original.
bb.   as: *Spider World, Book Two: The Tower*. New York: Ace Books, Jan. 1989, 181 p., paper. Comprises the second third of the original.
bc.   as: *Spider World, Book Three: The Fortress*. New York: Ace Books, July 1989, 149 p., paper. Comprises the final third of the original.

Dedication: "For Sally, Damon, and Rowan."

COMMENTS: This enormously entertaining fantasy novel follows the fortunes of Niall—a hero in the true sense of the word—as he battles against the tyrannical death spiders who rule the barren 25th-century Earth, and, in so doing, aids his personal evolution. Wilson here succeeds in integrating his philosophical ideas into the framework of a totally absorbing and gripping story which will not only satisfy his established readers, but also serve to introduce him to a whole new generation of enthusiasts.

The original manuscript was so large that it was split into two volumes, *The Tower* and *The Delta*; a third volume is promised in 1989 or 1990. This first part of the series is itself broken internally into three sections: "The Desert," "The Tower," and "The Fortress." For American publication, the two-volume British set was broken into four volumes.

SECONDARY SOURCES AND REVIEWS:

1. *British Book News* (Sept., 1987): 614.
2. *Fantasy Review* 10 (June, 1987): 42.
3. Farson, Daniel. "Outsider Comes in from the Cold." *Literary Review* no. 106 (April, 1987): 8-9.
4. Hutchinson, Tom. "Caught in a Silken Web of Words." *Hampstead and Highgate Express* (Feb. 28, 1987): .
5. *Observer* (Apr. 26, 1987): 26.
6. "Present Imperfect." *Time and Tide* (March, 1987): .
7. *Punch* 292 (Apr. 15, 1987): 66.
8. "When Insects Rule the Earth." *Manchester Evening News* (March 5, 1987): .
9. "Wilson into Sci-Fi." *Western Morning News* (Feb. 28, 1987): .

A87. **Spider World: The Delta.** London: Grafton, 1987, 304 p., cloth. Published simultaneously in trade paperback. The Spider World Trilogy, Volume 2. [novel]

ab. London: Grafton, 1988, 352 p., paper.
b. New York: Ace Books, Feb. 1990, p., paper.

COMMENTS: The continuation of Niall's epic struggle against the death spiders takes him to the very source of the Spider Lord's power, the mysterious Delta—an extraordinary landscape full of surprises. Wilson's imagination and inventiveness here prove equal to that of David Lindsay's *A Voyage to Arcturus*. The pace hardly ever slackens, and the philosophical message, although unobtrusive, is never far below the surface:

"The Delta has a habit of destroying those who are ready to be destroyed, and sparing those who refuse to become victims..." Toward the end of the book the comments about human nature and freedom are pure Wilson:

"For this, he could now see, was the central problem of human beings. When they are faced with perils and difficulties, they fought magnificently. But as soon as they had conquered, they lost all the ground they had gained; they sank into laziness and became the victims of triviality."

The answer, for Wilson, is for Man to cultivate *inner* freedom, and this ultimately is Niall's greatest problem:

"How do you teach them to do that?" he is asked.

"I don't know. Sooner or later, I'll find a way," is the optimistic reply.

SECONDARY SOURCES AND REVIEWS:

1. Hutchinson, Tom. *Times* (March 3, 1988): 21.
2. *Observer* (Dec. 27, 1987): 17.

A88. **Autobiographical Reflections.** Nottingham: Paupers' Press, 1988, 49 p., paper. [autobiography]

COMMENTS: Written in 1986, this highly readable extended essay summarizes and updates, but in no way replaces, his autobiography, *Voyage to a Beginning* (see A25). Essential reading for students and admirers, but also a valuable introduction to the work of a highly influential writer. Includes a three-page bibliography of selected autobiographical writings, and books about Wilson and his work, compiled by Colin Stanley.

SECONDARY SOURCES AND REVIEWS:

1. Wallis, Peter. "Two Booklets from Paupers' Press." *Lodestar* no. 9 (Summer, 1988): 22.

A89. **The Mammoth Book of True Crime,** by Colin Wilson, edited by Howard F. Dossor. London: Robinson Publishing, 1988, xvi, 630 p., paper. [crime]

b. New York: Carroll & Graf, Publishers, 1988, xvi, 630 p., paper.

COMMENTS: A huge book bringing together and reprinting most of Wilson's contributions to the part-work *Crimes and Punishments*, published by Phoebus between 1973-76 (see G1), into one alphabetical sequence. Unfortunately, the journalistic-style headings (designed in the original to break up the text, but clearly unnecessary here) are retained, giving the end product a false impression of superficiality.

Includes an interesting and illuminating eight-page introduction by Dossor. See also C97-C191.

SECONDARY SOURCES AND REVIEWS:

1. *Bloomsbury Review* 8 (Sept., 1988): 30.
2. Kinney, Eloise L. *Booklist* 84 (July, 1988): 1766.
3. *Kirkus Reviews* 56 (June 1, 1988): 822.
4. *Kliatt Young Adult Paperback Book Guide* 22 (Sept., 1988): 42.
5. *Library Journal* 113 (Sept. 15, 1988): 89.
6. *Publishers Weekly* 233 (June 10, 1988): 74.

A90. **The Misfits: A Study of Sexual Outsiders.** London: Grafton, 1988, 272 p., cloth. [psychology/sex/literature]

ab. London: Grafton, 1989, 272 p., paper.
b. New York: Carroll & Graf, Publishers, 1989, 272 p., cloth.

Includes an analytical table of contents, bibliography, and a seven-page index.

TABLE OF CONTENTS: Chapter One: The Secret of Charlotte Bach. Chapter Two: Charlotte and the Mysteries of Evolution. Chapter Three: Anarchy Incarnate. Chapter Four: Romantic Agonies. Chapter Five: Rebel Angel. Chapter Six: From Rebellion to Sex Crime. Chapter Seven: Victorian Misfits. Chapter Eight: Guilt and Defiance. Chapter Nine: Misfits or Mystics? Postscript: The Fifth Window.

COMMENTS: A fascinating and controversial work which, once again, got the critics in a tangle. Most of them, emboldened by Harry Ritchie's frenzied attack on Wilson in the book, *Success Stories* (see H25), which was published about the same time, reached for their knives. Wilson, unfortunately, left a few vulnerable spots in his text which were eagerly grasped, to the detriment of the central thesis of the book. Of the reviews listed below, only Baker and Burgess are worth reading, although the lampooning Wilson received in *Private Eye* (which includes a cartoon of the author dressed as a woman) is both spiteful and hilarious, in true *Eye* tradition.

SECONDARY SOURCES AND REVIEWS:

1. Baker, Roger. "Sexual Outsiders." *Gay Times* no. 114 (March, 1988): 40-42.
2. *Books* (Jan., 1988): 20.
3. *British Book News* (Jan., 1988): 52.
4. Burgess, Anthony. "Whips and Petticoats." *Observer* (Feb. 21, 1988): 27.
5. Clare, Anthony. "The Roots of Perversion." *Sunday Times* (March 6, 1988): G2.
6. "Come in, Outsider, Your Time's Up." *Bookseller* (Feb. 26, 1988): 787.
7. Fuller, Peter. "In Praise of Older Perverts." *Guardian* (Feb. 19, 1988): 24.
8. *Guardian Weekly* 138 (Mar. 6, 1988): 28.
9. *Kirkus Reviews* 56 (Nov. 1, 1988): 1596.
10. "Outside Loon." *Private Eye* no. 683 (Feb. 19, 1988): 24. A letter by M. G. Sherlock defending Wilson appeared in *Private Eye* no. 684 (March 4, 1988): 12.
11. Profumo, David. "How to Tumble Your Drier." *Literary Review* no. 117 (March, 1988): 26-28.
12. *Publishers Weekly* 234 (Dec. 9, 1988): 52.
13. *Punch* 294 (Feb. 12, 1989): 43.
14. *Times Literary Supplement* (Feb. 12, 1988): 158.

A91. **The Magician from Siberia.** London: Robert Hale, 1988, 224 p., cloth. [novel]

COMMENTS: The uncut version of "A Novelization of Events in the Life and Death of Grigori Efimovich Rasputin" (see B15), which was originally published in 1983 by Reader's Digest Association in *Tales of the Uncanny*. The Hale edition restores some 15,000 words believed excised from the anthology.

A92. **Beyond the Occult.** London, New York: Bantam Press, 1988, 381 p., cloth. [philosophy/occult]

COMMENTS: A new book on psychic phenomena.

A93. **Existentially Speaking: Essays on the Philosophy of Literature.** I.O. Evans Studies in the Philosophy and Criticism of Literature, No. 7. San Bernardino, CA: The Borgo Press, 1989, 144 p., cloth. [nonfiction collection]

ab. San Bernardino, CA: The Borgo Press, 1989, 144 p., paper.

Includes an index.

TABLE OF CONTENTS: Preface: "Colin Wilson, Literary High Flyer," by Colin Stanley (see I72); Introduction: "Affirmations of Faith," by Colin Wilson (an original essay; see D63); "Science Fiction and Existentialism: A Personal View" (see A54); "An Integrity Born of Hope: Notes on Christopher Isherwood" (see C210); "Michel Foucault" (see E110); "Arthur Koestler" (see E101); "Husserl and Evolution" (an original essay; see C339); "Wyndham Lewis: A Refracted Talent?" (see C197); "Robert Musil, the Man Without Qualities" (see C68); "The Decline and Fall of Existentialism" (an original essay; see C340); Index; About the Author.

COMMENTS: Another important retrospective collection, comprised largely of previously-published essays of existential criticism on various twentieth-century writers and movements.

A94. **The Decline and Fall of Leftism.** Nottingham: Paupers' Press, 1989,   p., paper. [political science]

A95. **The Untethered Mind,** by Colin Wilson, edited by Howard F. Dossor. Bath: Ashgrove Press, 1989,   p., cloth. Published simultaneously in trade paperback. [nonfiction collection]

COMMENTS: A collection of early essays.

A96. **Written in Blood: A History of Forensic Detection.** London: Education, 1989, [288] p., cloth. [criminology]

COMMENTS: A history of forensic medicine.

B.

SHORT FICTION

B1.   "The Interview: An Episode from an Unpublished Novel," in *London Magazine* 3 (no. 11, 1956): 33-46. [short story]

Contains a portrait of Wilson by Colin Spencer. The "unpublished novel" eventually became *Ritual in the Dark* (see also A4).

B2.   "The Frenchman," in *Evening Standard* (Aug. 22, 1957): . [short story]

A "Did it happen?" story challenging the reader's intelligence.

B3.   "Watching the Bird," in *Evening News* (Sept. 12, 1961): 4.

B4.   "Uncle Tom and the Police Constable," in *Evening News* (Oct. 23, 1961): 8.

B5.   "He Couldn't Fail," in *Evening News* (Dec. 29, 1961): 10.

B6.   "Uncle and the Lion," in *Evening News* (Sept. 28, 1962): 12.

B7.   "Hidden Bruise," in *Evening News* (Dec. 3, 1962): 6.

B8.   "The Wooden Cubes," in *Evening News* (June 27, 1963): 12.

B9.   "Margin of Darkness," in *Minnesota Review* 6 (1966): 268-295. [story]

An early draft of a section of *The Black Room* (see A30).

B10.   "The World of Violence," in *A Taste for Living: Young People in the Modern Novel*, edited by G. G. Urwin. London: Faber & Faber, 1967, cloth, p. 25-34. [extract]

A selection from the novel of the same name (see A10), plus criticism.

B11. **"The Return of the Lloigor,"** in *Tales of the Cthulhu Mythos*, edited by August Derleth. Sauk City, WI: Arkham House, 1969, cloth, p. 351-401. See also the expanded version, A42. [horror story]

   b. New York: Beagle Books, 1971, paper, Vol. 2, p. 205-269.
  bb. New York: Ballantine Books, 1973, paper, Vol. 2, p. 205-269.

B12. **"Sex and Fool's Gold,"** in *Mayfair* (Sept., 1970): 52-53. [extract]

Another section from *God of the Labyrinth* (see A26).

B13. **"God of the Labyrinth,"** in *A Strange Glory*, edited by Gerry Goldberg. Toronto: McClelland & Stewart, 1975, cloth, p. 134. [extract]

From the novel of the same name (see A26).

B14. **"Timeslip,"** in *Aries I*, edited by John Grant. Newton Abbot: David & Charles, 1979, cloth, p. 150-184. [short story]

A rarity from Wilson, a short piece of fiction that was not intended to be part of a novel. This science-fiction tale concerns the disappearance of Richard Bowen, and deals with split-brain psychology.

B15. **"A Novelization of Events in the Life and Death of Grigori Efimovich Rasputin,"** in *Tales of the Uncanny*. New York: Reader's Digest Association, 1983, cloth, 120 p. [short novel]

COMMENTS: Wilson mentions the problems involved in the writing of the original manuscript in his "Access to Inner Worlds" (pages 27-29): "Halfway through, it was clear that I wasn't going to succeed in compressing his life into 60,000 words—I had already done 40,000, and hadn't even got him as far as St. Petersburg....Eventually I finished it on time, 15,000 words too long—leaving *Reader's Digest* the problem of cutting..." I have seen and read the manuscript, but cannot say to what extent *Reader's Digest* edited it.

    The complete version of this work was published in 1988 as *The Magician from Siberia* (see A91).

C.

NONFICTION

C1. "A Writer's Prospect," in *London Magazine* 3 (no. 8, 1956): 48-55. [literature]

This article generated much comment, most of it uncomplimentary, the letters being published in the following issues: no. 10, p. 54-57 (P. W. Gaskell and Elizabeth Jennings); no. 11, p. 65-68 (Edwin Morgan, Pat Kavanagh, and Monk Gibbon); and no. 12, p. 59-61 (Dafydd Bond Thomas and Wilson himself).

C2. "Where Do We Go From Here: A Discourse," in *Zero Anthology of Literature and Art*, no. 8, edited by Themistocles Hoetis. London: Zero Press, 1956, cloth, p. 41-53. [literature]

C3. "On Margate Sands: An Autobiographical Fragment," in *Encounter* 8 (Jan., 1957): 25-33. [autobiography]

Watered-down version of Wilson's development from the age of 11. The circumstances of his discharge from the RAF were then considered "unprintable." For the full story, see *Voyage to a Beginning* (A25).

C4. "Beyond the Outsider," in *Declaration*, edited by Tom Maschler. London: MacGibbon and Kee, 1957, cloth, p. 29-59. [philosophy]

  b. New York: E. P. Dutton & Co., 1958, cloth, p. 29-59.
  c. Port Washington, NY: Kennikat Press, 1972, cloth, p. 29-59.

Wilson's personal vision of the world, as expressed in his critical works. Our "unheroic" age; The outsider: romantic or realist?; The decline of our civilization; Self-forget-fulness; The outsider and spiritual growth; The outsider and religion; The sceptical approach to religious belief; The bifurcation of philosophy and art; The evolution of the outsider; Critique of scientific materialism and abstract philosophy; Existentialism;

The evolution of a "higher type of man"; Wilson's personal contribution towards this end. "For me the instrument of philosophy is not the huge metaphysical tract, but the personal journal...or, best of all, the novel." An advocation of the artist-philosopher. "The job of the artist and of the philosopher is to widen the area of consciousness for the civilisation."

SECONDARY SOURCES AND REVIEWS:

1. *British Books News* (Dec., 1957):   .
2. Hamilton, Iain. "Enough of Their Guff," in *Spectator* (Oct. 18, 1957):   .
3. *Harper's Bazaar* (Dec., 1957):   .
4. Hobson, Harold. "Cross-Section of Discontent," in *Christian Science Monitor* (Apr. 17, 1958):   .
5. Lambert, J. W. "Young Lions," in *Sunday Times* (Oct. 13, 1957):   .
6. "Not the Cream But the Top of the Milk," in *Times Literary Supplement* (1957): 674. Response from Wilson on p. 689.
7. Pryce-Jones, Alan. "The Messiahs of the Milk Bars?" in *Listener* (Nov. 7, 1957):   .
8. Wilson, Angus. "Protest Meeting," in *Observer* (Oct. 13, 1957):   .

C5. **"The Writer in His Age,"** in *London Magazine* 4 (no. 5, 1957): 53-55. [literature]

C6. **"Colin Wilson Discusses Great Writing,"** in *New York Times Book Review* (Feb. 17, 1957): 2. [literature]

"Great writing is created when a mind with a positive and powerful bias starts taking a microscope to the substance of everyday life."

C7. **"Cause Without a Rebel,"** in *Encore* no. 9 (June/July, 1957): 13-35. [literature]

The Second Encore Symposium on British Play Writing, the full text of the meeting held at the Royal Court Theatre, Nov. 18, 1956. Panel: Benn W. Levy, Wolf Mankowitz, Arthur Miller, John Whiting, and Colin Wilson. Chairman: Kenneth Tynan. This verbatim transcription of the proceedings, complete with grunts, audience sounds, laughter, etc., remains readable and entertaining, thanks to Mankowitz, who seemed to be interested primarily in making points at the expense of Wilson. This be-

comes so blatant at times that the audience begins to partici-
pate, shouting: "Stick to the theatre, not an attack on Wilson!"
The debate, though lively, is largely ineffectual, and one gets
the feeling early on that no real conclusion would be reached.
Marilyn Monroe was in the audience, and people seemed to be
more interested in her than in the proceedings. During the
course of the discussion Wilson makes some controversial state-
ments regarding Shakespeare, calling him "a great poet but a
second-rate mind," thus infuriating Mankowitz even further.

C8.   "In Touch with Reality," in *Encore* no. 9 (June/July, 1957): 7-
9, 46. [literature]

The state of modern drama and how Wilson intends to put it
right.

C9.   "Existential Criticism and the Work of Aldous Huxley," in
London Magazine 5 (no. 9, 1958): 46-59. [literature]

b.   as: "Appendix 1," in *The Strength to Dream: Literature and the
Imagination*, by Colin Wilson.   London: Victor Gollancz,
1962, cloth, p.   . Expanded from the original.
bb.   as: "Appendix 1," in *The Strength to Dream: Literature and the
Imagination*, by Colin Wilson.   Boston: Houghton Mifflin
Co., 1962, cloth, p.   . Expanded from the original
bc.   as: "Appendix 1," in *The Strength to Dream: Literature and the
Imagination*, by Colin Wilson.   Westport, CT: Greenwood
Press, 1973, cloth, p.   . Expanded from the original.
bd.   as: "Appendix 1," in *The Strength to Dream: Literature and the
Imagination*, by Colin Wilson.   London: Abacus/Sphere,
1976, paper, p. 197-220. Expanded from the original.
c.   as: "   ," in *El Poder de Soñar*. Barcelona: Luis de Caralt,
1965, cloth, p.   . [Spanish]
d.   as: "   ," in *Munhaggwa Sangsangiyeog*. Seoul: Beomusa,
1978, cloth, p.   . [Korean]
e.   as: "   ," in *Yumeniru Chikara*. Tokyo: Takeuchi Shoten,
n.d., cloth, p.   . [Japanese]

C10.   "Shaw and Stringberg," in *The Shavian* no. 15 (June, 1959):
24. [literature]

C11.   "Existential Criticism," in *Chicago Review* 13 (Summer, 1959):
152-181. [literature]

b.   *Eagle and Earwig*. London: John Baker, 1965, cloth, p. 55-85.

c. as: "   ," in *Shinjidai no Bungaku.* Tokyo: Fukumura
Shuppan, 1976, cloth, p.   . [Japanese]

C12. **"The Writer and Publicity: A Reply to Critics,"** in *Encounter* 13
(Nov., 1959): 8-13. [literature]

Wilson outlines what happened to him and the other "Angry
Young Men" of the 1950s when they got caught in the vora-
cious jaws of the literary establishment's publicity machine.

b. *Eagle and Earwig.* London: John Baker, 1965, cloth, p. 242-
254.
c. as: "   ," in *Shinjidai no Bungaku.* Tokyo: Fukumura Shuppan, 1976, cloth, p.   . [Japanese]

C13. **"The Month,"** in *Twentieth Century* 166 (Dec., 1959): 492-498.
[autobiography]

C14. **"Country of the Blind,"** in *Protest*, edited by Gene Feldman
and Max Gartenburg. London: Souvenir Press, 1959, cloth,
p. 202-217. [philosophy]

An excerpt from *The Outsider.*

C15. **"What Makes a Sex Murderer?"** by Colin Wilson and Pat Pitman, in *Sunday Pictorial* (Jan. 17, 1960): 11. [crime]

C16. **"Strictly Personal,"** in *Education* (Jan. 29, 1960): 214-216.
[education]

Wilson writes about his experiences in the British educational
system.

C17. **"On the Bridge: A Memoir of the Fifties,"** in *Encounter* 14
(Apr., 1960): 17-23. [autobiography]

b. *The Bicameral Critic*, by Colin Wilson, edited by Howard Dossor. Bath, Avon: Ashgrove Press, 1985, paper, p. 257-269.
bb. *The Bicameral Critic*, by Colin Wilson, edited by Howard Dossor. Salem, NH: Salem House, 1985, cloth, p. 257-269.

Wilson's account of his involvement with the leaders of an ide-
alistic movement called "The Bridge," who were seeking disciples in London during the early 1950s. Wilson initially became
involved, gradually dissented, and finally broke with the group.
It was here that he first met Stuart Holroyd.

C18. "In a Vanishing London I Pick Up the Grim Trail of Murder," in *Evening Standard* (Aug. 8, 1960): 7. My Search for Jack the Ripper #1. [crime]

b. included in: *Unsolved! Classic True Murder Cases*, edited by Richard Glyn Jones. London: Xanadu, 1987, cloth, p. 11-32.

C19. "Amazing—How Luck Never Deserted the Killer," in *Evening Standard* (Aug. 9, 1960): 12. My Search for Jack the Ripper #2. [crime]

b. included in: *Unsolved! Classic True Murder Cases*, edited by Richard Glyn Jones. London: Xanadu, 1987, cloth, p. 11-32.

C20. "Always, a Woman Ready to Die," in *Evening Standard* (Aug. 10, 1960): 12. My Search for Jack the Ripper #3. [crime]

b. included in: *Unsolved! Classic True Murder Cases*, edited by Richard Glyn Jones. London: Xanadu, 1987, cloth, p. 11-32.

C21. "The Most Sensational Crime Night of Them All," in *Evening Standard* (Aug. 11, 1960): 12. My Search for Jack the Ripper #4. [crime]

b. included in: *Unsolved! Classic True Murder Cases*, edited by Richard Glyn Jones. London: Xanadu, 1987, cloth, p. 11-32.

C22. "Now the Final Question: Who Was the Ripper?" in *Evening Standard* (Aug. 12, 1960): 12. My Search for Jack the Ripper #5. [crime]

b. included in: *Unsolved! Classic True Murder Cases*, edited by Richard Glyn Jones. London: Xanadu, 1987, cloth, p. 11-32.

C23. "Alexis Kivi," in *Aylesford Review* 4 (Winter, 1960/61): 15-20. [literature]

An assessment of the work of the highly-rated Finnish writer, "...of such stature that every Englishman should be familiar with his novel from his schooldays...."

C24. "The Faust Outsider," in *Encyclopaedia of Murder*, by Colin Wilson and Pat Pitman. London: Arthur Barker, 1961, cloth, p. 559-561. [crime]

A discarded fragment from *The Outsider* discussing the "possessed" criminal and the man who commits crime for gain. Burke and Hare and Jack the Ripper are contrasted in this light. The Outsider is the man, Wilson says, who finds it impossible to become "possessed" because "his desires are not strong enough."

C25. **"The Study of Murder,"** in *Encyclopaedia of Murder*, by Colin Wilson and Pat Pitman. London: Arthur Barker, 1961, cloth, p. 17-44. [crime]

What can be learned from a study of crime?; Existentialism; The existential picture of man; Dürrenmatt's *The Pledge*; The lonely inn murder; The "abnormality" of murder; The crime of boredom; The psychology of motiveless crime; The problem of sex crime; The psychology of sexual murder; The criminal mentality; Capital punishment; A personal postscript.

C26. **"Friedrich Dürrenmatt: Heir of the Existential Tradition,"** in *London Magazine* 1 (June, 1961): 77-83. [literature]

 b. as: "Appendix 3," in *The Strength to Dream: Literature and the Imagination*, by Colin Wilson. London: Victor Gollancz, 1962, cloth, p. .
 bb. as: "Appendix 3," in *The Strength to Dream: Literature and the Imagination*, by Colin Wilson. Boston: Houghton Mifflin Co., 1962, cloth, p. .
 bc. as: "Appendix 3," in *The Strength to Dream: Literature and the Imagination*, by Colin Wilson. Westport, CT: Greenwood Press, 1973, cloth, p. .
 bd. as: "Appendix 3," in *The Strength to Dream: Literature and the Imagination*, by Colin Wilson. London: Abacus/Sphere, 1976, paper, p. 231-240.
 c. as: "   ," in *El Poder de Soñar*. Barcelona: Luis de Caralt, 1965, cloth, p. . [Spanish]
 d. as: "   ," in *Munhaggwa Sangsangiyeog*. Seoul: Beomusa, 1978, cloth, p. . [Korean]
 e. as: "   ," in *Yumeniru Chikara*. Tokyo: Takeuchi Shoten, n.d., cloth, p. . [Japanese]

C27. **"Can Art Help?"** in *Studio* 162 (Sept., 1961): 86-89. [art]

Written at the request of the Editor, who wanted an article on the role art can play in establishing a new "golden age" of civilization.

C28. "Henry Williamson," in *Aylesford Review* 4 (Autumn, 1961): 131-143. [literature]

C29. "Some Comments on the Beats and the Angries," in *Outsider Magazine* 1 (Fall, 1961): 57-60. [literature]

C30. "Nikos Kazantzakis," in *London Magazine* 1 (Dec., 1961): 80-89. [literature]

  b. as: "Appendix 2," in *The Strength to Dream: Literature and the Imagination*, by Colin Wilson. London: Victor Gollancz, 1962, cloth, p. .

  bb. as: "Appendix 2," in *The Strength to Dream: Literature and the Imagination*, by Colin Wilson. Boston: Houghton Mifflin Co., 1962, cloth, p. .

  bc. as: "Appendix 2," in *The Strength to Dream: Literature and the Imagination*, by Colin Wilson. Westport, CT: Greenwood Press, 1973, cloth, p. .

  bd. as: "Appendix 2," in *The Strength to Dream: Literature and the Imagination*, by Colin Wilson. London: Abacus/Sphere, 1976, paper, p. 221-230.

  c. as: " ," in *El Poder de Soñar*. Barcelona: Luis de Caralt, 1965, cloth, p. . [Spanish]

  d. as: " ," in *Munhaggwa Sangsangiyeog*. Seoul: Beomusa, 1978, cloth, p. . [Korean]

  e. as: " ," in *Yumeniru Chikara*. Tokyo: Takeuchi Shoten, n.d., cloth, p. . [Japanese]

C31. "I Write As I Please," in *John O'London's* 7 (1962): 52. [literature]

No. 2 in the series, "I Write As I Please." Discusses the problems of writing and getting published, the demands of publishers, and the problem of obscenity.

C32. "Some Notes on Grave's Prose," in *Shenandoah* 13 (Winter, 1962): 55-62. [literature]

  b. *Aylesford Review* 4 (Autumn, 1962): 270-276.
  c. *The Bicameral Critic*, by Colin Wilson, edited by Howard F. Dossor. Bath: Ashgrove Press, 1985, paper, p. 134-141.
  cb. *The Bicameral Critic*, by Colin Wilson, edited by Howard F. Dossor. Salem, NH: Salem House, 1985, cloth, p. 134-141.

C33. "This Filthy Literary Racket," in *John O'London's* 7 (1962): 147. [literature]

"I would like to see a thoroughly healthy cynicism on the part of the 'general public' towards fashionable literary opinion." Number 6 in the series, "I Write As I Please."

C34. **"Existential Temper of the Modern Novel,"** in *Christian Faith and the Contemporary Arts*, edited by Finlay Eversole. New York: Abingen Press, 1962, cloth, p. 115-120. [literature]

b. *Eagle and Earwig.* London: John Baker, 1965, cloth, p. 86-92.
c. as: "   ," in *Shinjidai no Bungaku.* Tokyo: Fukumura Shuppan, 1976, cloth, p.   . [Japanese]

C35. **"Thoughts on Being Biographed,"** in *John O'London's* 7 (1962): 243-244. [literature]

Thoughts on the publication of Sidney Campion's biography. "If being biographed at the age of 30 is a kind of success, then statistics indicate that chances are 10-1 I'm a bad writer." Number 10 in the series, "I Write As I Please."

C36. **"The Great Unrecognised,"** in *John O'London's* 7 (1962): 336. [literature]

Number 14 in the series, "I Write As I Please," this essay discusses important writers neglected during their own lifetimes. Henry Williamson and John Cowper Powys are cited as examples.

C37. **"Priestley Revalued,"** in *John O'London's* 7 (1962): 395-396. [literature]

Number 16 in the series, "I Write As I Please."

C38. **"The Paintings of D. H. Lawrence,"** in *Studio* 164 (Oct., 1962): 133-134. [art]

Wilson's reactions to four Lawrence paintings: "Fauns and Nymphs," "Rape of the Sabine Women," "The Kiss," and "The Dance."

C39. **"Introvert—Extrovert,"** in *John O'London's* 7 (1962): 555-556. [literature]

Number 23 in the series, "I Write As I Please," was instigated by a letter from J. B. Priestley suggesting that most fashionable writers of this century have been introverts. Wilson expounds on this theory.

C40. **"Going into Europe,"** in *Encounter* (Dec., 1962): 57. See also the sequel, "Going into Europe Again" (C71). [current affairs]

C41. **"The Weirdies,"** in *Time and Tide, with John O'London's* 44 (Feb., 1963): 21-22. [autobiography]

Wilson reveals some of the more eccentric contents of his mailbag.

C42. **"Scientific Establishment,"** in *Time and Tide, with John O'London's* 44 (Feb. 14-20, 1963): 23-24. [science]

C43. **"A Manifesto for the Young,"** in *Birmingham Bulletin* no. 2 (Autumn, 1963): . [philosophy]

C44. **"The Swamp and the Desert: Notes on Powys and Hemingway: 1. John Cowper Powys,"** in *Aylesford Review* 6 (Spring, 1964): 85-93. [literature]

    b. *Eagle and Earwig*. London: John Baker, 1965, cloth, p. 113-127.

    c. as: " ," in *Shinjidai no Bungaku*. Tokyo: Fukumura Shuppan, 1976, cloth, p. . [Japanese]

C45. **"Life and Living It,"** in *Nursing Mirror* (Aug. 21, 1964): 13, 16. [philosophy]

C46. **"The Swamp and the Desert: Notes on Powys and Hemingway: 2. Ernest Hemingway,"** in *Aylesford Review* 6 (Summer/Autumn, 1964): 129-135. [literature]

    b. *Eagle and Earwig*. London: John Baker, 1965, cloth, p. 113-127.

    c. as: " ," in *Shinjidai no Bungaku*. Tokyo: Fukumura Shuppan, 1976, cloth, p. . [Japanese]

Notes on Powys and Hemingway.

C47. **"The Ends of Pain,"** in *Town* (Dec., 1964): 47, 110. [psychology]

C48. **"Crimes of Freedom—and Their Cure,"** in *Twentieth Century* 173 (Winter, 1964/65): 25-31. [crime]

b. *The Bicameral Critic*, by Colin Wilson, edited by Howard F. Dossor. Bath: Ashgrove Press, 1985, paper, p. 220-227.

bb. *The Bicameral Critic*, by Colin Wilson, edited by Howard F. Dossor. Salem, NH: Salem House, 1985, cloth, p. 220-227.

The twentieth-century crime of boredom is brought about by "excess of freedom" and the lack of direction felt by some individuals in modern society. Maslow's work with alcoholics in America—effecting a cure by inducing "peak experiences"—is seen as a possible step towards understanding and, perhaps, even solving the problem.

C49. **"The Way of Knowledge,"** in *British Weekly* (Jan. 6, Jan. 13, and Jan. 20, 1966): . [philosophy]

A three-part credo.

C50. **"Big Universities Preclude Real Education,"** in *Daily Telegraph Magazine* (Jan. 21, 1966): 5. [education]

C51. **"Crime: The New Trend in Murder,"** in *Edgar Wallace Mystery Magazine* 3 (Dec., 1966): 47-54. [crime]

C52. **"Homage to E. H. Visiak,"** in *Aylesford Review* 8 (Winter, 1966/67): 221-236. [literature]

C53. **"Vietnam War,"** in *Authors Take Sides on Vietnam*, edited by Cecil Woolf and J. Bagguley. London: Peter Owen, 1967, cloth, p. 103-104. [current affairs]

C54. **"Existential Psychology: A Novelist's Approach,"** in *Challenges of Humanistic Psychology*, edited by James F. T. Bugental. New York: McGraw-Hill, 1967, cloth, p. 68-78. [psychology]

b. *The Bicameral Critic*, by Colin Wilson, edited by Howard F. Dossor. Bath: Ashgrove Press, 1985, paper, p. 38-54.

bb. *The Bicameral Critic*, by Colin Wilson, edited by Howard F. Dossor. Salem, NH: Salem House, 1985, cloth, p. 38-54.

Phenomenology; The "robot"; The "St. Neot's Margin"; The "orgasm experience"; The "robot" and the "real me"; Consciousness and habit; External stimulation and internal intentionality; "Faculty X"; The spirit/body duality; Beyond the "robot"; Conclusion: man's possible evolution.

C55. "Drought: An April Shower in the Literary Desert," in *Los Angeles Times Calendar Magazine* (Jan. 15, 1967): 1, 28. [literature]

C56. "Inside the Outsider," in *North-West Today* (Feb. 25, 1968): 4-5. [current affairs]

Impressions of the United States.

C57. "Writer in Residence," in *Encounter* 32 (June, 1969): 78-84. [autobiography/education]

   b. *The Bicameral Critic*, by Colin Wilson, edited by Howard F. Dossor. Bath: Ashgrove Press, 1985, paper, p. 241-256.
  bb. *The Bicameral Critic*, by Colin Wilson, edited by Howard F. Dossor. Salem, NH: Salem House, 1985, cloth, p. 241-256.

Amusing account of Wilson's experiences as writer-in-residence at Hollins Girls' College in America. "Americans sometimes say that England is the greenest country in the world, but I have never seen so much continuous, luxuriant greenness as between Hollins and Washington, D.C." He also seemed to enjoy the way of life there: "America has simply gone further in doing what all civilisation sets out to do: making life pleasant and convenient." But he was not unaware of poverty: "I wondered how it must feel for some young Negress to take a domestic job with the college and compare the lives of the faculty children with those of her own...."

C58. "Daphne du Maurier," in *Listener* 83 (1970): 787. [literature]

C59. "Lindsay As Novelist and Mystic," in *The Strange Genius of David Lindsay*, edited by J. B. Pick. Glendale, CA: Griffin, 1970, cloth, p. 33-91. [literature]

   b. London: John Baker, 1970, cloth, p. 33-91.

Revision of an essay first published in *Eagle and Earwig*, and later expanded to form the book, *The Haunted Man: The Strange Genius of David Lindsay* (see A55).

SECONDARY SOURCES AND REVIEWS:

1. *Books & Bookmen* 16 (Jan., 1971): 17.

2. *Times Literary Supplement* (1970): 1346. Follow-up letter published on page 1422.

C60. **"Prophets in Reverse,"** in *Daily Telegraph Colour Supplement* (Apr. 17, 1970): 18. [philosophy]

C61. **"A Universe That Thinks?"** in *Illustrated London News* 257 (July 20, 1970): 22-23. [philosophy]

C62. **"Strong Physick,"** in *Times* (July 20, 1970): 8. [literature]

Wilson seeks a publisher for E. H. Visiak's memoirs.

C63. **"The Image and the Truth,"** in *Illustrated London News* 257 (Aug. 22, 1970): 25. [current affairs]

On the distortion of the news by the media.

C64. **"The Former Life of Mrs. Smith,"** in *Man, Myth, and Magic* issue 91. Bristol: Purnell, 1970-72, cloth, p. . Frontiers of Belief Series. This series was issued in fascicles, then collected into permanent cloth volumes. [occult]

C65. **"Faculty X,"** in *Man, Myth, and Magic* issue 108. Bristol: Purnell, 1970-72, cloth, p. . Frontiers of Belief Series. This series was issued in fascicles, then collected into permanent cloth volumes. [philosophy]

A condensed version of ideas first expressed in *Poetry and Mysticism*, and expanded upon in *The Occult*.

C66. **"Occultism—The Future,"** in *Man, Myth, and Magic* issue 111. Bristol: Purnell, 1970-72, cloth, p. . Frontiers of Belief Series. This series was issued in fascicles, then collected into permanent cloth volumes. [occult]

Wilson, C. A. Burland, Rosalind Heywood, Rev. J. C. Neil-Smith, Patric Walker, and Dennis Wheatley discuss occultism.

C67. **"Angry? Who, Us?"** in *T.V. Times* 62 (Jan. 7, 1971): 6. [literature]

The "Angry Young Men" of the 1950s were never really angry in the first place.

C68. "Man Without Qualities," in *Books & Bookmen* 16 (Mar., 1971): 4-6. [literature]

The life and works of Robert Musil.

b. as: "Robert Musil, the Man Without Qualities," in *Existentially Speaking: Essays on the Philosophy of Literature*, by Colin Wilson. San Bernardino, CA: The Borgo Press, 1989, cloth, p. 105-110. Published simultaneously in trade paperback.

C69. "When Is a Neurotic Not a Neurotic?" in *Daily Telegraph Magazine* (Apr. 2, 1971): 7. [psychology]

"The correct definition of a neurotic is a man who is weak-minded enough to think he needs a psychiatrist."

C70. "Colin Wilson on Young People," in *Listener* 85 (1971): 482. [current affairs]

C71. "Going into Europe Again?" in *Encounter* (July, 1971): 24-25. [current affairs]

Britain's entry into the Common Market. A sequel to "Going into Europe" (C40).

C72. "Freud, Reich, and Nietzsche," in *The Humanist* 86 (July, 1971): 213-214. [psychology]

C73. "Getting Inside the Outsiders," in *T.V. Times* 65 (Oct. 21, 1971): 12. [psychology]

A re-examination of the frustrations of the human condition fifteen years later.

C74. "Bertrand Russell: Philosophical Partygoer," in *Books & Bookmen* 17 (Nov., 1971): 26-29. [philosophy]

C75. "To Be Or Not To Be: Sartre's Dilemma," in *The Humanist* 86 (Dec., 1971): 363-365. [philosophy]

C76. "Are You a Witch and Don't Know It?" in *T.V. Times* 66 (Dec. 30, 1971): 9 or 21 (depending on the regional edition in which it appeared). [occult]

C77. **"Love As an Adventure in Mutual Freedom,"** in *Love Today, a New Exploration*, edited by Herbert A. Otto. New York: Association Press, 1972, cloth, p. 49-65. [philosophy]

   b. *The Bicameral Critic*, by Colin Wilson, edited by Howard F. Dossor. Bath: Ashgrove Press, 1985, paper, p. 55-72.

  bb. *The Bicameral Critic*, by Colin Wilson, edited by Howard F. Dossor. Salem, NH: Salem House, 1985, cloth, p. 55-72.

C78. **"'Dual-Value Response': A New Key to Nietzsche,"** in *Malahat Review* 24 (Oct., 1972): 53-66. [philosophy]

   b. *The Bicameral Critic*, by Colin Wilson, edited by Howard F. Dossor. Bath: Ashgrove Press, 1985, paper, p. 95-109.

  bb. *The Bicameral Critic*, by Colin Wilson, edited by Howard F. Dossor. Salem, NH: Salem House, 1985, cloth, p. 95-109.

The enigma of Nietzsche; Heidegger on Nietzsche; Nihilism; The "dual-value response"; Examples of this in Nietzsche's life; The "bird's-eye view"; Nietzsche and sex; Parallels with the ideas of Husserl.

C79. **"Dominance and Sex,"** in *Sexual Behavior* 2 (Oct., 1972): . [psychology]

   b. *Sexual Behavior—Current Issues: An Interdisciplinary Prospective*, edited by L. Gross. New York: Spectrum Books, 1974, p. 127-135. [psychology]

With a commentary by Jessie Bernard.

C80. **"Wagner and Strauss,"** in *Audio* (Nov., 1972): 48-49, 52. [music]

C81. **"Brahms and Bax,"** in *Audio* (Dec., 1972): 48-49, 122. [music]

C82. **"Civilisation and Individual Fulfilment,"** in *Philosophy Forum* 12 (1973): 1-27. [philosophy]

   b. *The Bicameral Critic*, by Colin Wilson, edited by Howard F. Dossor. Bath: Ashgrove Press, 1985, paper, p. 11-37.

  bb. *The Bicameral Critic*, by Colin Wilson, edited by Howard F. Dossor. Salem, NH: Salem House, 1985, cloth, p. 11-37.

C83. **"Problems of Modern Music,"** in *Audio* (Mar., 1973): 44-45. [music]

C84. "The Decline of Modern Opera," in *Audio* (Apr., 1973): 44-45. [music]

C85. "One of the Greatest Intellectual Advances of the Twentieth Century: An Evaluation of the Work of Charlotte Bach," in *Time Out* no. 164 (Apr. 13-19, 1973): 13-15. [psychology]

C86. "The Essence of Berlioz," in *Audio* (May, 1973): 26-27. [music]

C87. "Korngold and Kurt Weill," in *Audio* (June, 1973): 36-37. [music]

C88. "Haydn—The World's Most Underrated Great Composer," in *Audio* (July, 1973): 36-38. [music]

C89. "Modern Music," in *Audio* (Aug., 1973): 42-43. [music]

Readers' reactions to modern music—"It's a fraud!" they claim. Wilson states his own point-of-view.

C90. "Bach Was a Bore," in *Audio* (Sept., 1973): 52-53. [music]

Wilson recalls his conversion to early music.

C91. "Tchaikovsky—The Karl Marx of Music?" in *Audio* (Oct., 1973): 89-91. [music]

How Tchaikovsky's music has earned him a party ticket.

C92. "History Cut on the Bias," in *Daily Telegraph Magazine* (Oct. 26, 1973): 85. [current affairs]

C93. "Silence of Jarvenpaa—The Rise and Fall of Sibelius," in *Audio* (Nov., 1973): 107-109. [music]

C94. "Gorran," in *My Cornwall*, edited by Michael Lyams. Bodmin: Bossiney Books, 1973, cloth, p. 68-82. [description and travel]

C95. "Doomed Society?" in *Journal of Human Relations* 21 (Fourth Quarter, 1973): 395-410. [philosophy]

C96. "Verdict on Verdi—Magnifico!" in *Audio* (Dec., 1973): 105, 107. [music]

C97. **"Ladykillers,"** in *Crimes and Punishment*. London: Phoebus Publications, 1973-75, paper, 6 vols., p. 1-6. [crime]

Wilson contributed one article per fascicle to this series, as listed below. Wilson's contributions were then gathered into one volume by Howard F. Dossor into one alphabetical sequence as *The Mammoth Book of True Crime* (see A89).

b. *The Mammoth Book of True Crime*, by Colin Wilson, edited by Howard F. Dossor. London: Robinson Publishing, 1988, paper, p. 343-351.

bb. *The Mammoth Book of True Crime*, by Colin Wilson, edited by Howard F. Dossor. New York: Carroll & Graf, 1988, paper, p. 343-351.

C98. **"Are You a Dominant Person?"** in *Ibid.*, p. 29-34. [crime]

b. as: "Dominance," in *The Mammoth Book of True Crime*, by Colin Wilson, edited by Howard F. Dossor. London: Robinson Publishing, 1988, paper, p. 142-149.

bb. as: "Dominance," in *The Mammoth Book of True Crime*, by Colin Wilson, edited by Howard F. Dossor. New York: Carroll & Graf, 1988, paper, p. 142-149.

C99. **"Greed,"** in *Ibid.*, p. 57-62. [crime]

b. *The Mammoth Book of True Crime*, by Colin Wilson, edited by Howard F. Dossor. London: Robinson Publishing, 1988, paper, p. 219-226.

bb. *The Mammoth Book of True Crime*, by Colin Wilson, edited by Howard F. Dossor. New York: Carroll & Graf, 1988, paper, p. 219-226.

C100. **"Kidnappers,"** in *Ibid.*, p. 85-90. [crime]

b. *The Mammoth Book of True Crime*, by Colin Wilson, edited by Howard F. Dossor. London: Robinson Publishing, 1988, paper, p. 326-333.

bb. *The Mammoth Book of True Crime*, by Colin Wilson, edited by Howard F. Dossor. New York: Carroll & Graf, 1988, paper, p. 326-333.

C101. **"Creatures That Thirst for Blood,"** in *Ibid.*, p. 113-118. [crime]

C102. **"Protection Rackets,"** in *Ibid.*, p. 141-146. [crime]

    b.   *The Mammoth Book of True Crime*, by Colin Wilson, edited by Howard F. Dossor. London: Robinson Publishing, 1988, paper, p. 493-501.

    bb. *The Mammoth Book of True Crime*, by Colin Wilson, edited by Howard F. Dossor. New York: Carroll & Graf, 1988, paper, p. 493-501.

C103. **"Witchcraft,"** in *Ibid.*, p. 169-174. [crime]

C104. **"Jealousy,"** in *Ibid.*, p. 197-204. [crime]

C105. **"The Alibis,"** in *Ibid.*, p. 225-230. [crime]

    b.   as: "Alibis," in *The Mammoth Book of True Crime*, by Colin Wilson, edited by Howard F. Dossor. London: Robinson Publishing, 1988, paper, p. 10-17.

    bb. as: "Alibis," in *The Mammoth Book of True Crime*, by Colin Wilson, edited by Howard F. Dossor. New York: Carroll & Graf, 1988, paper, p. 10-17.

C106. **"Rape,"** in *Ibid.*, p. 253-259. [crime]

C107. **"Triangle of Death,"** in *Ibid.*, p. 281-287. [crime]

    b.   as: "Vicious Triangles," in *The Mammoth Book of True Crime*, by Colin Wilson, edited by Howard F. Dossor. London: Robinson Publishing, 1988, paper, p. 597-604.

    bb. as: "Vicious Triangles," in *The Mammoth Book of True Crime*, by Colin Wilson, edited by Howard F. Dossor. New York: Carroll & Graf, 1988, paper, p. 597-604.

C108. **"Deadly Doctors,"** in *Ibid.*, p. 309-314. [crime]

    b.   as: "Doctors of Death," in *The Mammoth Book of True Crime*, by Colin Wilson, edited by Howard F. Dossor. London: Robinson Publishing, 1988, paper, p. 134-141.

    bb. as: "Doctors of Death," in *The Mammoth Book of True Crime*, by Colin Wilson, edited by Howard F. Dossor. New York: Carroll & Graf, 1988, paper, p. 134-141.

C109. **"Together They Slay,"** in *Ibid.*, p. 337-343. [crime]

b. as: "Killer Couples," in *The Mammoth Book of True Crime*, by Colin Wilson, edited by Howard F. Dossor. London: Robinson Publishing, 1988, paper, p. 334-342.

bb. as: "Killer Couples," in *The Mammoth Book of True Crime*, by Colin Wilson, edited by Howard F. Dossor. New York: Carroll & Graf, 1988, paper, p. 334-342.

C110. **"Human Beasts,"** in *Ibid.*, p. 365-370. [crime]

b. as: "Headless Corpses," in *The Mammoth Book of True Crime*, by Colin Wilson, edited by Howard F. Dossor. London: Robinson Publishing, 1988, paper, p. 235-242.

bb. as: "Headless Corpses," in *The Mammoth Book of True Crime*, by Colin Wilson, edited by Howard F. Dossor. New York: Carroll & Graf, 1988, paper, p. 235-242.

C111. **"Gangsters,"** in *Ibid.*, p. 393-398. [crime]

b. *The Mammoth Book of True Crime*, by Colin Wilson, edited by Howard F. Dossor. London: Robinson Publishing, 1988, paper, p. 202-209.

bb. *The Mammoth Book of True Crime*, by Colin Wilson, edited by Howard F. Dossor. New York: Carroll & Graf, 1988, paper, p. 202-209.

C112. **"Crooked Cops,"** in *Ibid.*, p. 421-426. [crime]

b. as: "Police Corruption," in *The Mammoth Book of True Crime*, by Colin Wilson, edited by Howard F. Dossor. London: Robinson Publishing, 1988, paper, p. 485-492.

bb. as: "Police Corruption," in *The Mammoth Book of True Crime*, by Colin Wilson, edited by Howard F. Dossor. New York: Carroll & Graf, 1988, paper, p. 485-492.

C113. **"Perverted Killers,"** in *Ibid.*, p. 449-454. [crime]

b. as: "Perverts," in *The Mammoth Book of True Crime*, by Colin Wilson, edited by Howard F. Dossor. London: Robinson Publishing, 1988, paper, p. 468-475.

bb. as: "Perverts," in *The Mammoth Book of True Crime*, by Colin Wilson, edited by Howard F. Dossor. New York: Carroll & Graf, 1988, paper, p. 468-475.

C114. **"Organised Crime,"** in *Ibid.*, p. 477-482. [crime]

b. as: "Underworlds," in *The Mammoth Book of True Crime*, by Colin Wilson, edited by Howard F. Dossor. London: Robinson Publishing, 1988, paper, p. 581-588.

bb. as: "Underworlds," in *The Mammoth Book of True Crime*, by Colin Wilson, edited by Howard F. Dossor. New York: Carroll & Graf, 1988, paper, p. 581-588.

C115. "Sex Scandals," in *Ibid.*, p. 505-512. [crime]

C116. "Con Men," in *Ibid.*, p. 533-539. [crime]

b. *The Mammoth Book of True Crime*, by Colin Wilson, edited by Howard F. Dossor. London: Robinson Publishing, 1988, paper, p. 104-110.

bb. *The Mammoth Book of True Crime*, by Colin Wilson, edited by Howard F. Dossor. New York: Carroll & Graf, 1988, paper, p. 104-110.

C117. "Mass Murderers," in *Ibid.*, p. 561-567. [crime]

b. *The Mammoth Book of True Crime*, by Colin Wilson, edited by Howard F. Dossor. London: Robinson Publishing, 1988, paper, p. 405-413.

bb. *The Mammoth Book of True Crime*, by Colin Wilson, edited by Howard F. Dossor. New York: Carroll & Graf, 1988, paper, p. 405-413.

C118. "Stranglers," in *Ibid.*, p. 589-594. [crime]

b. *The Mammoth Book of True Crime*, by Colin Wilson, edited by Howard F. Dossor. London: Robinson Publishing, 1988, paper, p. 548-555.

bb. *The Mammoth Book of True Crime*, by Colin Wilson, edited by Howard F. Dossor. New York: Carroll & Graf, 1988, paper, p. 548-555.

C119. "Vital Clues," in *Ibid.*, p. 617-622. [crime]

b. *The Mammoth Book of True Crime*, by Colin Wilson, edited by Howard F. Dossor. London: Robinson Publishing, 1988, paper, p. 614-622.

bb. *The Mammoth Book of True Crime*, by Colin Wilson, edited by Howard F. Dossor. New York: Carroll & Graf, 1988, paper, p. 614-622.

C120. "Killed on Duty," in *Ibid.*, p. 645-650. [crime]

b. as: "Cop Killers," in *The Mammoth Book of True Crime*, by Colin Wilson, edited by Howard F. Dossor. London: Robinson Publishing, 1988, paper, p. 111-118.

bb. as: "Cop Killers," in *The Mammoth Book of True Crime*, by Colin Wilson, edited by Howard F. Dossor. New York: Carroll & Graf, 1988, paper, p. 111-118.

C121. **"Scarlet Women,"** in *Ibid.*, p. 673-677. [crime]

b. as: "Female Murderers," in *The Mammoth Book of True Crime*, by Colin Wilson, edited by Howard F. Dossor. London: Robinson Publishing, 1988, paper, p. 175-182.

bb. as: "Female Murderers," in *The Mammoth Book of True Crime*, by Colin Wilson, edited by Howard F. Dossor. New York: Carroll & Graf, 1988, paper, p. 175-182.

C122. **"Fire-Raisers,"** in *Ibid.*, p. 701-706. [crime]

b. as: "Arson," in *The Mammoth Book of True Crime*, by Colin Wilson, edited by Howard F. Dossor. London: Robinson Publishing, 1988, paper, p. 27-35.

bb. as: "Arson," in *The Mammoth Book of True Crime*, by Colin Wilson, edited by Howard F. Dossor. New York: Carroll & Graf, 1988, paper, p. 27-35.

C123. **"Spy-Masters,"** in *Ibid.*, p. 729-734. [crime]

C124. **"One-Way Ticket,"** in *Ibid.*, p. 757-762. [crime]

b. as: "Train Murders," in *The Mammoth Book of True Crime*, by Colin Wilson, edited by Howard F. Dossor. London: Robinson Publishing, 1988, paper, p. 573-580.

bb. as: "Train Murders," in *The Mammoth Book of True Crime*, by Colin Wilson, edited by Howard F. Dossor. New York: Carroll & Graf, 1988, paper, p. 573-580.

C125. **"Parent Killers,"** in *Ibid.*, p. 785-791. [crime]

b. *The Mammoth Book of True Crime*, by Colin Wilson, edited by Howard F. Dossor. London: Robinson Publishing, 1988, paper, p. 460-467.

bb. *The Mammoth Book of True Crime*, by Colin Wilson, edited by Howard F. Dossor. New York: Carroll & Graf, 1988, paper, p. 460-467.

C126. "Sabotage," in *Ibid.*, p. 813-816. [crime]

b. *The Mammoth Book of True Crime*, by Colin Wilson, edited by Howard F. Dossor. London: Robinson Publishing, 1988, paper, p. 512-520.

bb. *The Mammoth Book of True Crime*, by Colin Wilson, edited by Howard F. Dossor. New York: Carroll & Graf, 1988, paper, p. 512-520.

C127. "Sleepwalkers," in *Ibid.*, p. 841-846. [crime]

b. as: "Sleep-Walking Slayers," in *The Mammoth Book of True Crime*, by Colin Wilson, edited by Howard F. Dossor. London: Robinson Publishing, 1988, paper, p. 530-539.

bb. as: "Sleep-Walking Slayers," in *The Mammoth Book of True Crime*, by Colin Wilson, edited by Howard F. Dossor. New York: Carroll & Graf, 1988, paper, p. 530-539.

C128. "There's a Corpse in the Cupboard," in *Ibid.*, p. 869-876. [crime]

b. as: "Houses of Death," in *The Mammoth Book of True Crime*, by Colin Wilson, edited by Howard F. Dossor. London: Robinson Publishing, 1988, paper, p. 269-277.

bb. as: "Houses of Death," in *The Mammoth Book of True Crime*, by Colin Wilson, edited by Howard F. Dossor. New York: Carroll & Graf, 1988, paper, p. 269-277.

C129. "Occult," in *Ibid.*, p. 897-902. [crime]

b. as: "Occult Detection," in *The Mammoth Book of True Crime*, by Colin Wilson, edited by Howard F. Dossor. London: Robinson Publishing, 1988, paper, p. 445-451.

bb. as: "Occult Detection," in *The Mammoth Book of True Crime*, by Colin Wilson, edited by Howard F. Dossor. New York: Carroll & Graf, 1988, paper, p. 445-451.

C130. "Jekyll and Hyde," in *Ibid.*, p. 925-930. [crime]

b. as: "Dual Personality," in *The Mammoth Book of True Crime*, by Colin Wilson, edited by Howard F. Dossor. London: Robinson Publishing, 1988, paper, p. 159-166.

bb. as: "Dual Personality," in *The Mammoth Book of True Crime*, by Colin Wilson, edited by Howard F. Dossor. New York: Carroll & Graf, 1988, paper, p. 159-166.

C131. "Blackmail," in *Ibid.*, p. 953-959. [crime]

    b. *The Mammoth Book of True Crime*, by Colin Wilson, edited by Howard F. Dossor. London: Robinson Publishing, 1988, paper, p. 70-77.

   bb. *The Mammoth Book of True Crime*, by Colin Wilson, edited by Howard F. Dossor. New York: Carroll & Graf, 1988, paper, p. 70-77.

C132. "War Crimes," in *Ibid.*, p. 981-985. [crime]

    b. *The Mammoth Book of True Crime*, by Colin Wilson, edited by Howard F. Dossor. London: Robinson Publishing, 1988, paper, p. 623-630.

   bb. *The Mammoth Book of True Crime*, by Colin Wilson, edited by Howard F. Dossor. New York: Carroll & Graf, 1988, paper, p. 623-630.

C133. "Imposters," in *Ibid.*, p. 1009-1015. [crime]

    b. *The Mammoth Book of True Crime*, by Colin Wilson, edited by Howard F. Dossor. London: Robinson Publishing, 1988, paper, p. 287-295.

   bb. *The Mammoth Book of True Crime*, by Colin Wilson, edited by Howard F. Dossor. New York: Carroll & Graf, 1988, paper, p. 287-295.

C134. "Left-Luggage Murders," in *Ibid.*, p. 1037-1043. [crime]

    b. *The Mammoth Book of True Crime*, by Colin Wilson, edited by Howard F. Dossor. London: Robinson Publishing, 1988, paper, p. 352-360.

   bb. *The Mammoth Book of True Crime*, by Colin Wilson, edited by Howard F. Dossor. New York: Carroll & Graf, 1988, paper, p. 352-360.

C135. "Celluloid Sinners," in *Ibid.*, p. 1065-1070. [crime]

C136. "Hired Killers," in *Ibid.*, p. 1093-1097. [crime]

    b. *The Mammoth Book of True Crime*, by Colin Wilson, edited by Howard F. Dossor. London: Robinson Publishing, 1988, paper, p. 251-259.

   bb. *The Mammoth Book of True Crime*, by Colin Wilson, edited by Howard F. Dossor. New York: Carroll & Graf, 1988, paper, p. 251-259.

C137. "Lonely-Hearts Killers," in *Ibid.*, p. 1121-1126. [crime]

    b. as: "Lonely Hearts Killers," in *The Mammoth Book of True Crime*, by Colin Wilson, edited by Howard F. Dossor. London: Robinson Publishing, 1988, paper, p. 378-386.

    bb. as: "Lonely Hearts Killers," in *The Mammoth Book of True Crime*, by Colin Wilson, edited by Howard F. Dossor. New York: Carroll & Graf, 1988, paper, p. 378-386.

C138. "Easy Prey," in *Ibid.*, p. 1149-1154. [crime]

    b. as: "Victims," in *The Mammoth Book of True Crime*, by Colin Wilson, edited by Howard F. Dossor. London: Robinson Publishing, 1988, paper, p. 605-613.

    bb. as: "Victims," in *The Mammoth Book of True Crime*, by Colin Wilson, edited by Howard F. Dossor. New York: Carroll & Graf, 1988, paper, p. 605-613.

C139. "Lethal Lawyers," in *Ibid.*, p. 1177-1184. [crime]

    b. *The Mammoth Book of True Crime*, by Colin Wilson, edited by Howard F. Dossor. London: Robinson Publishing, 1988, paper, p. 361-369.

    bb. *The Mammoth Book of True Crime*, by Colin Wilson, edited by Howard F. Dossor. New York: Carroll & Graf, 1988, paper, p. 361-369.

C140. "Monsters," in *Ibid.*, p. 1205-1212. [crime]

    b. *The Mammoth Book of True Crime*, by Colin Wilson, edited by Howard F. Dossor. London: Robinson Publishing, 1988, paper, p. 422-429.

    bb. *The Mammoth Book of True Crime*, by Colin Wilson, edited by Howard F. Dossor. New York: Carroll & Graf, 1988, paper, p. 422-429.

C141. "The Sound of Gunfire," in *Ibid.*, p. 1233-1237. [crime]

    b. as: "Gun Deaths," in *The Mammoth Book of True Crime*, by Colin Wilson, edited by Howard F. Dossor. London: Robinson Publishing, 1988, paper, p. 227-234.

    bb. as: "Gun Deaths," in *The Mammoth Book of True Crime*, by Colin Wilson, edited by Howard F. Dossor. New York: Carroll & Graf, 1988, paper, p. 227-234.

C142. "Air Crimes," in *Ibid.*, p. 1261-1267. [crime]

    b. *The Mammoth Book of True Crime*, by Colin Wilson, edited by Howard F. Dossor. London: Robinson Publishing, 1988, paper, p. 18-26.

    bb. *The Mammoth Book of True Crime*, by Colin Wilson, edited by Howard F. Dossor. New York: Carroll & Graf, 1988, paper, p. 18-26.

C143. "Robber Barons," in *Ibid.*, p. 1289-1293. [crime]

    b. *The Mammoth Book of True Crime*, by Colin Wilson, edited by Howard F. Dossor. London: Robinson Publishing, 1988, paper, p. 502-511.

    bb. *The Mammoth Book of True Crime*, by Colin Wilson, edited by Howard F. Dossor. New York: Carroll & Graf, 1988, paper, p. 502-511.

C144. "Murderous Families," in *Ibid.*, p. 1317-1322. [crime]

    b. as: "Families of Death," in *The Mammoth Book of True Crime*, by Colin Wilson, edited by Howard F. Dossor. London: Robinson Publishing, 1988, paper, p. 167-174.

    bb. as: "Families of Death," in *The Mammoth Book of True Crime*, by Colin Wilson, edited by Howard F. Dossor. New York: Carroll & Graf, 1988, paper, p. 167-174.

C145. "Seduction," in *Ibid.*, p. 1345-1350. [crime]

C146. "Bandits," in *Ibid.*, p. 1373-1377. [crime]

    b. *The Mammoth Book of True Crime*, by Colin Wilson, edited by Howard F. Dossor. London: Robinson Publishing, 1988, paper, p. 53-60.

    bb. *The Mammoth Book of True Crime*, by Colin Wilson, edited by Howard F. Dossor. New York: Carroll & Graf, 1988, paper, p. 53-60.

C147. "A Hard Day at the Office," in *Ibid.*, p. 1401-1406. [crime]

    b. as: "Office Crimes," in *The Mammoth Book of True Crime*, by Colin Wilson, edited by Howard F. Dossor. London: Robinson Publishing, 1988, paper, p. 452-459.

    bb. as: "Office Crimes," in *The Mammoth Book of True Crime*, by Colin Wilson, edited by Howard F. Dossor. New York: Carroll & Graf, 1988, paper, p. 452-459.

C148. "Homosexual Murders," *Ibid.*, p. 1429-1435. [crime]

    b. as: "Homosexual Murder," in *The Mammoth Book of True Crime*, by Colin Wilson, edited by Howard F. Dossor. London: Robinson Publishing, 1988, paper, p. 260-268.

    bb. as: "Homosexual Murder," in *The Mammoth Book of True Crime*, by Colin Wilson, edited by Howard F. Dossor. New York: Carroll & Graf, 1988, paper, p. 260-268.

C149. "High Cost of Libel," in *Ibid.*, p. 1457-1462. [crime]

    b. as: "Libel," in *The Mammoth Book of True Crime*, by Colin Wilson, edited by Howard F. Dossor. London: Robinson Publishing, 1988, paper, p. 370-377.

    bb. as: "Libel," in *The Mammoth Book of True Crime*, by Colin Wilson, edited by Howard F. Dossor. New York: Carroll & Graf, 1988, paper, p. 370-377.

C150. "Betrayed," in *Ibid.*, p. 1485-1489. [crime]

    b. as: "Betrayal," in *The Mammoth Book of True Crime*, by Colin Wilson, edited by Howard F. Dossor. London: Robinson Publishing, 1988, paper, p. 61-69.

    bb. as: "Betrayal," in *The Mammoth Book of True Crime*, by Colin Wilson, edited by Howard F. Dossor. New York: Carroll & Graf, 1988, paper, p. 61-69.

C151. "Law Changers," in *Ibid.*, p. 1513-1518. [crime]

C152. "Crimes of Passion," in *Ibid.*, p. 1541-1546. [crime]

    b. *The Mammoth Book of True Crime*, by Colin Wilson, edited by Howard F. Dossor. London: Robinson Publishing, 1988, paper, p. 127-133.

    bb. *The Mammoth Book of True Crime*, by Colin Wilson, edited by Howard F. Dossor. New York: Carroll & Graf, 1988, paper, p. 127-133.

C153. "Artists in Crime," in *Ibid.*, p. 1569-1573. [crime]

    b. as: "Artists' Crimes," in *The Mammoth Book of True Crime*, by Colin Wilson, edited by Howard F. Dossor. London: Robinson Publishing, 1988, paper, p. 36-43.

bb. as: "Artists' Crimes," in *The Mammoth Book of True Crime*, by Colin Wilson, edited by Howard F. Dossor. New York: Carroll & Graf, 1988, paper, p. 36-43.

C154. **"Drugs,"** in *Ibid.*, p. 1597-1602. [crime]

b. *The Mammoth Book of True Crime*, by Colin Wilson, edited by Howard F. Dossor. London: Robinson Publishing, 1988, paper, p. 150-158.

bb. *The Mammoth Book of True Crime*, by Colin Wilson, edited by Howard F. Dossor. New York: Carroll & Graf, 1988, paper, p. 150-158.

C155. **"Millionth Chance,"** in *Ibid.*, p. 1625-1629. [crime]

b. as: "Chance in a Million," in *The Mammoth Book of True Crime*, by Colin Wilson, edited by Howard F. Dossor. London: Robinson Publishing, 1988, paper, p. 86-94.

bb. as: "Chance in a Million," in *The Mammoth Book of True Crime*, by Colin Wilson, edited by Howard F. Dossor. New York: Carroll & Graf, 1988, paper, p. 86-94.

C156. **"The Forgers,"** in *Ibid.*, p. 1653-1658. [crime]

b. as: "Forgery," in *The Mammoth Book of True Crime*, by Colin Wilson, edited by Howard F. Dossor. London: Robinson Publishing, 1988, paper, p. 183-190.

bb. as: "Forgery," in *The Mammoth Book of True Crime*, by Colin Wilson, edited by Howard F. Dossor. New York: Carroll & Graf, 1988, paper, p. 183-190.

C157. **"Hit-Men,"** in *Ibid.*, p. 1681-1686. [crime]

b. as: "Stick-Up Men," in *The Mammoth Book of True Crime*, by Colin Wilson, edited by Howard F. Dossor. London: Robinson Publishing, 1988, paper, p. 540-548.

bb. as: "Stick-Up Men," in *The Mammoth Book of True Crime*, by Colin Wilson, edited by Howard F. Dossor. New York: Carroll & Graf, 1988, paper, p. 540-548.

C158. **"Justice in Slow Motion,"** in *Ibid.*, p. 1709-1714. [crime]

b. as: "Justice Delayed," in *The Mammoth Book of True Crime*, by Colin Wilson, edited by Howard F. Dossor. London: Robinson Publishing, 1988, paper, p. 317-325.

bb. as: "Justice Delayed," in *The Mammoth Book of True Crime*, by Colin Wilson, edited by Howard F. Dossor. New York: Carroll & Graf, 1988, paper, p. 317-325.

C159. **"Children Who Kill,"** in *Ibid.*, p. 1737-1743. [crime]

  b. *The Mammoth Book of True Crime*, by Colin Wilson, edited by Howard F. Dossor. London: Robinson Publishing, 1988, paper, p. 95-103.
  bb. *The Mammoth Book of True Crime*, by Colin Wilson, edited by Howard F. Dossor. New York: Carroll & Graf, 1988, paper, p. 95-103.

C160. **"The Husband Killers,"** in *Ibid.*, p. 1765-1769. [crime]

  b. as: "Husband Killers," in *The Mammoth Book of True Crime*, by Colin Wilson, edited by Howard F. Dossor. London: Robinson Publishing, 1988, paper, p. 278-286.
  bb. as: "Husband Killers," in *The Mammoth Book of True Crime*, by Colin Wilson, edited by Howard F. Dossor. New York: Carroll & Graf, 1988, paper, p. 278-286.

C161. **"Dangerous Millionaires,"** in *Ibid.*, p. 1793-1797. [crime]

  b. as: "Murderous Millionaires," in *The Mammoth Book of True Crime*, by Colin Wilson, edited by Howard F. Dossor. London: Robinson Publishing, 1988, paper, p. 437-444.
  bb. as: "Murderous Millionaires," in *The Mammoth Book of True Crime*, by Colin Wilson, edited by Howard F. Dossor. New York: Carroll & Graf, 1988, paper, p. 437-444.

C162. **"Suicide,"** in *Ibid.*, p. 1821-1825. [crime]

  b. *The Mammoth Book of True Crime*, by Colin Wilson, edited by Howard F. Dossor. London: Robinson Publishing, 1988, paper, p. 556-564.
  bb. *The Mammoth Book of True Crime*, by Colin Wilson, edited by Howard F. Dossor. New York: Carroll & Graf, 1988, paper, p. 556-564.

C163. **"Women Haters,"** in *Ibid.*, p. 1849-1854. [crime]

C164. **"Cannibalism,"** in *Ibid.*, p. 1877-1881. [crime]

b. *The Mammoth Book of True Crime*, by Colin Wilson, edited by Howard F. Dossor. London: Robinson Publishing, 1988, paper, p. 78-85.

bb. *The Mammoth Book of True Crime*, by Colin Wilson, edited by Howard F. Dossor. New York: Carroll & Graf, 1988, paper, p. 78-85.

C165. **"They Cheated the Gallows,"** in *Ibid.*, p. 1905-1910. [crime]

b. as: "Gallows Cheats," in *The Mammoth Book of True Crime*, by Colin Wilson, edited by Howard F. Dossor. London: Robinson Publishing, 1988, paper, p. 191-201.

bb. as: "Gallows Cheats," in *The Mammoth Book of True Crime*, by Colin Wilson, edited by Howard F. Dossor. New York: Carroll & Graf, 1988, paper, p. 191-201.

C166. **"Death from a Stranger,"** in *Ibid.*, p. 1933-1942. [crime]

C167. **"Good-Time Girls,"** in *Ibid.*, p. 1961-1965. [crime]

C168. **"Unwanted Lovers,"** in *Ibid.*, p. 1989-1994. [crime]

b. *The Mammoth Book of True Crime*, by Colin Wilson, edited by Howard F. Dossor. London: Robinson Publishing, 1988, paper, p. 589-596.

bb. *The Mammoth Book of True Crime*, by Colin Wilson, edited by Howard F. Dossor. New York: Carroll & Graf, 1988, paper, p. 589-596.

C169. **"Assassins,"** in *Ibid.*, p. 2017-2023. [crime]

b. as: "Assassination," in *The Mammoth Book of True Crime*, by Colin Wilson, edited by Howard F. Dossor. London: Robinson Publishing, 1988, paper, p. 44-52.

bb. as: "Assassination," in *The Mammoth Book of True Crime*, by Colin Wilson, edited by Howard F. Dossor. New York: Carroll & Graf, 1988, paper, p. 44-52.

C170. **"Sisters of Cain,"** in *Ibid.*, p. 2045-2049. [crime]

C171. **"Soldiers Who Slaughter,"** in *Ibid.*, p. 2073-2079. [crime]

b. as: "Military Murders," in *The Mammoth Book of True Crime*, by Colin Wilson, edited by Howard F. Dossor. London: Robinson Publishing, 1988, paper, p. 414-421.

bb. as: "Military Murders," in *The Mammoth Book of True Crime*, by Colin Wilson, edited by Howard F. Dossor. New York: Carroll & Graf, 1988, paper, p. 414-421.

C172. **"Blue-Blooded Murder,"** in *Ibid*., p. 2101-2106. [crime]

b. as: "High Society Murder," in *The Mammoth Book of True Crime*, by Colin Wilson, edited by Howard F. Dossor. London: Robinson Publishing, 1988, paper, p. 243-250.
bb. as: "High Society Murder," in *The Mammoth Book of True Crime*, by Colin Wilson, edited by Howard F. Dossor. New York: Carroll & Graf, 1988, paper, p. 243-250.

C173. **"Martyrs,"** in *Ibid*., p. 2129-2133. [crime]

b. *The Mammoth Book of True Crime*, by Colin Wilson, edited by Howard F. Dossor. London: Robinson Publishing, 1988, paper, p. 396-404.
bb. *The Mammoth Book of True Crime*, by Colin Wilson, edited by Howard F. Dossor. New York: Carroll & Graf, 1988, paper, p. 396-404.

C174. **"Crimes at Sea,"** in *Ibid*., p. 2157-2162. [crime]

C175. **"Motiveless Murder,"** in *Ibid*., p. 2185-2189. [crime]

b. *The Mammoth Book of True Crime*, by Colin Wilson, edited by Howard F. Dossor. London: Robinson Publishing, 1988, paper, p. 430-436.
bb. *The Mammoth Book of True Crime*, by Colin Wilson, edited by Howard F. Dossor. New York: Carroll & Graf, 1988, paper, p. 430-436.

C176. **"The Macabre Mind of the Poisoners,"** in *Ibid*., p. 2213-2218. [crime]

b. as: "Poisoners," in *The Mammoth Book of True Crime*, by Colin Wilson, edited by Howard F. Dossor. London: Robinson Publishing, 1988, paper, p. 476-484.
bb. as: "Poisoners," in *The Mammoth Book of True Crime*, by Colin Wilson, edited by Howard F. Dossor. New York: Carroll & Graf, 1988, paper, p. 476-484.

C177. **"Gentlemen Crooks,"** in *Ibid*., p. 2241-2246. [crime]

b. *The Mammoth Book of True Crime*, by Colin Wilson, edited by Howard F. Dossor. London: Robinson Publishing, 1988, paper, p. 210-218.

bb. *The Mammoth Book of True Crime*, by Colin Wilson, edited by Howard F. Dossor. New York: Carroll & Graf, 1988, paper, p. 210-218.

C178. **"Intolerance,"** in *Ibid.*, p. 2269-2275. [crime]

b. *The Mammoth Book of True Crime*, by Colin Wilson, edited by Howard F. Dossor. London: Robinson Publishing, 1988, paper, p. 308-316.

bb. *The Mammoth Book of True Crime*, by Colin Wilson, edited by Howard F. Dossor. New York: Carroll & Graf, 1988, paper, p. 308-316.

C179. **"Impeachment,"** in *Ibid.*, p. 2297-2303. [crime]

C180. **"Royalty,"** in *Ibid.*, p. 2325-2330. [crime]

C181. **"Pirates,"** in *Ibid.*, p. 2353-2358. [crime]

C182. **"Theft—The Super Thieves,"** in *Ibid.*, p. 2381-2386. [crime]

b. as: "Super Thieves," in *The Mammoth Book of True Crime*, by Colin Wilson, edited by Howard F. Dossor. London: Robinson Publishing, 1988, paper, p. 565-572.

bb. as: "Super Thieves," in *The Mammoth Book of True Crime*, by Colin Wilson, edited by Howard F. Dossor. New York: Carroll & Graf, 1988, paper, p. 565-572.

C183. **"Parliament,"** in *Ibid.*, p. 2409-2416. [crime]

C184. **"Country-Style Murder,"** in *Ibid.*, p. 2437-2442. [crime]

b. as: "Country Killings," in *The Mammoth Book of True Crime*, by Colin Wilson, edited by Howard F. Dossor. London: Robinson Publishing, 1988, paper, p. 119-126.

bb. as: "Country Killings," in *The Mammoth Book of True Crime*, by Colin Wilson, edited by Howard F. Dossor. New York: Carroll & Graf, 1988, paper, p. 119-126.

C185. **"Acquittals,"** in *Ibid.*, p. 2465-2470. [crime]

b. *The Mammoth Book of True Crime*, by Colin Wilson, edited by Howard F. Dossor. London: Robinson Publishing, 1988, paper, p. 1-9.

bb. *The Mammoth Book of True Crime*, by Colin Wilson, edited by Howard F. Dossor. New York: Carroll & Graf, 1988, paper, p. 1-9.

C186. **"Murderous Menials,"** in *Ibid.*, p. 2494-2500. [crime]

b. as: "Servants Who Murder," in *The Mammoth Book of True Crime*, by Colin Wilson, edited by Howard F. Dossor. London: Robinson Publishing, 1988, paper, p. 521-529.

bb. as: "Servants Who Murder," in *The Mammoth Book of True Crime*, by Colin Wilson, edited by Howard F. Dossor. New York: Carroll & Graf, 1988, paper, p. 521-529.

C187. **"Crimes by Gaslight,"** in *Ibid.*, p. 2521-2525. [crime]

C188. **"Inheritance,"** in *Ibid.*, p. 2549-2555. [crime]

b. as: "Inheritance Crime," in *The Mammoth Book of True Crime*, by Colin Wilson, edited by Howard F. Dossor. London: Robinson Publishing, 1988, paper, p. 296-307.

bb. as: "Inheritance Crime," in *The Mammoth Book of True Crime*, by Colin Wilson, edited by Howard F. Dossor. New York: Carroll & Graf, 1988, paper, p. 296-307.

C189. **"Conspirators,"** in *Ibid.*, p. 2577-2581. [crime]

C190. **"Death in the Tropics,"** in *Ibid.*, p. 2605-2613. [crime]

C191. **"Faith or Fantasy?"** in *Ibid.*, p. 2633-2637. [crime]

b. as: "Manic Messiahs," in *The Mammoth Book of True Crime*, by Colin Wilson, edited by Howard F. Dossor. London: Robinson Publishing, 1988, paper, p. 387-395.

bb. as: "Manic Messiahs," in *The Mammoth Book of True Crime*, by Colin Wilson, edited by Howard F. Dossor. New York: Carroll & Graf, 1988, paper, p. 387-395.

C192. **"The Steinheil Affair,"** in *Ibid.*, p. 2661-2670. [crime]

C193. **"Maurice,"** in *E. M. Forster: The Critical Heritage*, edited by Philip Gardner. London: Routledge & Kegan Paul, 1973, cloth, p. 453-456. [literature]

First printed as a review in *The Spectator* (see E58).

C194. **"Jack the Ripper,"** in *Illustrated Police News*, edited by Brian Lake. Great Newspapers Reprinted Series, no. 25. London: Peter Way Ltd., 1974, cloth, unnumbered. [crime]

C195. **"The Genius of Ronald Duncan,"** in *A Tribute to Ronald Duncan by His Friends*, edited by Harold Lockyear. Hartland, Devon: Hartland Press, 1974, cloth, p. 76-95. [literature]

   ba. as: "Ronald Duncan: A Self-Revealing Poet," in *Books & Bookmen* 19 (Aug., 1974): 66-68.

   bb. as: "Ronald Duncan: A Self-Revealing Poet 2," in *Books & Bookmen* 20 (Nov., 1974): 40-41.

   bc. as: "Ronald Duncan: A Self-Revealing Poet 3," in *Books & Bookmen* 20 (Apr., 1975): 61-62.

   bd. as: "Ronald Duncan: A Self-Revealing Poet 4," in *Books & Bookmen* 20 (June, 1975): 31-33.

   c. *The Bicameral Critic*, by Colin Wilson, edited by Howard F. Dossor. Bath: Ashgrove Press, 1985, paper, p. 196-219.

   cb. *The Bicameral Critic*, by Colin Wilson, edited by Howard F. Dossor. Salem, NH: Salem House, 1985, cloth, p. 196-219.

C196. **"Tales of Offenbach,"** in *Audio* (Jan., 1974): 93-94. [music]

C197. **"Wyndham Lewis: A Refracted Talent?"** in *Books & Bookmen* 19 (Feb., 1974): 44-48; (Mar., 1974): 51-52; and (Apr., 1974): 39-42. [literature]

   b. *Existentially Speaking: Essays on the Philosophy of Literature*, by Colin Wilson. San Bernardino, CA: The Borgo Press, 1989, cloth, p. 83-104. Published simultaneously in trade paperback.

C198. **"The Rise and Fall of Richard Strauss,"** in *Audio* (Feb., 1974): 65-66. [music]

C199. **"Was Mozart Murdered?"** in *Audio* 2 (Mar., 1974): 65-66. [music]

C200. **"Ill-Fated Genius,"** in *Audio* 2 (Apr., 1974): 71-72. [music]

Wilson recalls the financial torments of the great composers.

C201. **"Holst and Delius—Forty Years On,"** in *Audio* 2 (May, 1974): 64-65. [music]

A retrospective comparison of the contrasting careers and musical achievements of the two composers.

C202. "Discs for My Desert Island," in *Audio* 2 (May, 1974): 71-72. [music]

C203. "Charles Ives," in *Audio* 2 (June, 1974): 50-51. [music]

Why was Ives' music ignored for so long?

C204. "The Origin of Whiskey: A Speculation," in *A Treasury of Drinking Pleasure*. s.l.: Privately Published by Santori Ltd., 1974, cloth, p. 11-19. [history]

C205. "The Upside-Down Blessing That Sunk a Battleship," in *T.V. Times* 77 (Oct. 3, 1974): 38-39. [history]

C206. "Nazi Extermination of the Jews," in *Sunday Times* (Feb. 23, 1975): 6. [history]

C207. "Ken Russell: A Director in Search of a Hero," in *Sunday Times* (Mar. 30, 1975): 35. [film]

Later reprinted as a pamphlet (see A41).

C208. "A Dummy Run for Experience," in *New Fiction Magazine* no. 4 (July, 1975): 3. [literature]

An extract from *The Craft of the Novel* (see A45).

C209. "Miles Giffard of St. Austell," in *Murder in the West Country*, edited by Michael Williams. Bodmin: Bossiney Books, 1975, cloth, p. 129-143. [crime]

C210. "An Integrity Born of Hope: Notes on Christopher Isherwood," in *Twentieth Century Literature* 22 (Oct., 1976): 312-331. [literature]

   b. *The Bicameral Critic*, by Colin Wilson, edited by Howard F. Dossor. Bath: Ashgrove Press, 1985, paper, p. 110-133.
   bb. *The Bicameral Critic*, by Colin Wilson, edited by Howard F. Dossor. Salem, NH: Salem House, 1985, cloth, p. 110-133.
   c. *Existentially Speaking: Essays on the Philosophy of Literature*, by Colin Wilson. San Bernardino, CA: The Borgo Press,

1989, cloth, p. 33-52. Published simultaneously in trade paperback.

A view of Isherwood's work written for a special Isherwood issue: "He is one of the very few modern novelists I can think of who has escaped the slide into defeat or negation."

C211. **"The Outsider Twenty Years On,"** in *The Outsider*, by Colin Wilson. London: Pan Books, 1976, paper, p. 9-19. [autobiography]

b. *The Essential Colin Wilson*, by Colin Wilson. London: Harrap, 1985, cloth, p. 14-21.

An interesting autobiographical article about the writing of *The Outsider* and *Ritual in the Dark*. Also deals with the Wilson "revival" following publication of *The Occult*.

C212. **"A Personal Response to Wuthering Heights,"** in *The Art of Emily Brontë*, edited by Anne Smith. London: Vision Press, 1976, cloth, p. 223-237. [literature]

b. *The Bicameral Critic*, by Colin Wilson, edited by Howard F. Dossor. Bath: Ashgrove Press, 1985, paper, p. 172-186.
bb. *The Bicameral Critic*, by Colin Wilson, edited by Howard F. Dossor. Salem, NH: Salem House, 1985, cloth, p. 172-186.

In a controversial and thought-provoking article, Wilson sides with those critics who have found the novel repulsive. Brontë is labelled a "high dominance" woman, and the novel's hero a "brutal roughneck." See also the preface of *The Quest for Wilhelm Reich* for background material on the writing of this article.

C213. **"Just What I've Always Wanted: Father Christmas Gets His Orders,"** in *Punch* 271 (Dec. 1, 1976): 1022. [humor]

C214. **"The Flawed Superman,"** in *Beyond Baker Street: A Sherlockian Anthology*, edited by Michael Harrison. Indianapolis and New York: Bobbs-Merrill Co., 1976, cloth, p. 311-333. [philosophy]

"Even if Holmes is an intellectual superman, the superiority is only skin-deep; basically, he is as helpless and defeated as the rest of us."

C215. "The Male Menopause," in *The Male Menopause*, edited by Derek Bowskill and A. Linacre. London: Frederick Muller, 1976, cloth, p. 117-121. [sex]

C216. "Why I Belong: The London Library," in *Adam* 40 (1976/77): 94-95. [literature]

b. *The London Library*, edited by Miron Grindea. London: Boydell Press/Adam Books, 1978, cloth, p. 90-91.

C217. "Copland, Aaron," in *The Dictionary of Composers*, edited by Charles Osborne. London: Book Club Associates, 1977, cloth, p. 92-93. [music]

C218. "Glazunov, Alexander," in *Ibid.*, p. 141-143. [music]

C219. "Janacek, Leos," in *Ibid.*, p. 183-186. [music]

C220. "Martinu, Bohuslav," in *Ibid.*, p. 213-215. [music]

C221. "Mussorgsky, Modeste," in *Ibid.*, p. 243-245. [music]

C222. "Paganini, Niccolo," in *Ibid.*, p. 251-253. [music]

C223. "Rimsky-Korsakov, Nicolai," in *Ibid.*, p. 278-281. [music]

C224. "Old Stones, Ancient Vibrations," in *Radio Times* (June 13, 1977): 12. [occult]

David Humphries talks to Wilson about the mystical qualities of St. Michael's Mount, Cornwall.

C225. "The Standing Stones of Cornwall," in *South West Review* (England) no. 2 (Oct., 1977): 56-62. [occult]

C226. "Star Lores," in *Observer Magazine* (Oct. 2, 1977): 25, 27, 29-30. [occult]

C227. "Spinoza the Outsider," in *Speculum Spinozanum, 1677-1977*, edited by Siegfried Hessing. London: Routledge & Kegan Paul, 1977, cloth, p. 525-542. [philosophy]

b. *The Bicameral Critic*, by Colin Wilson, edited by Howard F. Dossor. Bath: Ashgrove Press, 1985, paper, p. 73-94.
bb. *The Bicameral Critic*, by Colin Wilson, edited by Howard F. Dossor. Salem, NH: Salem House, 1985, cloth, p. 73-94.

Why is Spinoza so important?; Early influences; Excommunication; General comments on Ethics; Nietzsche's objection to Spinoza; Spinoza the outsider; Spinoza's and Nietzsche's visions compared.

C228. **"The Making of a Playwright,"** in *Shaw Festival Programme 1977 (16th Season).* Niagara-on-the-Lake, Ontario: Shaw Festival, 1977, paper, unnumbered. [literature]

C229. **"The Observer Magazine Horoscope,"** in *Observer Magazine* (Nov., 1977-Apr. 2, 1978): . With Ruth Bartlett. [occult]

C230. **"How the Outsider Came in—To Cornwall,"** in The Countryman 83 (Spring, 1978): 27-32. [autobiography]

C231. **"Royalty and the Ripper,"** in *Royal Murder*, edited by Marc Alexander. London: Frederick Muller, 1978, cloth, p. 203-221. [crime]

C232. **"A Personal View,"** in *The Genius of Shaw*, edited by Michael Holroyd. New York: Holt, Rinehart & Winston, 1979, cloth, p. 223-229. [literature]

   b. *The Bicameral Critic*, by Colin Wilson, edited by Howard F. Dossor. Bath: Ashgrove Press, 1985, paper, p. 187-195.
  bb. *The Bicameral Critic*, by Colin Wilson, edited by Howard F. Dossor. Salem, NH: Salem House, 1985, cloth, p. 187-195.

C233. **"A New Look at the Paranormal,"** in *Bedside Book*, edited by Julian Schuckburgh. London: Windward, 1979, cloth, p. 176-192. [occult]

C234. **"The Occult Detectives,"** in *Genette Is Missing*, edited by John W. Tate. Newton Abbot: David & Charles, 1979, cloth, p. 100-140. [occult]

C235. **"Man Is Born Free, and He Is Everywhere in Chains,"** in *Lying Truths: A Critical Scrutiny of Current Beliefs and Conventions*, edited by Ronald Duncan and Miranda Weston-Smith. New York: Pergamon Press, 1979, cloth, p. 4-7. [philosophy]

An indictment of Rousseau's famous quotation; Wilson concludes that "freedom can only exist in conjunction with a sense of alertness."

C236. "The Right to Work," in *Ibid.*, p. 8-9. [philosophy]

Wilson calls upon De Sade, Marx, and Chesterton to expose this particular "lying truth," asserting that "the 'right to work' is a grotesque piece of illogicality amounting to a confidence trick."

C237. "The Truth That the Church Will Not Face," in *Evening News* (Mar. 7, 1979): 6. [religion]

The Church of England and life after death.

C238. "The Search for the Real Arthur," in *King Arthur Country in Cornwall*, edited by Brenda Duxbury and Michael Williams. Bodmin, Cornwall: Bossiney Books, 1979, cloth, p. 89-100. [mythology]

Arthur's grave; The story of his exhumation at Glastonbury; Did Arthur really live?; Who was Arthur?; Arthur in Cornwall; Excalibur and the Holy Grail: fact or myth?; Arthur's conquest: "Arthur's real conquest [was] the conquest of the European imagination."

C239. "Time in Disarray," in *The Book of Time*, edited by Colin Wilson and John Grant. Newton Abbot, Devon: Westbridge Books, 1980, cloth, p. 285-314. [philosophy]

Is time travel possible?; Time and mind; The divided brain; Faculty X and insight; A ladder of selves. An excellent introduction to Wilson's ideas.

C240. "Anti-Sartre [Part I]," in *Literary Review* no. 17 (May 2-May 15, 1980): 39-43. [philosophy and literature]

C241. "Anti-Sartre [Part II]," in *Literary Review* no. 18 (May 30-June 12, 1980): 40-42. [philosophy and literature]

C242. "Anti-Sartre [Part III]," in *Literary Review* no. 19 (June 27-July 10, 1980): 26-30. [philosophy and literature]

The above three essays were later incorporated as part of *Anti-Sartre, with an Essay on Camus* (see A60).

C243. "Colin Wilson's Ten Strangest Unsolved Murders in History," in *The People's Almanac Presents The Book of Lists #2*, edited by Irving Wallace, David Wallechinsky, Amy Wallace, Sylvia

Wallace. New York: William Morrow & Co., 1980, cloth, p. 51-54. [crime]

b. London: Elm Tree Books, 1980, cloth, p. 51-54.
c. Toronto, New York: Bantam Books, 1981, paper, p. 51-54.
d. London: Corgi Books, 1981, paper, p. 51-54.

C244. "An Alternative View," in *Literary Review* no. 31 (Dec. 18, 1980): 18-19. [films]

C245. "The Miracle of Life," in *The Unexplained*, Volume 1, Issue 9. London: Orbis Publishing Co., 1980, paper, p. 170-173. [science]

An essay about the origins of life.

C246. "A Seeker After Truth," in *The Unexplained*, Volume 3, Issue 29. London: Orbis Publishing Co., 1980, paper, p. 566-569. [occult]

Part I of a three-part article on dowser Tom Lethbridge.

C247. "The Master Dowser," in *The Unexplained*, Volume 3, Issue 31. London: Orbis Publishing Co., 1980, paper, p. 614-617. [occult]

Part II of an article on Tom Lethbridge.

C248. "The World of Uri Geller," in *The Unexplained*, Volume 3, Issue 32. London: Orbis Publishing Co., 1980, paper, p. 621-624. [occult]

Uri Geller's rise to fame—Part I of a three-part series.

C249. "Gateway to Other Worlds," in *The Unexplained*, Volume 3, Issue 33. London: Orbis Publishing Co., 1980, paper, p. 654-657. [occult]

The concluding segment of the Tom Lethbridge article.

C250. "Under the Eyes of Scientists," in *The Unexplained*, Volume 3, Issue 34. London: Orbis Publishing Co., 1980, paper, p. 666-669. [occult]

Continuation of the Geller article—the challenge of the skeptics.

C251. "The Psychic Superstar," in *The Unexplained*, Volume 3, Issue 35. London: Orbis Publishing Co., 1980, paper, p. 686-689. [occult]

The conclusion of the Geller article.

C252. "Spirit Guides at Glastonbury," in *The Unexplained*, Volume 5, Issue 50. London: Orbis Publishing Co., 1980, paper, p. 989-993. [occult]

First part of the story of Frederick Bligh Bond and his discoveries at Glastonbury.

C253. "A Career in Ruins," in *The Unexplained*, Volume 5, Issue 52. London: Orbis Publishing Co., 1980, paper, p. 1038-1040. [occult]

Wilson continues the story of Frederick Bond and how his unusual methods led to him being ostracized by his fellow archaeologists.

C254. "A Very Strange Place," in *The Unexplained*, Volume 5, Issue 53. London: Orbis Publishing Co., 1980, paper, p. 1046-1049. [occult]

The conclusion of Wilson's article on Frederick Bond.

C255. "In the Comet's Tail," in *The Unexplained*, Volume 5, Issue 60. London: Orbis Publishing Co., 1980, paper, p. 1181-1185. [occult]

Wilson examines the amazing theories put forward by Immanuel Velikovsky.

C256. "Catastrophe and Controversy," in *The Unexplained*, Volume 6, Issue 61. London: Orbis Publishing Co., 1980, paper, p. 1218-1220. [occult]

Part II of the story of Immanuel Velikovsky.

C257. "A Fair Hearing," in *The Unexplained*, Volume 6, Issue 62. London: Orbis Publishing Co., 1980, paper, p. 1226-1229. [occult]

The conclusion of the three-part series on Velikovsky.

C258. **"Puharich: Grey Eminence?"** in *The Unexplained*, Volume 12, Issue 133. London: Orbis Publishing Co., 1980, paper, p. 2654-2657. [occult]

Wilson looks at the research and the beliefs of the man behind Uri Geller.

C259. **"Geller's Guru,"** in *The Unexplained*, Volume 12, Issue 136. London: Orbis Publishing Co., 1980, paper, p. 2714-2717. [occult]

Part II of an article about Andrija Puharich.

C260. **"The Horrors of Healing,"** in *The Unexplained*, Volume 12, Issue 137. London: Orbis Publishing Co., 1980, paper, p. 2734-2737. [occult]

An account of the bizarre and horrific events that took place in the Paris churchyard of St. Médard between 1727-1732.

C261. **"Black Monk's Reign of Terror,"** in *The Unexplained*, Volume 13, Issue 150. London: Orbis Publishing Co., 1980, paper, p. 2986-2989. [occult]

Wilson investigates the Pontefract poltergeist.

C262. **"Sartre Obituary,"** in *Evening News* (Apr. 16, 1980): . [obituary]

b. *Anti-Sartre, with an Essay on Camus.* San Bernardino, CA: The Borgo Press, 1981, cloth, p. 45-47. Published simultaneously in trade paperback.

C263. **"Ancient Astronauts,"** in *The Directory of Possibilities*, edited by Colin Wilson and John Grant. Exeter, Devon: Webb & Bower, 1981, cloth, p. 29. [occult]

b. New York: Rutledge Press, 1981, cloth, p. 29.
c. New York: State Mutual Books, 1981, cloth, p. .
d. Toronto: John Wiley & Sons, 1981, paper, p. 29.
e. London: Corgi Books, 1982, paper, p. .

C264. **"Ancient Man,"** in *The Directory of Possibilities*, edited by Colin Wilson and John Grant. Exeter, Devon: Webb & Bower, 1981, cloth, p. 30-31. [occult]

b. New York: Rutledge Press, 1981, cloth, p. 30-31.
c. New York: State Mutual Books, 1981, cloth, p. .
d. Toronto: John Wiley & Sons, 1981, paper, p. 30-31.
e. London: Corgi Books, 1982, paper, p. .

C265. "Arthur," in *The Directory of Possibilities*, edited by Colin Wilson and John Grant. Exeter, Devon: Webb & Bower, 1981, cloth, p. 31-32. [occult]

b. New York: Rutledge Press, 1981, cloth, p. 31-32.
c. New York: State Mutual Books, 1981, cloth, p. .
d. Toronto: John Wiley & Sons, 1981, paper, p. 31-32.
e. London: Corgi Books, 1982, paper, p. .

C266. "Atlantis," in *The Directory of Possibilities*, edited by Colin Wilson and John Grant. Exeter, Devon: Webb & Bower, 1981, cloth, p. 32-33. [occult]

b. New York: Rutledge Press, 1981, cloth, p. 32-33.
c. New York: State Mutual Books, 1981, cloth, p. .
d. Toronto: John Wiley & Sons, 1981, paper, p. 32-33.
e. London: Corgi Books, 1982, paper, p. .

C267. "Book of the Dead," in *The Directory of Possibilities*, edited by Colin Wilson and John Grant. Exeter, Devon: Webb & Bower, 1981, cloth, p. 33-34. [occult]

b. New York: Rutledge Press, 1981, cloth, p. 33-34.
c. New York: State Mutual Books, 1981, cloth, p. .
d. Toronto: John Wiley & Sons, 1981, paper, p. 33-34.
e. London: Corgi Books, 1982, paper, p. .

C268. "Fertility Religion," in *The Directory of Possibilities*, edited by Colin Wilson and John Grant. Exeter, Devon: Webb & Bower, 1981, cloth, p. 35-36. [occult]

b. New York: Rutledge Press, 1981, cloth, p. 35-36.
c. New York: State Mutual Books, 1981, cloth, p. .
d. Toronto: John Wiley & Sons, 1981, paper, p. 35-36.
e. London: Corgi Books, 1982, paper, p. .

C269. "Glastonbury," in *The Directory of Possibilities*, edited by Colin Wilson and John Grant. Exeter, Devon: Webb & Bower, 1981, cloth, p. 36-37. [occult]

b. New York: Rutledge Press, 1981, cloth, p. 36-37.
c. New York: State Mutual Books, 1981, cloth, p. .
d. Toronto: John Wiley & Sons, 1981, paper, p. 36-37.
e. London: Corgi Books, 1982, paper, p. .

C270. **"Gog and Magog,"** in *The Directory of Possibilities*, edited by Colin Wilson and John Grant. Exeter, Devon: Webb & Bower, 1981, cloth, p. 37. [occult]

b. New York: Rutledge Press, 1981, cloth, p. 37.
c. New York: State Mutual Books, 1981, cloth, p. .
d. Toronto: John Wiley & Sons, 1981, paper, p. 37.
e. London: Corgi Books, 1982, paper, p. .

C271. **"Ley Lines,"** in *The Directory of Possibilities*, edited by Colin Wilson and John Grant. Exeter, Devon: Webb & Bower, 1981, cloth, p. 38-39. [occult]

b. New York: Rutledge Press, 1981, cloth, p. 38-39.
c. New York: State Mutual Books, 1981, cloth, p. .
d. Toronto: John Wiley & Sons, 1981, paper, p. 38-39.
e. London: Corgi Books, 1982, paper, p. .

C272. **"Megalithic Monuments,"** in *The Directory of Possibilities*, edited by Colin Wilson and John Grant. Exeter, Devon: Webb & Bower, 1981, cloth, p. 39. [occult]

b. New York: Rutledge Press, 1981, cloth, p. 39.
c. New York: State Mutual Books, 1981, cloth, p. .
d. Toronto: John Wiley & Sons, 1981, paper, p. 39.
e. London: Corgi Books, 1982, paper, p. .

C273. **"Pyramids,"** in *The Directory of Possibilities*, edited by Colin Wilson and John Grant. Exeter, Devon: Webb & Bower, 1981, cloth, p. 41-43. [occult]

b. New York: Rutledge Press, 1981, cloth, p. 41-43.
c. New York: State Mutual Books, 1981, cloth, p. .
d. Toronto: John Wiley & Sons, 1981, paper, p. 41-43.
e. London: Corgi Books, 1982, paper, p. .

C274. **"Rennes-le-Château, Mystery of,"** in *The Directory of Possibilities*, edited by Colin Wilson and John Grant. Exeter, Devon: Webb & Bower, 1981, cloth, p. 43-44. [occult]

b. New York: Rutledge Press, 1981, cloth, p. 43-44.

c. New York: State Mutual Books, 1981, cloth, p. .
d. Toronto: John Wiley & Sons, 1981, paper, p. 43-44.
e. London: Corgi Books, 1982, paper, p. .

C275. "Alchemy," in *The Directory of Possibilities*, edited by Colin Wilson and John Grant. Exeter, Devon: Webb & Bower, 1981, cloth, p. 48-49. [occult]

b. New York: Rutledge Press, 1981, cloth, p. 48-49.
c. New York: State Mutual Books, 1981, cloth, p. .
d. Toronto: John Wiley & Sons, 1981, paper, p. 48-49.
e. London: Corgi Books, 1982, paper, p. .

C276. "Doppelgängers," in *The Directory of Possibilities*, edited by Colin Wilson and John Grant. Exeter, Devon: Webb & Bower, 1981, cloth, p. 51-53. [occult]

b. New York: Rutledge Press, 1981, cloth, p. 51-53.
c. New York: State Mutual Books, 1981, cloth, p. .
d. Toronto: John Wiley & Sons, 1981, paper, p. 51-53.
e. London: Corgi Books, 1982, paper, p. .

C277. "Ghosts," in *The Directory of Possibilities*, edited by Colin Wilson and John Grant. Exeter, Devon: Webb & Bower, 1981, cloth, p. 53-54. [occult]

b. New York: Rutledge Press, 1981, cloth, p. 53-54.
c. New York: State Mutual Books, 1981, cloth, p. .
d. Toronto: John Wiley & Sons, 1981, paper, p. 53-54.
e. London: Corgi Books, 1982, paper, p. .

C278. "Healing," in *The Directory of Possibilities*, edited by Colin Wilson and John Grant. Exeter, Devon: Webb & Bower, 1981, cloth, p. 54-55. [occult]

b. New York: Rutledge Press, 1981, cloth, p. 54-55.
c. New York: State Mutual Books, 1981, cloth, p. .
d. Toronto: John Wiley & Sons, 1981, paper, p. 54-55.
e. London: Corgi Books, 1982, paper, p. .

C279. "Jinxes and Curses," in *The Directory of Possibilities*, edited by Colin Wilson and John Grant. Exeter, Devon: Webb & Bower, 1981, cloth, p. 55-57. [occult]

b. New York: Rutledge Press, 1981, cloth, p. 55-57.
c. New York: State Mutual Books, 1981, cloth, p. .

d. Toronto: John Wiley & Sons, 1981, paper, p. 55-57.

e. London: Corgi Books, 1982, paper, p. .

C280. **"Possession,"** in *The Directory of Possibilities*, edited by Colin Wilson and John Grant. Exeter, Devon: Webb & Bower, 1981, cloth, p. 57-58. [occult]

b. New York: Rutledge Press, 1981, cloth, p. 57-58.

c. New York: State Mutual Books, 1981, cloth, p. .

d. Toronto: John Wiley & Sons, 1981, paper, p. 57-58.

e. London: Corgi Books, 1982, paper, p. .

C281. **"Primitive Magic,"** in *The Directory of Possibilities*, edited by Colin Wilson and John Grant. Exeter, Devon: Webb & Bower, 1981, cloth, p. 58-60. [occult]

b. New York: Rutledge Press, 1981, cloth, p. 58-60.

c. New York: State Mutual Books, 1981, cloth, p. .

d. Toronto: John Wiley & Sons, 1981, paper, p. 58-60.

e. London: Corgi Books, 1982, paper, p. .

C282. **"Pyramid Power,"** in *The Directory of Possibilities*, edited by Colin Wilson and John Grant. Exeter, Devon: Webb & Bower, 1981, cloth, p. 60. [occult]

b. New York: Rutledge Press, 1981, cloth, p. 60.

c. New York: State Mutual Books, 1981, cloth, p. .

d. Toronto: John Wiley & Sons, 1981, paper, p. 60.

e. London: Corgi Books, 1982, paper, p. .

C283. **"Witchcraft,"** in *The Directory of Possibilities*, edited by Colin Wilson and John Grant. Exeter, Devon: Webb & Bower, 1981, cloth, p. 64, 81-82. [occult]

b. New York: Rutledge Press, 1981, cloth, p. 64, 81-82.

c. New York: State Mutual Books, 1981, cloth, p. .

d. Toronto: John Wiley & Sons, 1981, paper, p. 64, 81-82.

e. London: Corgi Books, 1982, paper, p. .

C284. **"Astrology,"** in *The Directory of Possibilities*, edited by Colin Wilson and John Grant. Exeter, Devon: Webb & Bower, 1981, cloth, p. 102-104. [occult]

b. New York: Rutledge Press, 1981, cloth, p. 102-104.

c. New York: State Mutual Books, 1981, cloth, p. .

d. Toronto: John Wiley & Sons, 1981, paper, p. 102-104.

e. London: Corgi Books, 1982, paper, p.   .

C285. **"Clairvoyance,"** in *The Directory of Possibilities*, edited by Colin Wilson and John Grant. Exeter, Devon: Webb & Bower, 1981, cloth, p. 105–107. [occult]

b. New York: Rutledge Press, 1981, cloth, p. 105–107.
c. New York: State Mutual Books, 1981, cloth, p.   .
d. Toronto: John Wiley & Sons, 1981, paper, p. 105–107.
e. London: Corgi Books, 1982, paper, p.   .

C286. **"Seers and Prophets,"** in *The Directory of Possibilities*, edited by Colin Wilson and John Grant. Exeter, Devon: Webb & Bower, 1981, cloth, p. 112–115. [occult]

b. New York: Rutledge Press, 1981, cloth, p. 112–115.
c. New York: State Mutual Books, 1981, cloth, p.   .
d. Toronto: John Wiley & Sons, 1981, paper, p. 112–115.
e. London: Corgi Books, 1982, paper, p.   .

C287. **"Time,"** in *The Directory of Possibilities*, edited by Colin Wilson and John Grant. Exeter, Devon: Webb & Bower, 1981, cloth, p. 115–116. [occult]

b. New York: Rutledge Press, 1981, cloth, p. 115–116.
c. New York: State Mutual Books, 1981, cloth, p.   .
d. Toronto: John Wiley & Sons, 1981, paper, p. 115–116.
e. London: Corgi Books, 1982, paper, p.   .

C288. **"Time-Slip,"** in *The Directory of Possibilities*, edited by Colin Wilson and John Grant. Exeter, Devon: Webb & Bower, 1981, cloth, p. 116–118. [occult]

b. New York: Rutledge Press, 1981, cloth, p. 116–118.
c. New York: State Mutual Books, 1981, cloth, p.   .
d. Toronto: John Wiley & Sons, 1981, paper, p. 116–118.
e. London: Corgi Books, 1982, paper, p.   .

C289. **"Acquired Characteristics,"** in *The Directory of Possibilities*, edited by Colin Wilson and John Grant. Exeter, Devon: Webb & Bower, 1981, cloth, p. 122–123. [occult]

b. New York: Rutledge Press, 1981, cloth, p. 122–123.
c. New York: State Mutual Books, 1981, cloth, p.   .
d. Toronto: John Wiley & Sons, 1981, paper, p. 122–123.
e. London: Corgi Books, 1982, paper, p.   .

The problem of evolution; Acquired characteristics or natural selection—Lamarck or Darwin?

C290. **"Acupuncture,"** in *The Directory of Possibilities*, edited by Colin Wilson and John Grant. Exeter, Devon: Webb & Bower, 1981, cloth, p. 123. [occult]

   b. New York: Rutledge Press, 1981, cloth, p. 123.
   c. New York: State Mutual Books, 1981, cloth, p. .
   d. Toronto: John Wiley & Sons, 1981, paper, p. 123.
   e. London: Corgi Books, 1982, paper, p. .

C291. **"Aura,"** in *The Directory of Possibilities*, edited by Colin Wilson and John Grant. Exeter, Devon: Webb & Bower, 1981, cloth, p. 123-125. [occult]

   b. New York: Rutledge Press, 1981, cloth, p. 123-125.
   c. New York: State Mutual Books, 1981, cloth, p. .
   d. Toronto: John Wiley & Sons, 1981, paper, p. 123-125.
   e. London: Corgi Books, 1982, paper, p. .

The electrical energy field that surrounds living creatures.

C292. **"Automatic Writing,"** in *The Directory of Possibilities*, edited by Colin Wilson and John Grant. Exeter, Devon: Webb & Bower, 1981, cloth, p. 125-126. [occult]

   b. New York: Rutledge Press, 1981, cloth, p. 125-126.
   c. New York: State Mutual Books, 1981, cloth, p. .
   d. Toronto: John Wiley & Sons, 1981, paper, p. 125-126.
   e. London: Corgi Books, 1982, paper, p. .

C293. **"Bio-Feedback,"** in *The Directory of Possibilities*, edited by Colin Wilson and John Grant. Exeter, Devon: Webb & Bower, 1981, cloth, p. 126. [occult]

   b. New York: Rutledge Press, 1981, cloth, p.126.
   c. New York: State Mutual Books, 1981, cloth, p. .
   d. Toronto: John Wiley & Sons, 1981, paper, p. 126.
   e. London: Corgi Books, 1982, paper, p. .

C294. **"Dianetics,"** in *The Directory of Possibilities*, edited by Colin Wilson and John Grant. Exeter, Devon: Webb & Bower, 1981, cloth, p. 126. [occult]

b. New York: Rutledge Press, 1981, cloth, p. 126.
c. New York: State Mutual Books, 1981, cloth, p.   .
d. Toronto: John Wiley & Sons, 1981, paper, p. 126.
e. London: Corgi Books, 1982, paper, p.   .

The conscious control of "automatic" body functions.

C295. **"Dowsing,"** in *The Directory of Possibilities*, edited by Colin Wilson and John Grant. Exeter, Devon: Webb & Bower, 1981, cloth, p. 126-127. [occult]

b. New York: Rutledge Press, 1981, cloth, p. 126-127.
c. New York: State Mutual Books, 1981, cloth, p.   .
d. Toronto: John Wiley & Sons, 1981, paper, p. 126-127.
e. London: Corgi Books, 1982, paper, p.   .

C296. **"Dreams and Visions,"** in *The Directory of Possibilities*, edited by Colin Wilson and John Grant. Exeter, Devon: Webb & Bower, 1981, cloth, p. 127-129. [occult]

b. New York: Rutledge Press, 1981, cloth, p. 127-129.
c. New York: State Mutual Books, 1981, cloth, p.   .
d. Toronto: John Wiley & Sons, 1981, paper, p. 127-129.
e. London: Corgi Books, 1982, paper, p.   .

C297. **"ESP,"** in *The Directory of Possibilities*, edited by Colin Wilson and John Grant. Exeter, Devon: Webb & Bower, 1981, cloth, p. 129-131. [occult]

b. New York: Rutledge Press, 1981, cloth, p. 129-131.
c. New York: State Mutual Books, 1981, cloth, p.   .
d. Toronto: John Wiley & Sons, 1981, paper, p. 129-131.
e. London: Corgi Books, 1982, paper, p.   .

C298. **"Gurdjieff, G. I.,"** in *The Directory of Possibilities*, edited by Colin Wilson and John Grant. Exeter, Devon: Webb & Bower, 1981, cloth, p. 132-134. [occult]

b. New York: Rutledge Press, 1981, cloth, p. 132-134.
c. New York: State Mutual Books, 1981, cloth, p.   .
d. Toronto: John Wiley & Sons, 1981, paper, p. 132-134.
e. London: Corgi Books, 1982, paper, p.   .

C299. **"Homeopathy,"** in *The Directory of Possibilities*, edited by Colin Wilson and John Grant. Exeter, Devon: Webb & Bower, 1981, cloth, p. 134. [occult]

b. New York: Rutledge Press, 1981, cloth, p. 134.
c. New York: State Mutual Books, 1981, cloth, p. .
d. Toronto: John Wiley & Sons, 1981, paper, p. 134.
e. London: Corgi Books, 1982, paper, p. .

C300. "Hypnosis," in *The Directory of Possibilities*, edited by Colin Wilson and John Grant. Exeter, Devon: Webb & Bower, 1981, cloth, p. 134-136. [occult]

b. New York: Rutledge Press, 1981, cloth, p. 134-136.
c. New York: State Mutual Books, 1981, cloth, p. .
d. Toronto: John Wiley & Sons, 1981, paper, p. 134-136.
e. London: Corgi Books, 1982, paper, p. .

C301. "Jung, Jungianism," in *The Directory of Possibilities*, edited by Colin Wilson and John Grant. Exeter, Devon: Webb & Bower, 1981, cloth, p. 136-137. [occult]

b. New York: Rutledge Press, 1981, cloth, p. 136-137.
c. New York: State Mutual Books, 1981, cloth, p. .
d. Toronto: John Wiley & Sons, 1981, paper, p. 136-137.
e. London: Corgi Books, 1982, paper, p. .

C302. "Kirlian Photography," in *The Directory of Possibilities*, edited by Colin Wilson and John Grant. Exeter, Devon: Webb & Bower, 1981, cloth, p. 137-138. [occult]

b. New York: Rutledge Press, 1981, cloth, p. 137-138.
c. New York: State Mutual Books, 1981, cloth, p. .
d. Toronto: John Wiley & Sons, 1981, paper, p. 137-138.
e. London: Corgi Books, 1982, paper, p. .

C303. "Levitation," in *The Directory of Possibilities*, edited by Colin Wilson and John Grant. Exeter, Devon: Webb & Bower, 1981, cloth, p. 138. [occult]

b. New York: Rutledge Press, 1981, cloth, p. 138.
c. New York: State Mutual Books, 1981, cloth, p. .
d. Toronto: John Wiley & Sons, 1981, paper, p. 138.
e. London: Corgi Books, 1982, paper, p. .

C304. "Life After Death," in *The Directory of Possibilities*, edited by Colin Wilson and John Grant. Exeter, Devon: Webb & Bower, 1981, cloth, p. 138-140. [occult]

b. New York: Rutledge Press, 1981, cloth, p. 138-140.
c. New York: State Mutual Books, 1981, cloth, p. .
d. Toronto: John Wiley & Sons, 1981, paper, p. 138-140.
e. London: Corgi Books, 1982, paper, p. .

C305. **"Mediums,"** in *The Directory of Possibilities*, edited by Colin Wilson and John Grant. Exeter, Devon: Webb & Bower, 1981, cloth, p. 140. [occult]

b. New York: Rutledge Press, 1981, cloth, p. 140.
c. New York: State Mutual Books, 1981, cloth, p. .
d. Toronto: John Wiley & Sons, 1981, paper, p. 140.
e. London: Corgi Books, 1982, paper, p. .

C306. **"Multiple Personality,"** in *The Directory of Possibilities*, edited by Colin Wilson and John Grant. Exeter, Devon: Webb & Bower, 1981, cloth, p. 140-142. [occult]

b. New York: Rutledge Press, 1981, cloth, p. 140-142.
c. New York: State Mutual Books, 1981, cloth, p. .
d. Toronto: John Wiley & Sons, 1981, paper, p. 140-142.
e. London: Corgi Books, 1982, paper, p. .

C307. **"Paranormal Photography,"** in *The Directory of Possibilities*, edited by Colin Wilson and John Grant. Exeter, Devon: Webb & Bower, 1981, cloth, p. 143. [occult]

b. New York: Rutledge Press, 1981, cloth, p. 143.
c. New York: State Mutual Books, 1981, cloth, p. .
d. Toronto: John Wiley & Sons, 1981, paper, p. 143.
e. London: Corgi Books, 1982, paper, p. .

C308. **"Peak Experience,"** in *The Directory of Possibilities*, edited by Colin Wilson and John Grant. Exeter, Devon: Webb & Bower, 1981, cloth, p. 143-144. [occult]

b. New York: Rutledge Press, 1981, cloth, p. 143-144.
c. New York: State Mutual Books, 1981, cloth, p. .
d. Toronto: John Wiley & Sons, 1981, paper, p. 143-144.
e. London: Corgi Books, 1982, paper, p. .

C309. **"Pineal Eye,"** in *The Directory of Possibilities*, edited by Colin Wilson and John Grant. Exeter, Devon: Webb & Bower, 1981, cloth, p. 144-145. [occult]

b. New York: Rutledge Press, 1981, cloth, p. 144-145.

c. New York: State Mutual Books, 1981, cloth, p. .

d. Toronto: John Wiley & Sons, 1981, paper, p. 144-145.

e. London: Corgi Books, 1982, paper, p. .

The "Third Eye."

C310. **"Plant Communication,"** in *The Directory of Possibilities*, edited by Colin Wilson and John Grant. Exeter, Devon: Webb & Bower, 1981, cloth, p. 145-146. [occult]

b. New York: Rutledge Press, 1981, cloth, p. 146-148.

c. New York: State Mutual Books, 1981, cloth, p. .

d. Toronto: John Wiley & Sons, 1981, paper, p. 146-148.

e. London: Corgi Books, 1982, paper, p. .

C311. **"Poltergeists,"** in *The Directory of Possibilities*, edited by Colin Wilson and John Grant. Exeter, Devon: Webb & Bower, 1981, cloth, p. 146-148. [occult]

b. New York: Rutledge Press, 1981, cloth, p. 146-148.

c. New York: State Mutual Books, 1981, cloth, p. .

d. Toronto: John Wiley & Sons, 1981, paper, p. 146-148.

e. London: Corgi Books, 1982, paper, p. .

C312. **"Reich, Wilhelm,"** in *The Directory of Possibilities*, edited by Colin Wilson and John Grant. Exeter, Devon: Webb & Bower, 1981, cloth, p. 148-149. [occult]

b. New York: Rutledge Press, 1981, cloth, p. 148-149.

c. New York: State Mutual Books, 1981, cloth, p. .

d. Toronto: John Wiley & Sons, 1981, paper, p. 148-149.

e. London: Corgi Books, 1982, paper, p. .

C313. **"Reincarnation,"** in *The Directory of Possibilities*, edited by Colin Wilson and John Grant. Exeter, Devon: Webb & Bower, 1981, cloth, p. 149-150. [occult]

b. New York: Rutledge Press, 1981, cloth, p. 149-150.

c. New York: State Mutual Books, 1981, cloth, p. .

d. Toronto: John Wiley & Sons, 1981, paper, p. 149-150.

e. London: Corgi Books, 1982, paper, p. .

C314. **"Revelations, Mystical,"** in *The Directory of Possibilities*, edited by Colin Wilson and John Grant. Exeter, Devon: Webb & Bower, 1981, cloth, p. 150-152. [occult]

b. New York: Rutledge Press, 1981, cloth, p. 150-152.
c. New York: State Mutual Books, 1981, cloth, p. .
d. Toronto: John Wiley & Sons, 1981, paper, p. 150-152.
e. London: Corgi Books, 1982, paper, p. .

C315. **"Rosicrucians,"** in *The Directory of Possibilities*, edited by Colin Wilson and John Grant. Exeter, Devon: Webb & Bower, 1981, cloth, p. 152. [occult]

b. New York: Rutledge Press, 1981, cloth, p. 152.
c. New York: State Mutual Books, 1981, cloth, p. .
d. Toronto: John Wiley & Sons, 1981, paper, p. 152.
e. London: Corgi Books, 1982, paper, p. .

C316. **"Spiritualism,"** in *The Directory of Possibilities*, edited by Colin Wilson and John Grant. Exeter, Devon: Webb & Bower, 1981, cloth, p. 152-154. [occult]

b. New York: Rutledge Press, 1981, cloth, p. 152-154.
c. New York: State Mutual Books, 1981, cloth, p. .
d. Toronto: John Wiley & Sons, 1981, paper, p. 152-154.
e. London: Corgi Books, 1982, paper, p. .

C317. **"Steiner, Rudolf,"** in *The Directory of Possibilities*, edited by Colin Wilson and John Grant. Exeter, Devon: Webb & Bower, 1981, cloth, p. 154. [occult]

b. New York: Rutledge Press, 1981, cloth, p. 154.
c. New York: State Mutual Books, 1981, cloth, p. .
d. Toronto: John Wiley & Sons, 1981, paper, p. 154.
e. London: Corgi Books, 1982, paper, p. .

C318. **"Stigmata,"** in *The Directory of Possibilities*, edited by Colin Wilson and John Grant. Exeter, Devon: Webb & Bower, 1981, cloth, p. 154-155. [occult]

b. New York: Rutledge Press, 1981, cloth, p. 154-155.
c. New York: State Mutual Books, 1981, cloth, p. .
d. Toronto: John Wiley & Sons, 1981, paper, p. 154-155.
e. London: Corgi Books, 1982, paper, p. .

C319. **"Tantrism,"** in *The Directory of Possibilities*, edited by Colin Wilson and John Grant. Exeter, Devon: Webb & Bower, 1981, cloth, p. 155. [occult]

b. New York: Rutledge Press, 1981, cloth, p. 155.

c. New York: State Mutual Books, 1981, cloth, p. .
d. Toronto: John Wiley & Sons, 1981, paper, p. 155.
e. London: Corgi Books, 1982, paper, p. .

C320. **"Transcendental Meditation,"** in *The Directory of Possibilities*, edited by Colin Wilson and John Grant. Exeter, Devon: Webb & Bower, 1981, cloth, p. 155-156. [occult]

b. New York: Rutledge Press, 1981, cloth, p. 155-156.
c. New York: State Mutual Books, 1981, cloth, p. .
d. Toronto: John Wiley & Sons, 1981, paper, p. 155-156.
e. London: Corgi Books, 1982, paper, p. .

C321. **"Yoga,"** in *The Directory of Possibilities*, edited by Colin Wilson and John Grant. Exeter, Devon: Webb & Bower, 1981, cloth, p. 156-157. [occult]

b. New York: Rutledge Press, 1981, cloth, p. 156-157.
c. New York: State Mutual Books, 1981, cloth, p. .
d. Toronto: John Wiley & Sons, 1981, paper, p. 156-157.
e. London: Corgi Books, 1982, paper, p. .

C322. **"Zen,"** in *The Directory of Possibilities*, edited by Colin Wilson and John Grant. Exeter, Devon: Webb & Bower, 1981, cloth, p. 157-158. [occult]

b. New York: Rutledge Press, 1981, cloth, p. 157-158.
c. New York: State Mutual Books, 1981, cloth, p. .
d. Toronto: John Wiley & Sons, 1981, paper, p. 157-158.
e. London: Corgi Books, 1982, paper, p. .

C323. **"Flat Earth,"** in *The Directory of Possibilities*, edited by Colin Wilson and John Grant. Exeter, Devon: Webb & Bower, 1981, cloth, p. 173. [occult]

b. New York: Rutledge Press, 1981, cloth, p. 173.
c. New York: State Mutual Books, 1981, cloth, p. .
d. Toronto: John Wiley & Sons, 1981, paper, p. 173.
e. London: Corgi Books, 1982, paper, p. .

C324. **"Relativity,"** in *The Directory of Possibilities*, edited by Colin Wilson and John Grant. Exeter, Devon: Webb & Bower, 1981, cloth, p. 196-197. [occult]

b. New York: Rutledge Press, 1981, cloth, p. 196-197.
c. New York: State Mutual Books, 1981, cloth, p. .

d. Toronto: John Wiley & Sons, 1981, paper, p. 196-197.
e. London: Corgi Books, 1982, paper, p. .

C325. "UFO's," in *The Directory of Possibilities*, edited by Colin Wilson and John Grant. Exeter, Devon: Webb & Bower, 1981, cloth, p. 198-201. [occult]

b. New York: Rutledge Press, 1981, cloth, p. 198-201.
c. New York: State Mutual Books, 1981, cloth, p. .
d. Toronto: John Wiley & Sons, 1981, paper, p. 198-201.
e. London: Corgi Books, 1982, paper, p. .

C326. "Utopia," in *The Directory of Possibilities*, edited by Colin Wilson and John Grant. Exeter, Devon: Webb & Bower, 1981, cloth, p. 220-221. [occult]

b. New York: Rutledge Press, 1981, cloth, p. 220-221.
c. New York: State Mutual Books, 1981, cloth, p. .
d. Toronto: John Wiley & Sons, 1981, paper, p. 220-221.
e. London: Corgi Books, 1982, paper, p. .

C327. **"Literature and Pornography,"** in *The Sexual Dimension in Literature*, edited by Alan Bold. London: Vision Press, 1982, cloth, p. . [literature]

Wilson points out the difficulty in drawing a line between literature and pornography. D. H. Lawrence's *Lady Chatterley's Lover*, the anonymous *My Secret Life* and *Josephine Mutzenbacher*, Fay Weldon's *Praxis*, Calder Willingham's *Eternal Fire*, are among the works considered. Pornography is attacked for presenting sex as a be-all and end-all: "...it is not questionable because it is about sex, but because it tells lies about sex...literature goes deeper; it is an attempt to tell the truth about human existence."

C328. **"H. P. Lovecraft, 1890-1937,"** in *Science Fiction Writers: Critical Studies of the Major Authors from the Early Nineteenth Century to the Present Day*, edited by E. F. Bleiler. New York: Charles Scribner's Sons, 1982, cloth, p. 131-137. [literature]

An essay on the life and career of America's premier horror writer of the early twentieth century. Includes Selected Bibliography.

C329. "A. E. van Vogt, 1912-   ," in *Science Fiction Writers: Critical Studies of the Major Authors from the Early Nineteenth Century to the Present Day*, edited by E. F. Bleiler. New York: Charles Scribner's Sons, 1982, cloth, p. 209-217. [literature]

On the life and career of this Canadian-American science fiction writer, with Selected Bibliography.

C330. "James Webb and the Occult," in *Light* 102 (Summer, 1982):   .
[occult]

C331. "The Real Charlotte," in Encounter 59 (Sept./Oct., 1982):   9-18. [psychology]

An important essay about Charlotte Bach, written after her death in June, 1981, when it was discovered that she was a man. Wilson reconsiders her sexual theories in light of this new and startling discovery.

C332. "Who Likes What: Colin Wilson," in *Mail on Sunday* (Apr. 10, 1983): 29. [literature]

Wilson outlines his reasons for considering David Lindsay's *A Voyage to Arcturus* "...one of the greatest...fantasy masterpieces ever written."

C333. "Multiple Personality," in *The Janus Murder Case*, by Colin Wilson. London: Granada, 1984, paper, p. 222-235. [crime]

Included as an appendix to Wilson's second Saltfleet novel, the author here covers all the classic cases discussed at greater length in *Mysteries* (see A52), plus a few others, including the fascinating stories of Lurancy Vennum/Mary Roff, and the conviction of murderer Alan Showery resulting from the evidence of the "spirit" of his victim speaking through a medium.

C334. "Peak Experience: The Schumacher Lecture 1982," in *The Schumacher Lectures, Volume 2*, edited by Kumar Satish. London: Blond & Briggs, 1984, cloth, p. 62-96. [psychology]

   b. *The Essential Colin Wilson*, by Colin Wilson. London: Harrap, 1985, cloth, p. 220-240.

C335. "Postscript: The Human Condition 1984," in *The Essential Colin Wilson*, by Colin Wilson. London: Harrap, 1985, cloth, p. 241-248. [psychology]

C336. **"Fantasy and Faculty X,"** in *How To Write Tales of Horror, Fantasy, and Science Fiction*, edited by J. N. Williamson. Cincinnati: Writer's Digest, 1987, cloth, p. 131-139. [literature]

C337. **"Wilson, Colin, 1931- : An Autobiographical Sketch,"** in *Contemporary Authors, Autobiography Series, Volume 5*, edited by Adele Sarkissian. Detroit: Gale Research Co., 1987, cloth, p. 311-331. Includes portraits and photos. [autobiography]

C338. **"Prurience: Who Really Dunnit?"** in *Literary Review* no. 125 (Nov., 1988): 23-24. [crime]

C339. **"Husserl and Evolution,"** in *Existentially Speaking: Essays on the Philosophy of Literature*, by Colin Wilson. San Bernardino, CA: The Borgo Press, 1989, cloth, p. 71-82. Published simultaneously in trade paperback. [philosophy]

Originally written for *How Does It Feel?*

C340. **"The Decline and Fall of Existentialism,"** in *Existentially Speaking: Essays on the Philosophy of Literature*, by Colin Wilson. San Bernardino, CA: The Borgo Press, 1989, cloth, p. 111-128. Published simultaneously in trade paperback. [philosophy]

D.

INTRODUCTIONS and AFTERWORDS

D1. "Foreword," in *The World of Colin Wilson*, by Sidney Campion. London: Frederick Muller, 1962, cloth, p. ix-xiv.

D2. "Introduction," in *A View of London*, by Edward Pagram. London: Hamish Hamilton, 1963, cloth, 2 unnumbered pages.

D3. "Introduction: Daniel Defoe and Moll Flanders," in *Moll Flanders*, by Daniel Defoe. London: Pan Books, 1965, paper, p. 5-16.

   b. *The Bicameral Critic*, by Colin Wilson, edited by Howard F. Dossor. Bath: Ashgrove Press, 1985, paper, p. 160-171.

  bb. *The Bicameral Critic*, by Colin Wilson, edited by Howard F. Dossor. Salem, NH: Salem House, 1985, cloth, p. 160-171.

D4. "Introduction," in *My Dear Times Waste*, by Brocard Sewell. Faversham, Kent: St. Albert's Press, 1966, cloth, p. vii-x.

D5. "Introduction," in *Juvenile Homosexual Experience and Its Effect on Adult Sexuality*, by Robert H. V. Ollendorff. London: Luxor Press, 1966, cloth, p. vii-xxi

D6. "Introduction," in *Life's Morning Hour*, by E. H. Visiak. London: John Baker, 1968, cloth, p. ix-xvii.

D7. "Introduction," in *The Search for Abraxas*, by Nevill Drury and Steven Skinner. Sudbury, Suffolk: Neville Spearman, 1972, cloth, p. xi-xxi.

D8. "Introduction," in *The Criminologist*, edited by Nigel Morland. New York: Library Press, 1972, cloth, p. i-xiii.

D9. "Introduction," in *The Magicians: Occult Stories*, edited by Peter Haining. London: Peter Owen, 1972, cloth, p. 15-26.

D10. "Introduction," in *Jack the Ripper: A Bibliography and Review of the Literature*, by Alexander G. Kelly. London: Association of Assistant Librarians, 1973, cloth, p.   .

D11. "Introduction," in *Unpopular Science*, by Art Rosenblum. Philadelphia: Running Press, 1974, cloth, 5 unnumbered pages.

D12. "Introduction," in *Geography of Consciousness*, by William Arkle. Sudbury, Suffolk: Neville Spearman, 1974, cloth, p. 5-22.

D13. "Introduction," in *Adventures of a Red Sea Smuggler*, by Henri de Monfreid, translated by Helen Buchanan Bell. New York: Hillstone Press, 1974, cloth, p. xi-xxix.

D14. "Foreword," in *The Roots of Witchcraft*, by Michael Harrison. Secaucus, NJ: Citadel Press, 1974, cloth, p. 23-24.

   b. London: Tandem Books, 1975, paper, p. 21-32.

D15. "Introduction," in *Murder in the West Country*, edited by Michael Williams. Bodmin, Cornwall: Bossiney Books, 1975, cloth, p. 9-20.

D16. "Preface," in *The Intelligent Universe*, by David Foster. New York: G. P. Putnam's Sons, 1975, cloth, p. 11-26.

D17. "Introduction," in *The Fiery Angel: A Sixteenth Century Romance*, by Valery Briussov.   Sudbury, Suffolk: Neville Spearman, 1975, cloth, p. vii-xxviii.

   b. *The Bicameral Critic*, by Colin Wilson, edited by Howard F. Dossor. Bath: Ashgrove Press, 1985, paper, p. 142-159.
   bb. *The Bicameral Critic*, by Colin Wilson, edited by Howard F. Dossor. Salem, NH: Salem House, 1985, cloth, p. 142-159.

D18. "Introduction," in *Knock*, by W. A. Harbinson. London: Intergroup Publishing, 1975, cloth, 7 unnumbered pages.

D19. "Introduction," in *The Complete Jack the Ripper*, by Donald Rumbelow. London: W. H. Allen, 1975, cloth, p. 11-29.

   b. New York: New York Graphic Society, 1975, cloth, p. 11-29.

D20. **"Introduction,"** in *An Occultist's Travels*, by Willy Reichel. Philadelphia: Running Press, 1975, paper, 6 unnumbered pages.

D21. **"Introduction,"** in *Heaven and Hell*, by Emanuel Swedenborg, translated by George F. Dole. New York: Pillar Books for the Swedenborg Foundation, 1976, cloth, p. 13-26.

D22. **"Foreword,"** in *The Power of the Pendulum*, by T. C. Lethbridge. London: Routledge & Kegan Paul, 1976, paper, p. ix-xx.

D23. **"Introduction,"** in *The Violet Apple and The Witch*, by David Lindsay. Chicago: Chicago Review Press, 1976, cloth, p. 1-18.

D24. **"Introduction,"** in *Briefing for a Landing on the Planet Earth*, by Stuart Holroyd. London: Corgi Books, 1977, paper, p. 9-14.

D25. **"Afterword,"** in *Glastonbury: Ancient Avalon, New Jerusalem*, edited by Anthony Roberts. London: Rider, 1978, cloth, p. 168-175.

D26. **"Foreword,"** in *Ritual Magic: An Occult Primer*, by David Conway. New York: E. P. Dutton, 1978, cloth, p. 15-27.

D27. **"Introduction,"** in *The Necronomicon*, edited by George Hay. Sudbury, Suffolk: Neville Spearman, 1978, cloth, p. 13-55.

   b. London: Corgi Books, 1980, paper, p. 13-55.

ANALYTICAL TABLE OF CONTENTS:
Lovecraft and the *Necronomicon*; Parallels with Crowley; Imagination and truth: Lovecraft and Machen; Wilson discovers Lovecraft; How *The Strength to Dream* was planned; Impressions of Lovecraft; Lovecraft and the dominant 5%; The influence of the subconscious mind on Lovecraft's work; Machen and "superconsciousness"; Machen and the Golden Dawn; A short biography of Lovecraft and criticism of his work; Lovecraft's romanticism; Kelley and Dee and the ancient Enochian language; The power of "will"; Wilson's experiences when writing *The God of the Labyrinth*; Were Lovecraft's literary "inventions" drawn from the collective unconscious?; A possible relationship between boredom and the development of cancer; How the *Necronomicon* was "found"; Was Lovecraft's father a

mason?; Dr. Hinterstoisser's "evidence"; Did Lovecraft have a copy of the *Necronomicon?*; Were the Cthulhu stories based on the *Necronomicon?*

D28. "Introduction," in *To Anger the Devil*, by Marc Alexander. London: Neville Spearman, 1978, cloth, p. 11-15.

D29. "Foreword," in *Murderer's Who's Who*, by J. H. H. Gaute and Robin Odell. London: Harrap, 1979, cloth, p. 7-13.

D30. "Introduction," in *Tarot Revelations*, by Joseph Campbell and Richard Roberts. San Francisco: Alchemy Books, 1979, cloth, p. 29-37.

D31. "Introduction," in *Truly Murderous*, by John Dunning. London: Hamlyn Paperbacks, 1979, paper, p. xi-xxiv.

Wilson outlines his interest in crime, and his association with Dunning, which began when he read an article by him in a "true detective" magazine.

D32. "Foreword," in *The Rosy Cross Unveiled: The History, Mythology, and Rituals of an Occult Order*, by Christopher McIntosh. Wellingborough, Northants.: Aquarian Press, 1980, paper, p. 9-16.

D33. "Foreword," in *The Essential T. C. Lethbridge*, edited by Tom Graves and Janet Hoult. London: Routledge & Kegan Paul, 1980, cloth, p. vii-xiv.

D34. "Foreword," in *The Dark Gods*, by Anthony Roberts and Jeff Gilbertson. London: Rider/Hutchinson, 1980, cloth, p. 13-24.

   b. *The Bicameral Critic*, by Colin Wilson, edited by Howard F. Dossor. Bath: Ashgrove Press, 1985, paper, p. 228-240.
   bb. *The Bicameral Critic*, by Colin Wilson, edited by Howard F. Dossor. Salem, NH: Salem House, 1985, cloth, p. 228-240.

D35. "Foreword," in *Cause of Death: The Story of Forensic Science*, by Frank Smyth. London: Orbis Publishing Co., 1980, cloth, p. 6-14.

D36. "Introduction," in *Clues to the Unknown*, by Robert Cracknell. London: Hamlyn Paperbacks, 1981, paper, p. 5-24.

D37. **"Postscript,"** *Ibid.*, p. 237-255.

D38. **"Foreword,"** in *The Life and Work of David Lindsay*, by Bernard Sellin. Cambridge: Cambridge University Press, 1981, cloth, p. xii-xvii.

D39. **"Foreword,"** in *Positive Magic*, by Marion Weinstein. British Columbia: Phoenix, 1981, paper, p. xiii-xix.

D40. **"Introduction,"** in *The Hidden Years*, by Alfred Reynolds. London: Cambridge International, 1981, paper, p. 1-16.

D41. **"Introduction: The New Science,"** in *The Directory of Possibilities*, edited by Colin Wilson and John Grant. Exeter, Devon: Webb & Bower, 1981, cloth, p. 11-22.

"...the human race could now be on the brink of its most important evolutionary development."

D42. **"Introduction,"** in *Like Black Swans: Some People and Themes*, by Brocard Sewell. Padstow, Cornwall: Tabb House, 1982, cloth, p. xiii-xviii.

D43. **"Foreword,"** in *Behind God's Back*, by Negley Farson. Fellham: Zenith, 1983, paper, p. 9-13.

D44. **"Introduction,"** in *Holistic Healing for Dowsers*, by Leonard Locker. U.K. (?) : Privately Printed, 1983, paper, 4 unnumbered pages.

D45. **"Introduction,"** in *Eccentrics in Cornwall*, by June Lander. Bodmin, Cornwall: Bossiney Books, 1983, paper, p. 4-7.

D46. **"The Age of Murder,"** in *Encyclopaedia of Modern Murder, 1962-82*, by Colin Wilson and Donald Seaman. London: Arthur Barker, 1983, cloth, p. ix-xx.

ANALYTICAL TABLE OF CONTENTS:
Motiveless aggression—the increasing trend in violence; Boredom; Resentment; Completely illogical "magical thinking"; Maslow's "hierarchy of needs"; The high IQ criminal; Critique of Rousseau's dictum, "Man is born free but he is everywhere in chains"; How this has helped create a reservoir of anti-authoritarian resentment; Crime as a way of dodging responsibility; The problem of obsession; The need to develop our mental states.

D47. "Introduction," in *The People of the Street*, by Ernest Scott. London: Octagon Press, 1983, cloth, p. 1-14.

D48. "Foreword," in *The Leap*, by Bill Hopkins. London: Deverell and Birdsey, 1984, cloth, p. v-xii.

D49. "Introduction," in *Jack the Ripper: A Bibliography and Review of the Literature, 2nd ed.*, by Alexander Kelly. London: Association of Assistant Librarians, 1984, cloth, p. 9-19.

D50. "Introduction," in *Interviews with Britain's Angry Young Men*, by Dale Salwak. San Bernardino, CA: The Borgo Press, 1984, cloth, p. 5-11. Published simultaneously in trade paperback.

D51. "Introduction," in *Westcountry Mysteries*, edited by Michael Williams. Bodmin, Cornwall: Bossiney Books, 1985, paper, p. 4-16.

D52. "Foreword," in *Witch Amongst Us*, by Lois Bourne. London: Robert Hale, 1985, cloth, p. 7-10.

D53. "Introduction," in *Multiple Man*, by Adam Crabtree. Toronto: Collins, 1985, cloth, 3 unnumbered pages.

D54. "Introduction," in *The Night Side of Nature*, by Catherine Crowe. Wellingborough, Northants.: Aquarian Press, 1986, paper, p. v-xii.

D55. "Introduction," in *Death-Bed Visions*, by Sir William Barrett. Wellingborough, Northants.: Aquarian Press, 1986, paper, p. vi-xxix.

D56. "Introduction," in *The Haunted Realm*, by Simon Marsden. Exeter: Webb & Bower, 1986, cloth, p. .

D57. "Introduction," in *The Goblin Universe*, by Ted Holiday. St. Paul: Llewellyn Press, 1986, paper, p. 1-42.

D58. "Introduction," in *After Death—What?* by Cesare Lombroso. Wellingborough, Northants.: Aquarian Press, 1988, paper, p. v-xiv.

D59. "Introduction," in *The Soul of Things*, by William Denton. Wellingborough, Northants.: Aquarian Press, 1988, paper, p. v-xiv.

D60. "Introduction," in *Sphinx*, by David Lindsay. London: Xanadu, 1988, cloth, p. 9-13.

   b. New York: Carroll & Graf, Publishers, 1988, cloth, p. 9-13.

D61. "Foreword," in *Perfect Murder*, by Bernard Taylor and Steven Knight. London: Grafton, 1988, paper, p. 7-8.

D62. "Foreword," in *The Aleister Crowley Scrapbook*, by Sandy Robertson. Berkeley, England: Foulsham, 1988, paper, p. 7.

D63. "Introduction: Affirmations of Faith," in *Existentially Speaking: Essays on the Philosophy of Literature*, by Colin Wilson. San Bernardino, CA: The Borgo Press, September 1989, cloth, p. 9-16. Published simultaneously in trade paperback.

D64. "Afterword: Inside Outside: Reflections on Being Bibliographed," in *The Work of Colin Wilson: An Annotated Bibliography & Guide*, by Colin Stanley. San Bernardino, CA: The Borgo Press, September 1989, cloth, p. 254-265. Published simultaneously in trade paperback.

E.

BOOK REVIEWS

E1. "The Dark Sun, by Graham Hough," in *Listener* 56 (1956): 951.

E2. "The Idiom of Contemporary Thought, by Crawford Knox," in *London Magazine* 4 (no. 1, 1957): 63-66.

E3. "The Dilemma of Being Modern, by J. P. Hodin," in *London Magazine* 4 (no. 1, 1957): 63-66.

E4. "The Tragic Philosopher: A Study of Nietzsche, by F. A. Lea," in *London Magazine* 4 (no. 8, 1957): 59-61.

E5. "Letters from Goethe, by Johann Wolfgang von Goethe," in *London Magazine* 4 (no. 8, 1957): 59-61.

E6. "Notebooks, Vol. I, by Samuel Taylor Coleridge, edited by Kathleen Coburn," in *London Magazine* 5 (no. 5, 1958): 75-79.

E7. "So I May Try To Be Hitler," in *News Chronicle* (May 28, 1958): . A review of *The Angry Decade*, by Kenneth Allsop.

E8. "Paintings and Poets," in *John O'London's* 1 (1959): 22. Reviews of *Poets in Their Letters*, by C. S. Emden; and *Concise History of Modern Painting*, by Herbert Read.

E9. "Ozymandias," in *John O'London's* 1 (1959): 182. A review of *James Joyce*, by Richard Ellmann. A follow-up letter by J. Kramer appears in *John O'London's* 2 (1960): 14.

E10. "Innocent Romance," in *John O'London's* 1 (1959): 321-322. Reviews of *Tender Tigress*, by Marjorie Vernon; *Moonlight Beguiling*, by Anne Trent; and *Isle of Whispers*, by Hilary Wayne.

E11. **"Semi-Darkness,"** in *Time and Tide* (Aug. 22, 1959): 898. A review of *Journey to the Ends of Time, Volume I: Lost in the Dark Woods*, by Sacheverell Sitwell.

E12. **"The Sleepwalkers, by Arthur Koestler,"** in *London Magazine* 6 (no. 4, 1959): 73-75.

E13. **"The Strange Case of James Ensor,"** in *John O'London's* 2 (1960): 119. A review of *James Ensor*, by Paul Haesaerts.

E14. **"The Possessed: A Play Adapted from F. M. Dostoyevsky's Novel, by Albert Camus,"** in *Listener* 64 (1960): 195.

E15. **"Documentary Novels,"** in *John O'London's* 2 (1960): 280. Reviews of *Two Persons Singular*, by Joyce Howard; *The Learning Lark*, by Glyn Jones; and *Peppercorn Days*, by Jon Rose.

E16. **"Finnegans Wake,"** in *John O'London's* 2 (1960): 428. A review of *Excerpts from* Finnegans Wake: *James Joyce*, read by Siobhan McKenna and Cyril Cusack, directed by Howard Sackler [LP record].

E17. **"Quality Paperbacks,"** in *John O'London's* 3 (1960): 708. Reviews of *Tales of Hoffmann*, by E. T. A. Hoffmann; and *The Achievement of T. S. Eliot*, by F. O. Matthiessen.

E18. **"Less Reverence for Beethoven,"** in *John O'London's* 3 (1960): 763. A review of *Beethoven and Human Destiny*, by Burnett James.

E19. **"Vagaries of Mathematics,"** in *John O'London's* 4 (1961): 34. Reviews of *The World of Mathematics*, edited by James Newman; and *Mathematics in the Making*, by Lancelot Hogben.

E20. **"Thomas Mann—the Bourgeois Outsider,"** in *John O'London's* 4 (1961): 76. A review of *A Sketch of My Life*, by Thomas Mann.

E21. **"Nijinsky, by Françoise Reiss,"** in *Listener* 65 (1961): 279.

E22. **"The Memoirs of Casanova,"** in *John O'London's* 4 (1961): 260.

E23. **"Diary, by Søren Kierkegaard, edited by Peter Rohde,"** in *Listener* 65 (1961): 842, 845.

E24. "Angry Mood," in *Education* (May 19, 1961): 1133. A review of *A Mirror for Anglo-Saxons*, by Martin Green.

E25. "The Corvo Problem," in *Aylesford Review* 4 (Summer, 1961): 95-99. A review of *Corvo: 1860-1960; Centenary Essays*, edited by Cecil Woolf and Brocard Sewell.

E26. "This Business of Living: A Journal, 1935-50, by Cesare Pavese," in *Listener* 66 (1961): 104-105.

E27. "The Missing Link," in *John O'London's* 7 (1962): 482. A review of *African Genesis*, by Robert Ardrey. No. 20 in the series, "I Write As I Please."

E28. "The Letters of Fyodor Dostoyevsky, translated by Ethel Coburn Mayne," in *Listener* 67 (1962): 437.

E29. "The Unknowable Gurdjieff, by Margaret Anderson," in *Listener* 68 (1962): 526-527.

E30. "The Nets of Politics," in *Aylesford Review* 4 (Spring, 1962): 229-231. Reviews of *The Fascists in Britain*, by Colin Cross, and *Mosley, Right or Wrong?* by Sir Oswald Mosley.

E31. "O'Neill's Impact," in *Yorkshire Post* (Nov. 8, 1962): . A review of *O'Neill*, by Arthur and Barbara Gelb.

E32. "Doderer's The Demons," in *Aylesford Review* 5 (Winter, 1962/63): 25-29. A review of *The Demons*, by H. von Doderer.

E33. "Catlin's Systematic Politics," in *Time and Time, with John O'London's* 44 (Jan. 10-16, 1963): 24. A review of *Systematic Politics*, by George Catlin.

E34. "Cost of Lust," in *Yorkshire Post* (July 4, 1963): . A review of *Prostitution in Europe and the New World; Volume 2 of Prostitution in Society*, by Fernando Henriques.

E35. "Angry Man's Curses," in *Yorkshire Post* (Mar. 27, 1964): . A review of *All Men Are Islands*, by Ronald Duncan.

E36. "Where East Meets West," in *Yorkshire Post* (Aug. 27, 1964): . Reviews of *The Christian Debate*, by Geoffrey Parrinder; and *Myths of Creation*, by Philip Freund.

E37. "Carrington: Letters and Extracts from Her Diaries, edited by David Garnett," in *Spectator* 225 (Nov. 14, 1970): 601.

E38. "'Dear Miss Weaver': Harriet Shaw Weaver, 1876-1961, by Jane Lidderdale and Mary Nicholson," in *Spectator* 225 (Nov. 14, 1970): 601.

E39. "Oscar Wilde: The Critical Heritage, edited by Karl Beckson," in *Spectator* 225 (Dec. 26, 1970): 846.

E40. "A Superior Liberal," in *Books & Bookmen* 16 (Jan., 1971): 28-29. A review of *Russell Remembered*, by Rupert Crawshay-Williams.

E41. "A Dictionary of British Folk Tales, Part B: Folk Legends, by Katherine M. Briggs," in *Spectator* 226 (May 15, 1971): 669-670.

E42. "An Autobiography, Volume 2, by George Bernard Shaw, edited by Stanley Weintraub," in *Spectator* 226 (May 22, 1971): 706.

E43. "The Bodley Head Bernard Shaw: Collected Plays, Vol. 2," in *Spectator* 226 (May 22, 1971): 706.

E44. "Two Guests for Swedenborg, by March Cost," in *Spectator* 226 (May 29, 1971): 739-741.

E45. "The Passions of the Mind: A Novel of the Life and Work of Sigmund Freud, by Irving Stone," in *Spectator* 226 (May 29, 1971): 739-741.

E46. "Lie Down in Me, by Andrew Jolly," in *Spectator* 226 (May 29, 1971): 739-741.

E47. "Social History of the Third Reich, by Richard Grunberger," in *Books & Bookmen* 16 (June, 1971): 56-57. A follow-up letter by Christopher Hibbs appears in *Books & Bookmen* (August, 1971): 4.

E48. "Gazetteer of British Ghosts, by Peter Underwood," in *Books & Bookmen* 16 (July, 1971): 56-57.

E49. "Breakthrough: An Amazing Experiment in Electronic Communication with the Dead, by Konstantin Raudive," in *Hi-Fi News* (July, 1971): .

E50. "Snobbery with Violence, by Colin Watson," in *Spectator* 227 (July 24, 1971): 140-141.

E51. "Journey to Heartbreak: The Crucible Years of Bernard Shaw, 1914-1918, by Stanley Weintraub," in *New York Times Book Review* (Aug. 8, 1971): 3, 10.

   b. *Books & Bookmen* 19 (Nov., 1973): 110.

E52. "Bound Upon a Course, by John Stewart Collis," in *Spectator* 227 (Aug. 21, 1971): 280.

E53. "Youth in the Twenties, by Ethel Mannin," in *Spectator* 227 (Aug. 21, 1971): 280.

E54. "Pilgrim Son, by John Masters," in *Spectator* 227 (Aug. 21, 1971): 280.

E55. "My Lives, by Francis Meynell," in *Spectator* 227 (Aug. 21, 1971): 280.

E56. "The Disciple and His Devil, by Valerie Pascal," in *Spectator* 227 (Sept. 11, 1971): 375. A review of a biography of Gabriel Pascal by his widow.

E57. "A Sort of Life, by Graham Greene," in *Spectator* 227 (Sept. 18, 1971): 413-414.

"An excellent little book, beautifully written...," writes Wilson, but he obviously struggles to find common ground with Greene's pessimism. Many of the arguments introduced in *The Strength to Dream* are employed.

E58. "Maurice, by E. M. Forster," in *Spectator* 227 (Oct. 9, 1971): 512. See also: C193.

E59. "Girl 20, by Kingsley Amis," in *Spectator* 227 (Oct. 30, 1971): 623-624.

E60. "Kathleen and Frank, by Christopher Isherwood," in *Spectator* 227 (Nov. 27, 1971): 767-768.

E61. **"The Devil and All His Works; The Ravishing of Lady Mary Ware, by Dennis Wheatley,"** in *Spectator* 227 (Dec. 11, 1971): 851-852. Reviews of two books.

E62. **"Sartre, by Philip Thody,"** in *Mediterranean Review* (Winter, 1972): 38-40.

E63. **"The Wolf Man and Sigmund Freud, by Muriel Gardner,"** in *Spectator* 228 (Jan. 29, 1972): 159-160.

E64. **"Make Your Own Magic,"** in *Books & Bookmen* 17 (Mar., 1972): 44-45. Reviews of *Sexuality, Magic, and Perversion: Astral Projection, Magic, and Alchemy*, by Francis King; and *Magic: An Occult Primer*, by David Conway.

E65. **"One Man's Music, by Peter Gammond,"** in *Hi-Fi News* (Mar., 1972): .

E66. **"Dawn and the Darkest Hour: A Study of Aldous Huxley, by George Woodcock,"** in *Spectator* 228 (Mar. 25, 1972): 480-481.

E67. **"Shaviana,"** in *Books & Bookmen* 17 (Apr., 1972): 32-33. Reviews of *Shavian Playground*, by Marjorie M. Morgan; and *Shaw the Dramatist*, by Lewis Crompton.

E68. **"The New Optimism,"** in *Books & Bookmen* 17 (Apr., 1972): 40. A review of *Human Hope and the Death Instinct*, by David Holbrook.

E69. **"The Children on the Hill: The Story of an Extraordinary Family, by Michael Deakin,"** in *Spectator* 228 (May 27, 1972): 814-815.

E70. **"The Cult of the Fact, by Liam Hudson,"** in *Spectator* 228 (June 17, 1972): 938-939.

E71. **"Ordeal of an Actor,"** in *Books & Bookmen* 17 (July, 1972): 57. Reviews of *The Ordeal of Philip Yale Drew*, by Richard Whittington-Egan; and *They Hanged My Saintly Billy*, by Robert Graves.

E72. **"Letters from the Golden Age,"** in *Spectator* 229 (July 22, 1972): 138-139. A review of *Letters, 1904-1914*, by George Bernard Shaw.

E73. "Shaw in His Letters," in *Books & Bookmen* 17 (Sept., 1972): 26-27. Reviews of *Collected Letters: 1898-1910*, by George Bernard Shaw, edited by Dan H. Laurence; and *Bernard Shaw: His Life, Work, and Friends*, by St. John Irvine.

E74. "Never Say Die," in *Books & Bookmen* 18 (Jan., 1973): 64-65. Reviews of *Blueprint for Immortality*, by Harold Saxton Burr; *Einstein and Dostoyevsky*, by Boris Kusnetsov; and *Total Man*, by Stan Gooch.

  b. *Undercurrents* no. 6 (Mar./Apr., 1974): 43-45. Includes the review of *Total Man* only.

E75. "Behaviourist Bias," in *Books & Bookmen* 18 (Feb., 1973): 50-51. A review of *Encyclopaedia of Psychology*, by H. J. Eysenck *et al.*

E76. "What <u>Was</u> Wrong with Adolf Hitler?" in *Books & Bookmen* 18 (May, 1973): 88. A review of *The Mind of Adolf Hitler*, by Walter C. Langer.

E77. "A Time for Wells," in *Books & Bookmen* 18 (July, 1973): 54-56. A review of *The Time Traveller: The Life of H. G. Wells*, by Norman & Jenny Mackenzie.

E78. "Borges and Nostalgia," in *Books & Bookmen* 18 (Aug., 1973): 36-39. Reviews of *Conversations with Borges*, by Richard Bergin; and *Labyrinths*; *Extraordinary Tales*; *Other Inquisitions, 1937-52*; *Dream Tigers*; *Book of Imaginary Beings*, by Jorge Luis Borges.

E79. "Negley Farson's World," in *Books & Bookmen* 18 (Sept., 1973): 64-65. A review of *Wanderlust*, by Negley Farson.

E80. "Supernature, by Lyall Watson," in *Spectator* 231 (Sept. 8, 1973): 314-315.

E81. "Magic and the Millennium: A Sociological Study of Religious Movements of Protest Among Tribal and Third World Peoples, by Bryan R. Wilson," in *Spectator* 231 (Sept. 29, 1973): 410.

E82. "Inside Crime," in *Books & Bookmen* 19 (Oct., 1973): 87. Reviews of *Camps on Crimes*, by Francis Camps; *The Sex War and Others*, by Rayner Heppenstall; and *Sounds of Murder*, by Percy Hoskins.

E83. "The Mind Possessed, by William Sargent," in *Spectator* 231 (Dec. 8, 1973): 754-755.

E84. "Observation of Psychology," in *Books & Bookmen* 19 (Jan., 1974): 28-29. A review of *The Experimental Study of Freudian Theories*, by H. J. Eysenck and Glenn D. Wilson.

"...one of my earlier full-scale attacks on Freud..."—Colin Wilson, in a letter to Colin Stanley.

E85. "The Dark Side of the Mind," in *Undercurrents* no. 6 (March/April, 1974): 43-45. A review of *Total Man*, by Stan Gooch.

E86. "The Occult Flood," in *Books & Bookmen* 19 (May, 1974): 75-78. Reviews of *A History of the Devil*, by William Woods; *Worlds in Collision* and *Ages in Chaos*, by Immanuel Velikovsky; *The Morning of the Magicians*, by Louis Pauwels and Jacques Bergier; *Our Haunted Planet*, by John A. Keele; *A Foot in Both Worlds*, by Arthur Guirdham; *Path of the Chameleon*, by Nevill Drury; and *Mysteries of the Earth*, by Jacques Bergier.

E87. "The Fuehrer in Perspective [Part I]," in *Books & Bookmen* 20 (Oct., 1974): 18-19. A review of *Hitler*, by Joachim Fest.

E88. "The Fuehrer in Perspective [Part II]," in *Books & Bookmen* 20 (Nov., 1974): 28. A review of *Hitler*, by Joachim Fest.

E89. "The Grand Tradition, by J. B. Steane," in *Audio* (Dec., 1974): 50.

E90. "Memoirs, by Cardinal Mindszenty," in *Spectator* 234 (Mar. 29, 1975): 379-380.

E91. "Appreciating Dumas," in *Books & Bookmen* 20 (Sept., 1975): 38-39. A review of *Horror at Fontenay*, by Alexandre Dumas, translated by Alan Hull Walton.

E92. "Rippers Galore," in *Books & Bookmen* 21 (June, 1976): 52-53. A review of *A Casebook on Jack the Ripper*, by Richard Whittington-Egan.

E93. "The Bitter Side of Life," in *Books & Bookmen* 21 (Aug., 1976): 54-55. A review of *The Agents of Love*, by Rudolf Nassauer.

E94. "Not So Elementary," in *Books & Bookmen* 22 (Feb., 1977): 52-54. Reviews of *Sleeping Murder*, by Agatha Christie; *The American Rivals of Sherlock Holmes*, edited by Hugh Greene; *Adventures of Sherlock Holmes*, by Charles Hyams; *The Sherlock Holmes File*, by Michael Pointer; and *The Encyclopaedia of Mystery and Detection*, by Chris Steinbrunner and Otto Pensler.

E95. "Curiouser and Curiouser," in *Books & Bookmen* 22 (July, 1977): 56-57. A review of *The Geller Phenomena*, by Stuart Holroyd.

E96. "The Mystery of Things," in *Books & Bookmen* 23 (Nov., 1977): 35-37. Reviews of *New Atlantis*, by Colin Amery; *A History of Magic*, by Richard Cavendish; and *The Undiscovered Country*, by Steven Jenkins.

E97. "Science and Seance," in *Books & Bookmen* 23 (July, 1978): 43. A review of *The Paranormal*, by Stan Gooch.

E98. "Mystery of Menstruation," in *Books & Bookmen* 23 (Sept., 1978): 44-45. A review of *The Wise Wound*, by Penelope Shuttle and Peter Redgrove.

E99. "Cowper Powys's Private World," in *Books & Bookmen* 23 (Feb., 1979): 44-45. A review of *The Saturnian Quest: John Cowper Powys, a Study of His Prose Works*, by G. Wilson Knight.

E100. "Riddle of the Sweet Potato," in *Evening News* (Feb. 19, 1979): 7. A review of *Lifetide*, by Lyall Watson.

E101. "Koestler, God, and the Right Brain," in *Literary Review* 2 (Mar., 1980): 7-12. A review of *Bricks to Babel*, by Arthur Koestler.

   b.   as: "Arthur Koestler," in *Existentially Speaking: Essays on the Philosophy of Literature*, by Colin Wilson. San Bernardino, CA: The Borgo Press, 1989, cloth, p. 60-70. Published simultaneously in trade paperback.

E102. "Tales of Suicide," in *Books & Bookmen* 25 (Mar., 1980): 36-38. A review of *Suicides*, by Jean Baechler.

E103. **"Brought Back to Earth by Life Out There,"** in *Evening News* (Mar. 24, 1980): 7. A review of *Extraterrestrial Civilizations*, by Isaac Asimov.

E104. **"Magicians,"** in *Books & Bookmen* 25 (Apr., 1980): 29-31. Reviews of *The Confessions of Aleister Crowley: An Autobiography*, edited by John Symonds and Kenneth Walker; *Gurdjieff: A Study of His Teaching*, by Kenneth Walker; and *The Reappearance of Christ and the Masters of Wisdom*, by Benjamin Creme.

E105. **"Would We Be Better Off Without T.V.?"** in *Evening News* (Apr. 22, 1980): . A review of *Four Arguments for the Elimination of Television*, by Jerry Mander.

E106. **"If Only These Chimps Could Talk Back,"** in *Evening News* (June 16, 1980): 7. A review of *Nim*, by Herbert Terris.

E107. **"Mind-Bending Tales of the Unexpected,"** in *Evening News* (June 30, 1980): 7. A review of *Science and the Supernatural*, by John Taylor.

E108. **"Henry Williamson,"** in *Literary Review* no. 29 (Nov. 14, 1980): 16-21. A review of *Henry Williamson: The Man, the Writings: A Symposium*, edited by Brocard Sewell.

E109. **"Love and Conquest,"** in *Literary Review* no. 30 (Nov. 28, 1980): 23-24. Reviews of *The Kama Sutra*, translated by Indra Sinha; and *Men in Love*, by Nancy Friday.

E110. **"Michel Foucault,"** in *Literary Review* no. 38 (July, 1981): 27-29. Reviews of *Power/Knowledge: Selected Interviews and Other Writings, 1972-1977*, by Michel Foucault, and *Michel Foucault: The Will to Truth*, by Alan Sheridan.

b. *Existentially Speaking: Essays on the Philosophy of Literature*, by Colin Wilson. San Bernardino, CA: The Borgo Press, 1989, cloth, p. 53-59. Published simultaneously in trade paperback. Rewritten for this book. [philosophy]

E111. **"An Architectural Handbook of Glastonbury Abbey, by Frederick Bligh Bond,"** in *Light* 101 (Autumn, 1981): 129-130.

E112. **"Delightful and Indiscreet,"** in *Book Choice* no. 11 (Nov., 1981): 14-16. Reviews of *The Hite Report on Male Sexuality*, by Shere Hite; *The Book Browser's Guide to Erotica*, by Roy

Harley Lewis; *The Manuscript Murders*, by Roy Harley Lewis; and *Great Lovers*, by George Melly and Walter Dorin.

E113. "The Science in Science Fiction, edited by Peter Nicholls," in *Mail on Sunday* (Nov. 7, 1982):   .

E114. "The Awakening Earth: Our Next Evolutionary Leap, by Peter Russell," in *Books & Bookmen* no. 327 (Dec., 1982): 31.

E115. "Orage with Gurdjieff in America, by Louise Welch," in *Light* 103 (Spring, 1983):   .

E116. "Up from Eden, by Ken Wilber," in *Light* 103 (Summer, 1983):.

E117. "Rappings and Hauntings," in *Books & Bookmen* no. 335 (Aug., 1983): 9-10. A review of *The Spiritualists: The Passion for the Occult in the Nineteenth and Twentieth Centuries*, by Ruth Brandon.

E118. "Brazen Romantic," in *Books & Bookmen* no. 338 (Nov., 1983): 17. A review of *Bax: A Composer and His Times*, by Lewis Foreman.

E119. "Money and Muses," in *Books & Bookmen* no. 348 (Sept., 1984): 27. A review of *Between Moon and Moon: Selected Letters of Robert Graves, 1946-72*, edited by Paul O'Prey.

E120. "The Great Seducer," in *Books & Bookmen* no. 373 (Nov., 1986): 10-11. Reviews of *Bernard Shaw: The Diaries, 1885-1897*, edited by Stanley Weintraub; *The Unexpected Shaw*, by Stanley Weintraub; *Shaw on Dickens*, edited by Dan H. Laurence and Martin Quinn; *Agitations: Shaw's Letters to the Press, 1875-1950*, edited by Dan H. Laurence and James Rambeau.

E121. "Gin Doesn't Stain," in *Literary Review* no. 113 (Nov., 1987): 31-32. A review of *Soho in the Fifties*, by Daniel Farson.

E122. "A Rather Juvenile Offender...," in *Yorkshire Post* (Feb. 25, 1988):   . A review of *Success Stories: Literature and the Media in England, 1950-59*, by Harry Ritchie.

E123. "The Author Has Not Yet Read My Masterpiece," in *Literary Review* no. 118 (Apr., 1988): 50-51. A review of *Success Stories: Literature and the Media in England, 1950-59*, by Harry Ritchie.

E124. **"Shy, But Not Cock-Shaw,"** in *Literary Review* no. 123 (Sept., 1988): 25-26. A review of *Bernard Shaw: The Search for Love, 1856-1898*, by Michael Holroyd.

E125. **"He Put a Shine on Shoe,"** in *Literary Review* no. 130 (Apr., 1989): 10. A review of *Shoe: The Odyssey of a Sixties Survivor*, by Jonathan Guinness.

F.

OTHER MEDIA

NOTE: Wilson has also been involved in many television projects, as consultant, playwright, and creator, primarily for BBC Southwest, I.T.V. Westward, and, more recently, for T.V. Southwest. Details of these programs are not available.

F1. **The New Analytic Philosophy.** Big Sur, CA: Big Sur Recordings, March 1967, 8 cassettes (no. 3440). [audio cassettes]

"The author develops phenomenological insights into a practical Western discipline toward the pursuit of higher consciousness."

F2. **Human Evolution and a New Psychology.** Big Sur, CA: Big Sur Recordings, 1968, 4 cassettes (nos. 4040, 4050). Recorded in San Francisco on January 31 and February 1, 1968. [audio cassette]

"In a series of vignettes from his English middle-class upbringing and 'total-trap' environment, the author develops his 'evolution by will' theory as presented in his book, The Outsider."

F3. **The Outsider: Twenty Years On.** London: Seminar Cassettes, 1976 (University Series SS125), 1 cassette.

Wilson, speaking from the comfort of his own home, talks to John Warrington about his philosophical ideas.

F4. **"Beyond the Outsider."** Side A of a cassette, *Man, Science, and His Environment*, produced by Speakers International Agency Ltd. The lecture was given by Wilson at the Festival for Mind and Body, Jubilee Exhibition, April 19-24, 1977.

F5. **Symphony No. 8 and 14,** by Havergal Brian. CA: Aries Records, n.d. Supposedly a recording of Wilson conducting the Wales Symphony Orchestra (but Wilson denies it). [recording]

F6. **Symphony No. 18, 19, and 22,** by Havergal Brian. CA: Aries Records, n.d. Supposedly a recording of Wilson conducting the Wales Symphony Orchestra (but Wilson denies it). [recording]

F7. **Symphony No. 9, 23, and 12,** by Havergal Brian. CA: Aries Records, n.d. Supposedly a recording of Wilson conducting the Wales Symphony Orchestra (but Wilson denies it). [recording]

F8. **The Essential Colin Wilson.** Wyastone Leys, Monmouth: Nimbus Records, 1988, 1 compact disc (#N15124).

An excellent record of Wilson reading extracts from his work, combined with a spontaneous commentary. In just over 67 minutes, Wilson explains the basic theme of all his books, goes into his association with Abraham Maslow (with particular reference to "Peak Experiences"), and examines the "Self-Image Concept" which he so effectively dramatized in his novel, The Personality Surgeon.

G.

EDITORIAL CREDITS

NOTE: See also the one-volume work, *The Book of Time*, for which Wilson served as Consultant Editor (A56).

G1. **Crimes and Punishment.** Colin Wilson, Consultant Editor. London: Phoebus Publishing Co., 1973-75, 6 v., cloth.

Issued in fascicles, which were later combined to form the six-volume set. Wilson also contributed one article per issue, which were later collected together and published as *The Mammoth Book of True Crime* (see A89).

G2. **The Unexplained.** Colin Wilson, Consultant Editor. London: Orbis Publishing Co., 1980-1983, 13 v., cloth.

An open-ended, multi-volume set on unexplained phenomena. Wilson was one of several editors on this massive project, and also contributed several articles to it.

G3. **The Colin Wilson Library of the Paranormal.** Wellingborough, Northants.: Aquarian Press, 1986-   , v., paper.

Each book in this series of classic reprints of the occult includes a new introduction by Wilson, and is packaged with a distinctive series cover design. No series number appears on the books themselves.

1. *The Night Side of Nature*, by Catherine Crowe. 1986, 451 p.
2. *Death-Bed Visions*, by Sir William Barrett. 1986, 173 p.
3. *After Death—What?*, by Cesare Lombroso. 1988, 364 p.
4. *The Soul of Things*, by William Denton. 1988, 370 p.

G4. **The Supernatural Library.** London: Xanadu, 1988- , v., cloth. New York: Carroll & Graf, Publishers, 1988- , v., cloth.

Each book includes a new introduction by Wilson.

1. *Sphinx*, by David Lindsay. 1988, 287 p.

H.

ABOUT THE AUTHOR

Monographs

NOTE: See also Wilson's 1969 autobiography, *Voyage to a Beginning: A Preliminary Autobiography* (A25).

H1. **Thoughts in the Wilderness,** by J. B. Priestley. London: Heinemann, 1957, 242 p., cloth.

b. New York: Harper & Row, 1957, viii, 242 p., cloth.
c. Port Washington, NY: Kennikat Press, 1971, viii, 242 p., cloth.

The chapter entitled *"The Outsider"* (p. 174-180) comments on Wilson's first book, and on John Osborne's play, *Look Back in Anger*, and is reprinted in *Colin Wilson: A Celebration* (H26).

H2. **The Angry Decade: A Survey of the Cultural Revolt of the Nineteen Fifties,** by Kenneth Allsop. London: Peter Owen, 1958, 212 p., cloth. Indexed.

b. New York: British Book Centre, 1958, 212 p., cloth.
c. Third Edition. London: Peter Owen, 1964, 220 p., cloth. Reprinted 1969.
d. Third Edition. Port Washington, NY: Kennikat Press, 1964, 220 p., cloth.
e. Wendover, England: John Goodchild, 1985, 212 p., cloth.

TABLE OF CONTENTS:
Part One: The dissentient mood. Part Two: The neutralists. Part Three: The emotionalists. Part Four: The law-givers. Part Five: The end of innocence.

COMMENTS: Wilson is discussed in detail in Part Four, but mentioned or alluded to throughout. Particular attention is given to the period between publication of his first two books, and the way in which adverse publicity helped to swing the critics against him. Allsop tries to give the impression that he is unbiased, but, in the final analysis, cannot resist jumping on the bandwagon himself. In so doing, I cannot help feel that he has missed the point somewhere along the line: "It is not Wilson's *pessimism* that bothers me at all—that seems to me comparatively mild and justifiable as far as it goes. It is his reasons for optimism which are *not only morally unacceptable*, but which should be *seen not to be accepted*...His solution...is not for me, and I hope won't be for most people here" (the italics are mine).

I can do no more than leave the reader to study the two works Allsop had at his disposal—*The Outsider* and *Religion and the Rebel*—and reach his or her own conclusions. I feel that he simply took Wilson's work too much in the context of the "spirit" of the Fifties (inevitably, as the title of his work suggests), whereas the volumes concerned were designed as part of an overall thesis which stretched well into the Sixties, and indeed, forms the core of his message even today.

H3.   **Modern Gloom and Christian Hope**, by Hilda Graef. Chicago: Henry Regnery Co., 1959, 143 p., cloth.

Wilson is mentioned in passing.

H4.   **The World of Colin Wilson**, by Sidney Campion. London: Frederick Muller, 1962, xvii, 254 p., cloth. Includes several black-and-white photographs.

TABLE OF CONTENTS:
    Foreword, by Colin Wilson. Introduction. Chapter One: How we met. Chapter Two: The unusual boy. Chapter Three: "Shaw's natural successor?" Chapter Four: The civil service. Chapter Five: The Royal Air Force. Chapter Six: Extracts from a journal. Chapter Seven: The "*wanderjahre*." Chapter Eight: Marriage and London. Chapter Nine: Extracts from a journal. Chapter Ten: Anarchism and amateur dramatics. Chapter Eleven: Writing *The Outsider*. Chapter Twelve: The problems of notoriety. Chapter Thirteen: The cocktail party. Chapter Fourteen: Comments on reviewers. Chapter Fifteen: Success and anti-success. Chapter Sixteen: The books. Chapter Seventeen: *The Age of Defeat*. Chapter Eighteen: *Ritual in the Dark*. Chapter Nineteen: Studio conversations. Chapter Twenty: The plays. Chapter Twenty-One: Work in progress. Chapter

Twenty-Two: Towards the new existentialism. Chapter Twenty-Three: "The possibility of a poetic burial." Index.

COMMENTS: A curious hodgepodge of a book written by an established writer who, coincidentally, Wilson had read in his youth. Wilson had mixed feelings about the book, as he explains in his Foreword: "I would prefer that it completely ignored the biography, and concentrated on my work. Why should anybody be interested in the biographical facts about any man under the age of eighty?" Further reservations are expressed in an article which appeared in *John O'London's*. However, Campion's book is interesting in that it includes extracts from Wilson's early journals. Also, the critic's analysis of Wilson's first books shows a genuine enthusiasm and understanding of the material. He also supplies some fascinating background details concerning the stages *Ritual in the Dark* went through before publication. A sequel, *The Sound Barrier*, was never published (see K2). Chapter 18 is reprinted in *Colin Wilson: A Celebration* (H26).

SELECTED REVIEWS:

1. *John O'London's* 7 (September 20, 1962): .
2. "Nothing Could Stop Genius Flowering," in *Yorkshire Evening Post* (October 13, 1962): .
3. "Re-Write," in *Daily Mail* (August 31, 1962): .
4. *Times* (Oct. 5, 1962): 17.
5. Wordsworth, Christopher. "Whither Wilson?" in *Guardian* (Sept. 21, 1962): .

H5.   **Postwar British Fiction: New Accents and Attitudes**, by James Gindin. Berkeley, CA: University of California Press, 1962, xii, 246 p., cloth.

ab. Berkeley, CA: University of California Press, xii, 246 p., paper.
b. London: Cambridge University Press, 1962, xii, 246 p., cloth.
c. Westport, CT: Greenwood Press, 1976, xii, 246 p., cloth.

Wilson's first two novels, *Ritual in the Dark* and *Adrift in Soho*, are given short shrift, along with Wilson's friend Bill Hopkins' *Divine and the Decay*, on pages 222-225, under the Chapter entitled "Current Fads." Wilson's characters are accused of being "...irrational and violent..." but later "...innocents, seeking to understand all the violence and irrationality they find around

them." They also, apparently, "...reflect something about contemporary Britain: the interest in violence and perversion..." I
leave the reader to draw his or her own conclusions.

H6. **The Literary Rebel,** by Kingsley Widmer. Carbondale and
     Evansville, IL: Southern Illinois University Press, 1965, x,
     261 p., cloth.

     Wilson is mentioned throughout the chapter entitled,
     "Ambiguous Rebels on Literature," p. 159-174.

H7. **Time to Murder and Create: The Continental Novel in Crisis,**
     by John W. Aldridge. New York: David McKay Co., 1966,
     xviii, 264 p., cloth.

  b. Freeport, NY: Books for Libraries Press, 1972, xviii, 264 p.,
     cloth.

     Wilson is mentioned on pages 233-236.

H8. **The Neophiliacs: A Study of the Revolution in English Life in
     the Fifties and Sixties,** by Christopher Booker. London:
     Collins, 1969, 381 p., cloth.

  b. Boston: Gambit, 1970, xvi, 414 p., cloth.

     Wilson is mentioned in passing.

H9. **Jack the Ripper,** by Daniel Farson. London: Michael Joseph,
     1972, 144 p., cloth.

  b. London: Sphere Books, 1973, 157 p., paper.

     Wilson is mentioned throughout, and the book is dedicated to
     Wilson, "the most generous of friends and authors."

H10. **The Sexual Revolution in Modern English Literature,** by
     Charles I. Glicksberg. The Hague: Martinus Nijhoff, 1973,
     xxii, 201 p., cloth.

     Wilson is mentioned in passing.

H11.　**Out of Step,** by Daniel Farson.　London:　Michael Joseph, 1974, 252 p., cloth.

Wilson is again mentioned at length in this highly readable autobiography.　The chapter entitled, "A Meeting in Archer's Bookshop" (p. 129-137), is specifically about Wilson.　Farson's first television assignment was interviewing Wilson.

H12.　**Colin Wilson,** by John A. Weigel.　Boston:　Twayne Publishers, 1975, 157 p., cloth.　Twayne English Authors Series, No. 181.

ANALYTICAL TABLE OF CONTENTS:
　　Chapter One: The Outsider As Phenomenon.　*Voyage to a Beginning*; Early years; Young adulthood; "A major writer at 24"—immediate reaction to *The Outsider*; The massacre—aftermath of *The Outsider*; Productive years—a brief summary through the 1960s to 1974.　Chapter Two: The Outsider As Philosopher I.　*The Outsider*; *Religion and the Rebel*; *The Age of Defeat*.　Chapter Three: The Outsider As Philosopher II.　*Strength to Dream*; *Origins of the Sexual Impulse*; *Beyond the Outsider*.　Chapter Four: The Outsider As Novelist I.　*Ritual in the Dark*; *Adrift in Soho*; *World of Violence*; *Man Without a Shadow*.　Chapter Five: The Outsider As Novelist II.　*Necessary Doubt*; *The Glass Cage*; *The Mind Parasites*; *The Philosopher's Stone*; *The Killer*; *God of the Labyrinth*; *The Black Room*; The outsider as novelist: guilty or innocent?; Wilson has "...become a competent novelist worthy of being read on his own terms."　Chapter Six: The Outsider As Critic-of-All-Trades.　Existential criticism; *Eagle and Earwig*; Music; Murder—an evaluation of Wilson's murder trilogy; Biography; Drama; Mysticism; Critic of all trades: the paradox.　Chapter Seven: The Outsider As a New Existentialist: An Evaluation.　*Introduction to the New Existentialism*; The 1% that counts—assessment of Wilson's essay in *Challenges of Humanist Psychology*; *New Pathways in Psychology*; "As a new existentialist he is his own best witness that he is a good man."

COMMENTS:　A fairly well-balanced and sensibly structured account of Wilson's work through *The Schoolgirl Murder Case* in 1974.　Contains a brief chronology, eight pages of useful notes and references, a selected bibliography, and index.

H13. **Contraries: A Personal Progression,** by Stuart Holroyd. London: Bodley Head, 1975, 174 p., cloth.

COMMENTS: An autobiographical sketch by Wilson's friend and fellow writer, dealing mainly with the author's love-life. Wilson is mentioned in passing throughout. Essential reading for anyone wishing to get a flavor of the mid-Fifties British literary scene, the thoughts and actions of its principal characters, and the reaction to these writers by the establishment. Also essential to any would-be Wilson biographer, as there are anecdotes about him which I had not previously seen, and some fairly lengthy contemporaneous quotations. An interesting view of Wilson on a personal level.

H14. **The Twentieth-Century English Novel: An Annotated Bibliography of Criticism,** by A. F. Cassis. New York: Garland Publishing Co., 1977, xxiii, 413 p., cloth.

Wilson's novels are included along with those of many other authors.

H15. **Gollancz: The Story of a Publishing House, 1928-1978,** by Sheila Hodges. London: Victor Gollancz, 1978, 256 p., cloth.

Wilson is mentioned on pages 188-190.

H16. **The Fifties,** by Peter Lewis. London: Heinemann, 1978, 256 p., cloth.

b. New York: J. B. Lippincott, 1978, 256 p., cloth.
c. as: *The Fifties: Portrait of an Age, Second Edition.* London: Cupid, 1988, 256 p., paper.

Wilson is mentioned on pages 165-170, with photo. The index mistakenly lists Wilson as being on pages 155-158.

H17. **Colin Wilson: The Outsider and Beyond,** by Clifford P. Bendau. The Milford Series: Popular Writers of Today, Volume 21. San Bernardino, CA: The Borgo Press, 1979, 63 p., cloth.

ab. San Bernardino, CA: The Borgo Press, 1979, 63 p., paper.

ANALYTICAL TABLE OF CONTENTS:
Introduction: The Colin Wilson Phenomenon. Chapter One: The New Existentialism. The paradoxical notion of freedom; Meaning and value in human existence; The evolution of will. Chapter Two: Perception and Imagination. Glimpses of meaning: the creative process; The imagination: tool of perception. Chapter Three: Literature, Imagination, and Human Values. The existential hero; The strength to dream: the problem; Existential realism; Existential criticism. Chapter Four: The Critics. Colin Wilson and the Angry Young Men; Wilson and the critics; Wilson reassessed. Chapter Five: A Critical Chronology. Chapter Six: Conclusion. "He is a mature writer who has been writing prolifically and well for over two decades."

COMMENTS: Published four years after Weigel's assessment, Bendau's book has a completely different approach, both in style and structure. The first four chapters attempt to pin down the essence of Wilson's work, dealing exclusively with the more important nonfiction, from *The Outsider* to *New Pathways in Psychology*. Chapters 5 and 6 form a straightforward critical chronology which, although not written in as much depth as Weigel's book, nonetheless takes into account the smaller books and pamphlets published in the early Seventies. Thus, it has the advantage, despite its size, of being more comprehensive. Bendau is also not afraid to dismiss a work if he does not consider it important to the central theme of Wilson's message: "*Sex and the Intelligent Teenager* is one of Wilson's least significant works, and it is sufficient to mention here that it was published" (page 41). On the whole, however, he is sympathetic to Wilson's philosophy and message: "Wilson's literary distinction lies in his exceptional insight into the nature of things" (page 59). Includes a brief bibliography of Wilson's works.

SELECTED REVIEWS:

1. *Choice* 16 (Jan., 1980): 1439.
2. Wilgus, Neal. *Science Fiction Review* 9 (Feb., 1980): 37-38.

H18. **In Anger: Culture in the Cold War, 1945-60,** by Robert Hewison. London: Weidenfeld & Nicolson, 1981, 230 p., cloth.

b. New York: Oxford University Press, 1981, 230 p., cloth.
c. Revised Edition. London: Methuen, 1988, [240] p., cloth.

Wilson and the other so-called "angry young men" are the subject of Chapter 5, "Declaration."

H19. **The British Museum in Fiction: A Check-List,** by Edward F. Ellis. Buffalo, NY: [Anthoensen Press], 1981, xiv, 193 p., paper.

Wilson has mentioned the British Museum in ten of his novels and short stories; they are all cited here (p. 175-177), in this privately published, but very well produced, bibliography.

H20. **The Novels of Colin Wilson,** by Nicolas Tredell. London: Vision Press; Totowa, NJ: Barnes & Noble Books, 1982, 157 p., cloth.

ANALYTICAL TABLE OF CONTENTS:
Chapter One: A Writer's Development. Early years—information taken mostly form *Voyage to a Beginning* and the earlier books published about Wilson. Chapter Two: Evolutionary Existentialism. Wilson's philosophy. Chapter Three: Novel Approaches. Wilson's attitudes toward the novel. Chapter Four: Metaphysical Thriller. *Ritual in the Dark.* Chapter Five: Novels of Transition. *Adrift in Soho; The World of Violence; Man Without a Shadow.* Chapter Six: Unofficial Detectives. *Necessary Doubt* and *The Glass Cage.* Chapter Seven: Arrows to the Farther Shore. *The Mind Parasites* and *The Philosopher's Stone.* Chapter Eight: Murder, Sex, and Spying. *The Killer; God of the Labyrinth; The Black Room.* Chapter Nine: The Story So Far. *The Schoolgirl Murder Case; The Space Vampires;* Works in progress; Conclusion.

COMMENTS: A long overdue study of Wilson's fiction, updating and expanding Dillard's short critique (see I25), based upon the author's thesis, *Existence and Evolution—A Study of Colin's Wilson's Novels,* completed while he was a student at East Susses College of Higher Education. Detailed notes follow every chapter. The bibliography is divided into three parts: novels, nonfiction, and studies of Wilson, but is very selective. A good, balanced criticism of the early novels, although the later works are given short shrift.

SELECTED REVIEWS:

1. *Journal of Modern Literature* 10 (1983): 591.

H21. **Henry: An Appreciation of Henry Williamson**, by Daniel Farson. London: Michael Joseph, 1982, x, 245 p., cloth.

b. as: *Henry Williamson—A Portrait*. London: Robinson, 1986, 246 p., paper.

Wilson is mentioned throughout this biography of one of the most underrated of English writers. His friendship with Williamson and Daniel Farson's father, Negley, is highlighted. See also Farson's earlier book, *Out of Step* (H11).

H22. **An Odyssey to Freedom: Four Themes in Colin Wilson's Novels**, by K. Gunnar Bergström. Acta Universitatis Upsaliensis, Studia Anglistica Upsaliensia, no. 47. Uppsala, Sweden: University of Uppsala, 1983, 160 p., paper.

ANALYTICAL TABLE OF CONTENTS:
Introduction: How this work differs from the other critical works on Wilson; Chronological table of Wilson's novels and the "most important" critical-philosophical works.

Chapter One: The Philosophical Background. 1) Existentialism: Kierkegaard, Nietzsche, Husserl, Heidegger, and Sartre. 2) New existentialism: Wilson's "Outsider Cycle"; His books on murder; "Faculty X."

Chapter Two: The Outsider Hero. The relationship between Wilson's novels and his works of nonfiction; The "intellectual" hero—Gerard Sorme, Hugh Greene, Harry Preston, and Karl Zweig; The "visionary" hero—Damon Reade; The "superman" hero—Gilbert Austin and Howard Lester; The "insider-outsider" hero—Chief Superintendent Saltfleet and Commander Carlsen.

Chapter Three: The Outsider Criminal. Arthur Lingard; George Gaylord Sundheim.

Chapter Four: Sex—A Glimpse of the Powers Within. Gerard Sorme in *Man Without a Shadow*, and Gerard Sorme/Esmond Donelly in *God of the Labyrinth*.

Chapter Five: Faculty X—The Key to Man's Hidden Potentialities. *The Philosopher's Stone* and *The Black Room*.

Summary and Conclusion: Wilson's use of different genres as "symbolic forms"; The author's reservations about Wilson's work: "The strength of Colin Wilson's novels lies in their message, in their philosophical content."

COMMENTS: An interesting assessment of Wilson's fiction, with the connection between his novels and critical/philosophical works clearly stressed. The author has relied on several earlier critiques for help, but does not seem to be aware of Bendau's book. It is interesting to compare his approach to that of Tredell, whose book was published just one year previously. Bergström does provide a good, in-depth assessment of *The Philosopher's Stone*, but his critique contains a few printing and typographical errors, including a misspelling of Wilson's name (p. 141), and two missed references to Howard Lester as Henry Howard (p. 146). Written in English as a doctoral thesis at Uppsala University. Includes a selective bibliography divided into three sections—works by Wilson, criticism on Wilson, and other works cited; and a good five-page index.

H23. **Interviews with Britain's Angry Young Men**, by Dale Salwak. Literary Voices, No. 2. The Milford Series: Popular Writers of Today, Vol. 39. San Bernardino, CA: The Borgo Press, 1984, 96 p., cloth.

ab. San Bernardino, CA: The Borgo Press, 1984, 96 p., paper.

TABLE OF CONTENTS:
Introduction, by Colin Wilson. The literary depression after World War II; John Wain's *Hurry on Down*; Kingsley Amis' *Lucky Jim*; Iris Murdoch's *Under the Net*; The writing and publication of *The Outsider*; John Osborne's *Look Back in Anger*; The press creates the "Angry Young Men" movement, and then sets about destroying it; The Beat Generation in America; The effects of the "Angry Young Men" publicity on its protagonists.
Chapter One: Kingsley Amis: Mimic and Moralist. Chapter Two: John Braine: The Man at the Top. Chapter Three: Bill Hopkins: Looking for the Revolutionary. Chapter Four: John Wain: Man of Letters. Chapter Five: Colin Wilson: The Man Behind *The Outsider*. Index.

COMMENTS: A fascinating collection of interviews with some of the "Angry Young Men," illustrated with black-and-white photographs of the participants. It lacks, however, the voices of two important characters: John Osborne and Stuart Holroyd, but compensates somewhat by achieving a rare interview with the enigmatic Bill Hopkins, who faded quickly from the literary scene after his novel, *The Divine and the Decay* (recently reprinted as *The Leap*), was savaged by critics in the "Angry Young Men" backlash of the late 1950s. The interview with Wilson is an important one, particularly the second half, where he begins discussing his work and its philosophical implications.

SELECTED REVIEWS:

1. *Booklist* 81 (Oct. 1, 1984): 183.
2. *Modern Fiction Studies* 31 (Summer, 1985): 365.
3. *World Literature Today* 59 (Summer, 1985): 435.

H24. **The Colin Wilson Collection of Howard F. Dossor**, by Howard F. Dossor. Melbourne: Privately Printed, 1986, 107 p., paper.

A catalog of a remarkable collection of Wilson's works by the editor of *The Bicameral Critic* (see A72), perhaps the best assemblance of its kind in existence, more comprehensive, even, than Wilson's own. This booklet lists the fruits of thirty years of collecting, which culminated in three visits by the author to the United States and Great Britain during the past decade in search of new material. The catalog is divided into twenty-two sections, and includes audio and video tapes, posters, photographs, and all manner of Wilson-related material. Not commercially available. With the author's permission, I have used his list of Colin Wilson books in translation to add some material to the first section of this bibliography.

H25. **Success Stories: Literature and the Media in England, 1950-59**, by Harry Ritchie. London: Faber & Faber, 1988, 257 p., cloth.

COMMENTS: An extraordinary book, meticulously researched by the author, who must have spent weeks in the Newspaper Library examining press coverage of the "Angry Young Men" phenomenon. The main problem, however, is that Ritchie somewhat naively seems to have assimilated the worst of the 1950s' criticism of this movement, which he then regurgitates in Chapters 7-8 in one of the most vituperative attacks on Wilson's work of the last two decades.

In the course of his critique, Ritchie accuses Wilson of lacking "thoroughness" and "insight," the very qualities he himself demonstrates in failing to assess fairly the enormous breadth and depth of Wilson's thirty years of publishing. The "highbrow" critics followed Ritchie's lead and allowed his comments to go unchallenged. Wilson himself responded with admirable restraint in the reviews cited below.

While this is not a work I can recommend to the serious student of Colin Wilson, it is a prime example of the type of unjustified and generally unsupported attack which has dogged the author from the beginning of his career. The twenty-four pages of notes at the end of the book are, however, extremely valuable.

SELECTED REVIEWS:

1. Campbell, James. "That Old Sensation," in *Times Literary Supplement* (Feb. 19-25, 1988): 184.
2. Dyer, Geoff. "More in Anger," in *New Statesman* 115 (Feb. 19, 1988): 35.
3. Morrison, Blake. "Rebels Without a Cause," in *Observer* (Feb. 7, 1988): 24.
4. Rutherford, Malcolm. "Raging Success," in *Financial Times* (Feb. 20, 1988): xviii.
5. Wain, John. "Mr. Wain Waxes Angry About the Angries," in *Sunday Times* (Mar. 6, 1988): G3.
6. Wilson, Colin. "A Rather Juvenile Offender...," in *Yorkshire Post* (Feb. 25, 1988):   .
7. Wilson, Colin. "The Author Has Not Yet Read My Masterpiece," in *Literary Review* no. 118 (April, 1988): 50-51.

H26. **Colin Wilson, a Celebration: Essays and Recollections**, edited by Colin Stanley. London: Cecil Woolf, 1988, 256 p., cloth.

CONTENTS: "Foreword," by Angus Wilson; "Editor's Preface," by Stanley; 1. "The Even-Tempered Guide," by Jonathan Guinness; 2. "Colin: Still an Outsider?" by Donald Seaman; 3. "Shared Experiences," by Tom Greenwell; 4. "Angry Young Mania and Beyond," by Stuart Holroyd; 5. "Aiming for a Likeness," by Bill Hopkins; 6. "'So Much Work To Do'," by John Rety; 7. "A Literary Incident," by Allen Ginsberg; 8. "Crisis and Revelation: Some Personal Experiences," by Colin Stanley; 9. "*Floreat* Colin Wilson," by Brocard Sewell; 10. "A Tribute to Colin Wilson," by Renate Rasp; 11. "Colin Wilson," by June O'Shea; 12. "Colin Wilson," by A. E. van Vogt; 13. "Colin Wilson, the Best of Friends," by Daniel Farson; 14. "Coming in from the Outside," by Daniel Farson; 15. "The Human Future," by Nicolas Tredell;

16. "Writing *Ritual in the Dark*," by Sidney Campion; 17. "Introduction to *The Outsider*," by Marilyn Ferguson; 18. "Murder As Existential Act," by Howard F. Dossor; 19. "Control of Consciousness: Mental Freedom, Not Bliss: Colin Wilson's Ultimate Objective," by K. Gunnar Bergström; 20. "Wilson's Occult," by Alan Hull Watson; 21. "Colin Wilson's *Magnum Opus*," by Alan Hull Walton; 22. "Toward an Existential Realism: The Novels of Colin Wilson," by R. H. W. Dillard; 23. "The Novels of Colin Wilson," by John A. Weigel; 24. "Introduction to *The Philosopher's Stone*," by Joyce Carol Oates; 25. "The Sage of Tetherdown," by H. D. Purcell; 26. "Interview with Colin Wilson," by Pete Barraclough; and "Five Reviews of *The Outsider*, 1956-7": 27. "Loser Take All," by Cyril Connolly; 28. "Unlucky Jims," by Philip Toynbee; 29. "Thoughts on *The Outsider*," by J. B. Priestley; 30. "*The Outsider*," by Kenneth Walker; 31. "Colin Wilson's *The Outsider*," by Sir Oswald Mosley; 32. "Postscript," by Uri Geller; Bibliography, by Colin Stanley and Howard F. Dossor; Notes on the Contributors; Index.

COMMENTS: To mark the thirty-two years which have elapsed since the original publication of *The Outsider*, Stanley gathered this volume of thirty-three mainly unpublished essays by various authors, on Wilson's life and remarkable achievements.   The contributions fall roughly into two categories: candid recollections by friends and colleagues of Wilson, and critical assessments by recognized scholars of Wilson's work.   A number of entries combine the two.   Also included are a number of biographical pieces which place the reader on intimate terms with Wilson's background and origins.   As Tom Greenwell writes: "Wilson does not just write books; he shares experiences with his readers.   He uses ideas—good ones and bad ones, new ones and old ones—as a climber uses footholds and handholes to zig-zag his way to the ultimate goal.   Sometimes Wilson falters, slips back a bit, and finds new paths around obstacles; but the general progress is upwards and towards the sunlight."

A storehouse of memoirs and critiques.

H27.   Colin Wilson: Two Essays: The English Existentialist and Spiders and Outsiders (Including an Interview with the Author), by John Moorhouse and Paul Newman, edited by Colin Stanley. Nottingham: Paupers' Press, 1989, 49 p., paper.

COMMENTS: Two essays, one biographical, the other critical, plus an interesting interview with Wilson conducted by Newman in 1986.

H28. The Work of Colin Wilson: An Annotated Bibliography & Guide, by Colin Stanley, edited by Boden Clarke. Bibliographies of Modern Authors, No. 1. San Bernardino, CA: The Borgo Press, 1989, 312 p., cloth. [bibliography]

ab. San Bernardino, CA: The Borgo Press, 1989, 312 p., paper.

CONTENTS: Acknowledgments and Note; Introduction: "The Quest for Colin Wilson"; A Colin Wilson Chronology; A. Books; B. Short Fiction; C. Nonfiction; D. Introductions and Afterwords; E. Book Reviews; F. Other Media; G. Editorial Credits; H. About the Author: Monographs; I. About the Author: Critiques, Profiles, Interviews; J. About the Author: Short Bio-Bibliographies; K. About the Author: Other Materials; L. Miscellanea; Quoth the Critics; Afterword: "Inside Outside: Reflections on Being Bibliographed," by Colin Wilson (an original essay); About Colin Stanley; Title Index to Colin Wilson's Works; Subject Index with Author/Title Index.

I.

ABOUT THE AUTHOR
Critiques, Profiles, Interviews

NOTE: See also Wilson's own lengthy essay, "An Autobiographical Sketch" (C337).

I1.   "The Inside Story of The Outsider," by David Wainwright, in *Evening News* (London) (May 28, 1956): 4. Information for a hungry public about England's hottest new literary property. [profile]

I2.   "Reader's Indigestion," by Dwight MacDonald, in *New Yorker* (Oct. 13, 1956): 187-199. An extended review of *The Outsider*. [review]

I3.   "Authentic Voices," by W. J. Morgan, in *Twentieth Century* 161 (1957): 138-144. [critique]

I4.   "Colin Wilson Explains: 'My Genius'," by Daniel Farson, in *Books and Art* (October, 1957): 24-25. [interview]

I5.   "Getting to Know Mr. Wilson," by Daniel Farson, in *Books and Art* (October, 1957): 25. [profile]

I6.   "No Man's Land," by Bonamy Dobree, in *Sewanee Review* 65 (part 2, 1957): 309-326. A review of *The Outsider* and other important works of the time. [review article]

I7.   "What Is Wrong with the Snipers and Outsiders," by Derek Stanford, in *Church of England Newspaper* (Jan. 3, 1958): 7. Wilson is referred to as "...a sort of expresso-bar encyclopaedist." [critique]

I8.   "Men of Anger," by Kenneth Tynan, in *Holiday* 23 (April, 1958): 92-93. [critique]

I9. **"England's Angry Young Men—Mystics, Provincials, and Radicals,"** by Robert Weaver, in *Queen's Quarterly* 65 (Summer, 1958): 183-194. Wilson classified as a "mystic." [critique]

I10. **"Why All This Anger?"** by Hilda Graef, in *Catholic World* 188 (November, 1958): 122-128. [critique]

I11. **"The Man Outside,"** by Coral Taylor, in *Yorkshire Post* (Dec. 4, 1958): . An assessment of Wilson's first two books, with a brief biography. [profile]

I12. **"Profile with Pencil—Colin Wilson,"** by Stanley Parker, in *John O'London's* 1 (1959): 382. One of a series of weekly profiles of famous personalities. [profile]

I13. **"Ripe for Ruin,"** by G. Cloyne, in *Times* (Oct. 29, 1959): 15. Concerning publicity and the writer. [critique]

I14. **"The Painless Heroism of Mr. Colin Wilson,"** by Sir Arnold Lunn, in *Month* (March, 1960): 142-146. An extended review of *The Age of Defeat*, with heavy Christian bias. [review article]

I15. **"The Outsider Revisited,"** by J. C. Mihalick, in *Four Quarters* 9 (March, 1960): 26-30. [critique]

I16. **"The Two Colin Wilsons,"** by Tom Greenwell, in *Books & Bookmen* 5 (March, 1960): 9. "Colin Wilson, social provocateur, serious literary figure..." With a photo of Wilson on the front cover, and a portrait with his wife Joy inside. Published to coincide with publication of *Ritual in the Dark*. [profile]

I17. **"The Struggle Continues: Some Comments on English Modern Esthetics,"** by V. V. Evashova, in *Zeitschrift für Anglistik und Amerikanistik* 8 (1960): 409-421. A translation by John Mitchell of an article which appeared originally in the Russian journal, *Inostrannaia Literatura* (no. 5, 1959). A communist view of modern English writers. [critique]

I18. **"The Infallibility of Colin Wilson,"** by Sir Arnold Lunn, in *Month* (November, 1961): 278-286. An extended review of *Religion and the Rebel*, with heavy Christian bias. [review article]

I19. "Colin Wilson Talks Freely to Tom Greenwell: Part One: The Outsider and After," by Tom Greenwell, in *Yorkshire Post* (Mar. 20, 1962): . [interview]

I20. "Colin Wilson Talks Freely to Tom Greenwell: Part Two: Is Man a God or a Worm?" by Tom Greenwell, in *Yorkshire Post* (Mar. 21, 1962): . [interview]

I21. "Creators in Cornwall," by Denys Val Baker, in *New Strand* (November, 1962): . About writers and artists in Cornwall. [profile]

I22. "Violence in the Modern Novel," by Derek Stanford, in *Critic* 22 (August/September, 1963): 32-36. [critique]

I23. "The Angry Young Men Revisited," by Leslie Paul, in *Kenyon Review* 27 (Spring, 1965): 344-352. [critique]

I24. "The World of Violence," in *Taste for Living: Young People in the Modern Novel*, edited by G. G. Urwin. London: Faber & Faber, 1967, cloth, p. . An extract from *The World of Violence*, plus commentary. [critique]

I25. "Toward an Existential Realism: The Novels of Colin Wilson," by R. H. W. Dillard, in *Hollins Critic* 4 (October, 1967): 1-12. An important pioneering essay on Wilson's novels, heavily referred to by later critics. Covers the early novels through *The Mind Parasites*, which is described by Dillard as "an apocalyptic parable of Wilson's insight into the nature of things." [critique]

b. *The Sounder Few: Essays from* The Hollins Critic. Athens, GA: University of Georgia Press, 1971, cloth, p. 283-304.
c. *Colin Wilson, a Celebration: Essays and Recollections*, edited by Colin Stanley. London: Cecil Woolf, 1988, cloth, p. 137-149.

I26. "The Analysis of an 'Outsider'," by Charles Savage *et al.*, in *The Psychoanalytic Forum, Volume 3*, edited by John A. Lindon. New York: Science House, 1969, cloth, p. 275-303. [critique]

I27. "Colin Wilson: Author in Search of Immortality," by Pete Barraclough, in *Leicester Chronicle* (May 29, 1970): 4-5, 24. [profile]

128. **"Interview with Colin Wilson,"** uncredited, in *Torque* 2 (Autumn, 1970): 5-12. [interview]

129. **"The Wilson Age: The Outsider at 40,"** by R. C. Churchill, in *Birmingham Post* (October 3, 1970): . Includes reviews of *Poetry and Mysticism*, *The Killer*, *Voyage to a Beginning*, and *God of the Labyrinth*. [review article]

130. **"The Curious Case of Colin Wilson,"** by Christopher Hibbs, in *Books & Bookmen* 16 (January, 1971): 16-17. An assessment of Wilson's work, with special reference to his article, "Lindsay As Novelist and Mystic" (later expanded into *The Haunted Man: The Strange Genius of David Lindsay*). [critique]

131. **"Colin Wilson, the Permanent Outsider,"** by Tim Wilson, in *Guardian* (May 24, 1971): 8. [profile]

132. **"The Outsider at Forty,"** by R. C. Churchill, in *Humanist* 87 (March, 1972): 83-84. [profile]

133. **"Colin Wilson,"** by Paddy Kitchen, in *Time Out* (June 16-22, 1972): . A short biography and bibliography. [bio-bibliography]

134. **"Conversation with Colin Wilson,"** by Daniel Grotta, in *Oui* 2 (Dec., 1973): 71, 74, 92, 129-130. [interview]

135. **"Colin Wilson and the Occult,"** by Martha Eckman, in *The Contemporary Literary Scene 1973*, edited by Frank N. Magill. Englewood Cliffs, NJ: Salem Press, 1974, cloth, p. 62-72. [critique]

136. **"Introduction,"** by Joyce Carol Oates, in *The Philosopher's Stone*, by Colin Wilson. New York: Warner Books, 1974, paper, p. 7-15. Wilson is equated with John Fowles, Doris Lessing, and Margaret Drabble. [introduction]

   b. *Colin Wilson, a Celebration: Essays and Recollections*, edited by Colin Stanley. London: Cecil Woolf, 1988, cloth, p. 161-167.

137. An article, title unknown, by Joy Wilson, in *A Meal for All Seasons*. Bodmin, Cornwall: Bossiney Books, 1975, cloth, p. 32. On Wilson's eating habits, with a recipe for French onion soup. [profile]

138. "Novel News," by David Hughes, in *New Fiction Magazine* no. 4 (July, 1975): 1. "Years ago I put him [Wilson] mentally down for a masterpiece. When it arrives I hope we'll recognise it..." [review article]

139. "Colin Wilson, 1931- ," in *Contemporary Literary Criticism: Excerpts from Criticism of the Works of Today's Novelists, Poets, Playwrights, and Other Creative Writers, Volume 3*, edited by Carolyn Riley. Detroit: Gale Research Co., 1975, cloth, p. 536-538. [excerpted critiques]

140. "Conversation with Colin Wilson," by Joyce Carol Oates, in *Ontario Review* no. 4 (Spring/Summer, 1976): 7-15. [interview]

141. "Chris Simons Talks to Colin Wilson," by Chris Simons, in *Writer's Review* (February/March, 1979): 10-16. [interview]

142. "Colin Wilson: Of Unwearied Fancy," by Joan Revill, in *Prediction* 45 (May, 1979): 4-6. [astrological profile]

143. "The Mind Parasites," by Timothy O'Reilly, in *Survey of Science Fiction Literature*, edited by Frank N. Magill. Englewood Cliffs, NJ: Salem Press, 1979, Vol. 3, p. 1401-1406. [critique]

144. "The Philosopher's Stone," by Brian Stableford, in *Survey of Science Fiction Literature*, edited by Frank N. Magill. Englewood Cliffs, NJ: Salem Press, 1979, Vol. 4, p. 1674-1677. [critique]

145. "Wilson, Colin," in *A Spectrum of Fantasy: The Bibliography and Biography of a Collection of Fantastic Literature*, by George Locke. London: Ferret Fantasy, 1980, cloth, p. 233. [bibliography]

    A bibliographical description of, and guide to, first edition information on *The Mind Parasites* and *The Philosopher's Stone*.

146. "Colin Wilson: The Outsider," by Jeffrey M. Elliot, in *Fantasy Newsletter* 3 (Nov., 1980): 4-7, 31. [interview]

147. "Coming in from the Outside," by Daniel Farson, in *Sunday Telegraph Magazine* no. 219 (December 7, 1980): 30-36. About Wilson and his Cornwall home. [profile]

b. *Colin Wilson, a Celebration: Essays and Recollections*, edited by Colin Stanley. London: Cecil Woolf, 1988, cloth, p. 83-87.

I48. "Colin Wilson," in *Contemporary Literary Criticism: Excerpts from Criticism of the Works of Today's Novelists, Poets, Playwrights, and Other Creative Writers, Volume 14*, edited by Dedria Bryfonski and Laurie Lanzen Harris. Detroit: Gale Research Co., 1980, cloth, p. 583-590. [excerpted critiques]

I49. "A Cornish Diary," by "Pendennis," in *Observer* (December 7, 1980): 26. Impressions of a visit to Wilson's home. [profile]

I50. "Marcel Aymé and Colin Wilson on the Bourgeois, the Outlaw, and Poetry," by Camille R. Labossière," in *Dalhousie Review* 61 (1981): 103-112. The author cites four of Wilson's works: *Beyond the Outsider, The Outsider, Casebook of Murder*, and *Poetry and Mysticism*. [critique]

I51. "Wilson, Colin (U.K.). The Mind Parasites," by Joe De Bolt and John R. Pfeiffer, in *Anatomy of Wonder: A Critical Guide to Science Fiction, Second Edition*, edited by Neil Barron. New York & London: R. R. Bowker Co., 1981, cloth, p. 299-300. [critique]

I52. "Wilson, Colin (U.K.). The Mind Parasites," by Gary William Crawford, in *Horror Literature: A Core Collection and Reference Guide*, edited by Marshall B. Tymn. New York & London: R. R. Bowker Co., 1981, cloth, p. 346. [critique]

I53. "Colin Wilson," in *British Novel Explication, Supplement II*, by Christian J. W. Kloesel and Jeffrey R. Smitten. Hamden, CT: Shoe String Press, 1981, cloth, p. 261-262. [bibliography]

I54. "Things That Go Bump in the Night," by Fred Newman, in *Book Choice* no. 13 (Jan., 1982): 25. Newman talks to Wilson about his book, *Poltergeist*. [interview]

I55. "Voyage to a Beginning—Colin Wilson and Me," by Colin Stanley, in *Tentacles* no. 28 (Spring, 1982): 10-15. [profile]

I56. "Colin Wilson," by John A. Weigel, in *British Novelists Since 1960*, edited by Jay L. Halio. The Dictionary of Literary Biography, Volume 14. Detroit: Gale Research Co., 1983, cloth, p. 780-787. Weigel here condenses his ideas about Wilson's work into an encyclopedia article. [critique]

b. *Colin Wilson, a Celebration: Essays and Recollections*, edited by Colin Stanley. London: Cecil Woolf, 1988, cloth, p. 150-160.

I57. **"Interview: Colin Wilson,"** by Lisa Tuttle, in *Twilight Zone* 3 (March/April, 1983): 24-28. [interview]

I58. **"Do Psychics Really Solve Crimes?"** by Suzanne Thomas, in *Woman* (Jan. 7, 1984): 46-47. Published to coincide with release of *Psychic Detectives*. [interview]

I59. **"Ready for Fame Second Time Round,"** by Anna Cooknell, in *Leicester Mercury* (Apr. 6, 1984): 34. Wilson briefly talks about his rise to fame in the Sixties, and his subsequent condemnation. With typical optimism, he sees the tide turning once more, and is determined to be ready for fame this time. [interview]

I60. **"Big Screen First for Sci-Fi Novelist,"** by Lois Rogers, in *Leicester Mercury* (July 18, 1984): 11. A superficial article rushed into print when it was announced that *Space Vampires* was being filmed (the film was released under the title, *Lifeforce*). Wilson mentions that A. E. van Vogt gave him the idea for the book. [interview]

I61. **"The New Age Interview: Colin Wilson,"** by Robert Anton Wilson, in *New Age Journal* (April, 1985): 59-66. [interview]

A lengthy and readable interview in which Wilson restates his ideas about peak experiences, split brain psychology, and the need for all of us to work upon ourselves in order to evolve. This is only possible when the right and left brain work in harmony, controlled by the "I." He concludes: "So sex is great, and relaxing into the right brain is great, and peak experiences are great, but *meaning* is only found when you are in the driver's seat, when the transcendental ego is awake and aware."

I62. **"Indoors...with the Outsider,"** by Jim Gould, in *Leicester Mercury* (July 19, 1985): 15. Resume of the ups and downs of Wilson's career for the readers of his home town newspaper. [profile]

I63. **"Colin Wilson: The Case for Optimism,"** by Howard F. Dossor, in *The Bicameral Critic*, by Colin Wilson, edited by Howard F. Dossor. Bath: Ashgrove Press, 1985, paper, p. 1-10. Dossor pinpoints an essential aspect of Wilson's work, its optimism. [critique]

I64. **"Lifeforce and Space Vampires: A Comparison,"** by Dale Skran, Jr., in *Lan's Lantern* no. 18 (Dec., 1985): 12-14. [critique]

I65. **"Lifeforce,"** in *FutureVisions: The New Golden Age of the Science Fiction Film*, by Douglas Menville and R. Reginald, with Mary A. Burgess. North Hollywood, CA: A Greenbriar Book, Newcastle Publishing Co. Inc., 1985, paper, p. 180, 186. Includes a still from the original film. [film critique]

   b. San Bernardino, CA: The Borgo Press, 1985, cloth, p. 180, 186.

"[Tobe] Hooper would have done better to stick more closely to Wilson's original [idea], which at least made sense."

I66. **"Colin Wilson Interview,"** by Diana Cooper-Clark, in *Interviews with Contemporary Novelists*. New York: St. Martin's Press, 1986, cloth, p. 212-238. London: Macmillan, 1986, cloth, p. 212-238. [interview]

A lively and outspoken interview with Wilson, in which he concludes: "I suspect that I probably am the greatest writer of the twentieth century...I'd be very interested to find somebody who was greater...because I'd really want to know what they had to say."

I67. **"Slaves of the Death Spiders: Colin Wilson and Existentialist Science Fiction,"** by Brian Stableford, in *Foundation* no. 38 (Winter, 1986/87): 63-67. [critique]

I68. **"Colin Wilson: Checklist of American Editions, Articles and Selected Reference Material, 1956-1982,"** by Jerome Drost, in *Bulletin of Bibliography* 44 (March, 1987): 3-9. [bibliography]

A brief listing of books and articles in one alphabetical sequence, with a general introduction.

I69. **"Keeping up with the Outsider,"** by Colin Stanley, in *Cornish Scene* 2 (May/June, 1987): 32-33. Discusses the author's association with Wilson. [profile]

A follow-up letter appears in *Cornish Scene* 3 (July/August, 1987): 13.

I70. "Colin Wilson: Psychology, Sex, and Science Fiction," by Stephen Jones, in *Locus, the Newspaper of the Science Fiction Field* 20 (June, 1987): 31. [profile]

I71. "Wilson, Colin (U.K.). The Mind Parasites," by Brian Stableford, in *Anatomy of Wonder: A Critical Guide to Science Fiction, Third Edition*, edited by Neil Barron. New York & London: R. R. Bowker Co., 1987, cloth, p. 315. [critique]

Also covers *The Philosopher's Stone* and *The Space Vampires*.

I72. "Preface: Colin Wilson, Literary High Flyer," by Colin Stanley, in *Existentially Speaking: Essays on the Philosophy of Literature*, by Colin Wilson. San Bernardino, CA: The Borgo Press, 1989, cloth, p. 5-8. Published simultaneously in trade paperback. [critical introduction]

I73. "Introduction: The Quest for Colin Wilson," in *The Work of Colin Wilson: An Annotated Bibliography & Guide*, by Colin Stanley. San Bernardino, CA: The Borgo Press, 1989, cloth, p. 5-9. Published simultaneously in trade paperback. [critical introduction]

J.

ABOUT THE AUTHOR
Short Bio-Bibliographies

NOTE: Wilson has has been listed in well over a hundred biographical and literary directories. The list below, while probably not complete, represents all the titles that could be easily located.

J1. "Wilson, Colin Henry," in *Who's Who: An Annual Biographical Directory 1958*. London: Adam & Charles Black, 1958, cloth, p. 3279.

J2. "Wilson, Colin Henry," in *Who's Who: An Annual Biographical Directory 1959*. London: Adam & Charles Black, 1959, cloth, p. 3291.

J3. "Wilson, Colin Henry," in *Who's Who: An Annual Biographical Directory 1960*. London: Adam & Charles Black, 1960, cloth, p. 3270.

J4. "Wilson, Colin Henry," in *Who's Who: An Annual Biographical Directory 1961*. London: Adam & Charles Black, 1961, cloth, p. 3298-3299.

J5. "Wilson, Colin Henry," in *Who's Who: An Annual Biographical Directory 1962*. London: Adam & Charles Black, 1962, cloth, p. 3321.

J6. "Wilson, Colin, 1931- ," in *Contemporary Authors: A Bio-Bibliographical Guide to Current Authors and Their Works, Volume 3*, edited by James M. Ethridge. Detroit: Gale Research Co., 1963, cloth, p. 215.

J7. "Wilson, Colin (Henry)," in *Current Biography Yearbook 1963*, edited by Charles Moritz. New York: H. W. Wilson Co., 1963, cloth, p. 469-471. Includes a photo of the author. [biography]

J8. "Wilson, Colin Henry," in *Who's Who: An Annual Biographical Directory 1963*. London: Adam & Charles Black, 1963, cloth, p. 3309.

J9. "Wilson, Colin," in *The Author's and Writer's Who's Who, [Fifth Edition]*. Darien, CT: Hafner Publishing Co., 1963, cloth, p. 525.

J10. "Wilson, Colin Henry," in *Who's Who: An Annual Biographical Directory 1964*. London: Adam & Charles Black, 1964, cloth, p. 3307.

J11. "Wilson, Colin," in *Who's Who in America: A Biographical Directory of Notable Living Men and Women, Volume 33 (1964-1965)*. Chicago: Marquis Who's Who, 1964, cloth, p. 2180.

J12. "Wilson, Colin (1931-)," in *The Reader's Encyclopedia, Second Edition*, by William Rose Benét. New York: Thomas Y. Crowell Co., 1965, cloth, p. 1094.

J13. "Wilson, Colin Henry," in *Who's Who: An Annual Biographical Directory 1965*. London: Adam & Charles Black, 1965, cloth, p. 3325.

J14. "Wilson, Colin," in *Modern British Literature*, compiled and edited by Ruth Z. Temple and Martin Tucker. New York: Frederick Ungar Publishing Co., 1966, cloth, p. .

J15. "Wilson, Colin Henry," in *Who's Who: An Annual Biographical Directory 1966*. London: Adam & Charles Black, 1966, cloth, p. 3325.

J16. "Wilson, Colin," in *Who's Who in America: A Biographical Directory of Notable Living Men and Women, Volume 34 (1966-1967)*. Chicago: Marquis Who's Who, 1966, cloth, p. 2319.

J17. "Wilson, Colin, 1931- ," in *Contemporary Authors: A Bio-Bibliographical Guide to Current Authors and Their Works, Volumes 1-4, First Revision*, edited by James M. Ethridge and Barbara Kopala. Detroit: Gale Research Co., 1967, cloth, p. 1010-1011.

J18. "Wilson, Colin," in *The New Century Handbook of English Literature, Revised Edition*, edited by Clarence L. Barnhart and

William D. Halsey. New York: Appleton-Century-Crofts, 1967, cloth, p. .

J19. "Wilson, Colin Henry," in *Who's Who: An Annual Biographical Directory 1967-68*. London: Adam & Charles Black, 1967, cloth, p. 3331-3332.

J20. "Wilson, Colin, 1931- ," in *Twentieth Century British Literature: A Reference Guide and Bibliography*, by Ruth Z. Temple and Martin Tucker. New York: Frederick Ungar Publishing Co., 1968, cloth, p. 253.

J21. "Wilson, Colin Henry," in *Who's Who: An Annual Biographical Directory 1968-69*. London: Adam & Charles Black, 1968, cloth, p. 3331.

J22. "Wilson, Colin," in *Who's Who in America: A Biographical Directory of Notable Living Men and Women, Volume 35 (1968-1969)*. Chicago: Marquis Who's Who, 1968, cloth, p. 2367.

J23. "Wilson, Colin Henry," in *Who's Who: An Annual Biographical Directory 1969-70*. London: Adam & Charles Black, 1969, cloth, p. 3359-60.

J24. "Wilson, Colin," in *Longman Companion to Twentieth Century Literature*, by A. C. Ward. London: Longman Group, 1970, cloth, p. 576.

J25. "Wilson, Colin Henry," in *Who's Who: An Annual Biographical Directory 1970-71*. London: Adam & Charles Black, 1970, cloth, p. 3381.

J26. "Wilson, Colin," in *Who's Who in America: A Biographical Directory of Notable Living Men and Women, Volume 36 (1970-1971)*. Chicago: Marquis Who's Who, 1970, cloth, p. 2470.

J27. "Wilson, Colin," in *Who's Who in the World, 1st Edition, 1971-1972*. Chicago: Marquis Who's Who, 1970, cloth, p. 960.

J28. "Wilson, Colin (Henry)," in *The Writers Directory, 1971-73*, edited by A. G. Seaton. Chicago, London: St. James Press, 1971, cloth, p. 496.

J29. "Wilson, Colin," in *The Author's and Writer's Who's Who, Sixth Edition*. Darien, CT: Hafner Publishing Co., 1971, cloth, p. .

J30. "Wilson, Colin," in *Twentieth Century Writing: A Reader's Guide to Contemporary Literature*, edited by Kenneth Richardson. Levittown, NY: Transatlantic Arts, 1971, cloth, p.   .

J31. "Wilson, Colin Henry," in *Who's Who: An Annual Biographical Directory 1971-72.* London: Adam & Charles Black, 1971, cloth, p. 3425.

J32. "Wilson, Colin (Henry)," by John A. Weigel, in *Contemporary Novelists*, edited by James Vinson. New York: St. Martin's Press, 1972, cloth, p. 1377-1381.

J33. "Wilson, Colin Henry," in *Who's Who: An Annual Biographical Directory 1972-73.* London: Adam & Charles Black, 1972, cloth, p. 3470.

J34. "Wilson, Colin," in *Who's Who in America, 37th Edition, 1972-1973.* Chicago: Marquis Who's Who, 1972, cloth, Vol. 2, p. 3437.

J35. "Wilson, Colin Henry," in *International Who's Who, Thirty-Sixth Edition, 1972-73.* London: Europa Publications, 1972, cloth, p. 1805.

J36. "Wilson, Colin," in *Cassell's Encyclopaedia of World Literature*, edited by S. H. Steinberg and J. Buchanan-Brown. New York: William Morrow & Co., 1973, cloth, Vol. 3, p. 749.

J37. "Wilson, Colin," in *Who's Who in the World, 2nd Edition, 1974-1975.* Chicago: Marquis Who's Who, 1973, cloth, p. 1066.

J38. "Wilson, Colin Henry," in *Who's Who: An Annual Biographical Directory 1973.* London: Adam & Charles Black, 1973, cloth, p. 3512.

J39. "Wilson, Colin (Henry)," in *The Writers Directory, 1974-76.* London: St. James Press; New York: St. Martin's Press, 1973, cloth, p. 887.

J40. "Wilson, Colin Henry," in *International Who's Who, Thirty-Seventh Edition, 1973-74.* London: Europa Publications, 1973, cloth, p. 1826.

J41. "Wilson, Colin Henry," in *International Who's Who, Thirty-Eighth Edition, 1974-75*. London: Europa Publications, 1974, cloth, p. 1870.

J42. "Wilson, Colin Henry," in *Who's Who: An Annual Biographical Directory 1974*. London: Adam & Charles Black, 1974, cloth, p. 3552.

J43. "Wilson, Colin," in *Modern British Literature, Supplement*, compiled and edited by Martin Tucker and Rita Stein. New York: Frederick Ungar Publishing Co., 1975, cloth, p. .

J44. "Wilson, Colin," in *Longman Companion to Twentieth Century Literature, Second Edition*, by A. C. Ward. London: Longman Group, 1975, cloth, p. .

J45. "Wilson, Colin (Henry)," in *World Authors, 1950-1970: A Companion to Twentieth Century Authors*, edited by John Wakeman. New York: H. W. Wilson Co., 1975, cloth, p. 1554-1556.

J46. "Wilson, Colin Henry," in *International Who's Who, Thirty-Ninth Edition, 1975-76*. London: Europa Publications, 1975, cloth, p. 1870.

J47. "Wilson, Colin Henry," in *Who's Who: An Annual Biographical Directory 1975*. London: Adam & Charles Black, 1975, cloth, p. 3424.

J48. "Wilson, Colin (Henry)," in *The Blue Book: Leaders of the English-Speaking World, 1976 Edition*. London: St. James Press; New York: St. Martin's Press, 1976, cloth, p. .

  b. Detroit: Gale Research Co., 1979, cloth, Vol. 2, p. . Reprinted in two volumes.

J49. "Wilson, Colin (Henry)," by John A. Weigel, in *Contemporary Novelists, Second Edition*, edited by James Vinson. London: St. James Press; New York: St. Martin's Press, 1976, cloth, p. 1518-1522.

J50. "Wilson, Colin (Henry)," in *The Writers Directory, 1976-78*. London: St. James Press; New York: St. Martin's Press, 1976, cloth, p. 1163.

J51. "Wilson, Colin (Henry)," in *International Authors and Writers Who's Who, Seventh Edition*, edited by Ernest Kay. Cambridge: Melrose Press, 1976, cloth, p. .

J52. "Wilson, Colin," in *Who's Who in the World, 3rd Edition, 1976-1977*. Chicago: Marquis Who's Who, 1976, cloth, p. .

J53. "Wilson, Colin Henry," in *International Who's Who, Fortieth Edition, 1976-77*. London: Europa Publications, 1976, cloth, p. 1855.

J54. "Wilson, Colin Henry," in *Who's Who: An Annual Biographical Directory 1976*. London: Adam & Charles Black, 1976, cloth, p. 2581.

J55. "Colin Wilson," in *Who's Who in Horror and Fantasy Fiction*, by Mike Ashley. London: Elm Tree Books, 1977, cloth, p. 184-185. Published simultaneously in trade paperback.

   b. New York: Taplinger Publishing Co., 1977, cloth, p. 184-185. Published simultaneously in trade paperback.

J56. "Wilson, Colin (Henry)," in *International Authors and Writers Who's Who, Eighth Edition*, edited by Adrian Gaster. Cambridge: International Biographical Centre, 1977, cloth, p. 1097.

J57. "Wilson, Colin Henry," in *International Who's Who, Forty-First Edition, 1977-78*. London: Europa Publications, 1977, cloth, p. 1862.

J58. "Wilson, Colin Henry," in *Who's Who: An Annual Biographical Directory 1977*. London: Adam & Charles Black, 1977, cloth, p. 2621.

J59. "Wilson, Colin," in *The Lincoln Library of Language Arts, Third Edition*. Columbus, OH: Frontier Press Co., 1978, cloth, Vol. 2, p. .

J60. "Wilson, Colin," in *Encyclopedia of Occultism and Parapsychology, Update Issue Number 1*, edited by Leslie Shepard. Detroit: Gale Research Co., 1978, paper, p. .

J61. "Wilson, Colin," in *Who's Who in the World, 4th Edition, 1978-1979*. Chicago: Marquis Who's Who, 1978, cloth, p. 1003-1004.

J62. "Wilson, Colin Henry (1931-)," in *A Dictionary of Literature in the English Language from 1940 to 1970*, edited by Robin Myers. Oxford: Pergamon Press, 1978, cloth, p. 332-333.

J63. "Wilson, Colin Henry," in *International Who's Who, Forty-Second Edition, 1978-79*. London: Europa Publications, 1978, cloth, p. 1851.

J64. "Wilson, Colin (26 June 1931-)," in *The Encyclopedia of Science Fiction and Fantasy Through 1968*, edited by Donald H. Tuck. Chicago: Advent:Publishers, 1978, cloth, Vol. 2, p. 463.

J65. "Wilson, Colin Henry," in *Who's Who: An Annual Biographical Directory 1978*. London: Adam & Charles Black, 1978, cloth, p. 2662.

J66. "Wilson, Colin (1931-)," by John Clute, in *The Encyclopedia of Science Fiction: An Illustrated A to Z*, edited by Peter Nicholls and John Clute. London: Grenada, 1979, cloth, p. 657. Published simultaneously in trade paperback.

   b. *The Science Fiction Encyclopedia*, edited by Peter Nicholls and John Clute. Garden City, NY: Doubleday & Co., 1979, cloth, p. 657.

J67. "Wilson, Colin (Henry)," in *The Writers Directory, 1980-82*. New York: St. Martin's Press, 1979, cloth, p. 1346-1347.

J68. "Colin Wilson," in *Science Fiction and Fantasy Literature: A Checklist, 1700-1974, with Contemporary Science Fiction Authors II*, by R. Reginald. Detroit: Gale Research Co., 1979, cloth, Vol. 1, p. 563-564, and Vol. 2, p. 1130.

J69. "Wilson, Colin Henry," in *The International Who's Who, Forty-Third Edition, 1979-1980*. London: Europa Publications, 1979, cloth, p. 1346.

J70. "Wilson, Colin Henry," in *Who's Who: An Annual Biographical Directory 1979*. London: Adam & Charles Black, 1979, cloth, p. 2717-2718.

J71. "Wilson, Colin (1931)," in *Novels and Novelists: A Guide to the World of Fiction*, edited by Martin Seymour-Smith. New York: St. Martin's Press, 1980, cloth, p. 237.

J72. "Wilson, Colin," in *The Macmillan Family Encyclopaedia.* London: Macmillan, 1980, cloth, Vol. 20, p. 164.

J73. "Wilson, Colin (Henry)," by John A. Weigel, in *Twentieth-Century Crime and Mystery Writers,* edited by John M. Reilly. New York: St. Martin's Press, 1980, cloth, p. 1502-1505.

J74. "Wilson, Colin Henry," in *The International Who's Who, Forty-Fourth Edition, 1980-1981.* London: Europa Publications, 1980, cloth, p. 1366.

J75. "Wilson, Colin Henry," in *Who's Who: An Annual Biographical Directory 1980.* London: Adam & Charles Black, 1980, cloth, p. 2764.

J76. "Wilson, Colin, 1931- ," in *Contemporary Authors: A Bio-Bibliographical Guide to Current Writers in Fiction, General Nonfiction, Poetry, Journalism, Drama, Motion Pictures, Television, and Other Fields, New Revision Series, Volume 1,* edited by Ann Evory. Detroit: Gale Research Co., 1981, cloth, p. 709-711.

J77. "Wilson, Colin," in *Longman Companion to Twentieth Century Literature, Third Edition,* by A. C. Ward, revised by Maurice Hussey. London: Longman Group, 1981, cloth, p. 577-578.

J78. "Wilson, Colin (Henry)," in *The Writers Directory, 1982-84.* Detroit: Gale Research Co., 1981, cloth, p. 1016.

J79. "Wilson, Colin Henry," in *The International Who's Who, Forty-Fifth Edition, 1981-1982.* London: Europa Publications, 1981, cloth, p. 1382.

J80. "Wilson, Colin (Henry)," by John R. Pfeiffer, in *Twentieth-Century Science-Fiction Writers,* edited by Curtis C. Smith. New York: St. Martin's Press, 1981, cloth, p. 589-591.

J81. "Wilson, Colin Henry," in *Who's Who: An Annual Biographical Directory 1981.* London: Adam & Charles Black, 1981, cloth, p. 2814.

J82. "Wilson, Colin (Henry)," by John A. Weigel, in *Contemporary Novelists, Third Edition,* edited by James Vinson. New York: St. Martin's Press, 1982, cloth, p. 705-708.

J83.   "Wilson, Colin," in *The International Authors and Writers Who's Who, Ninth Edition*, edited by Adrian Gaster.   Cambridge: International Biographical Centre, 1982, cloth, p. 696.

J84.   "Wilson, Colin Henry," in *The International Who's Who, Forty-Sixth Edition, 1982-1983*.   London: Europa Publications, 1982, cloth, p. 1415.

J85.   "Wilson, Colin Henry," in *Who's Who in America, 42nd Edition, 1982-1983*.   Chicago: Marquis Who's Who, 1982, cloth, p. 3590.

J86.   "Wilson, Colin Henry," in *Who's Who: An Annual Biographical Directory 1982*.   London: Adam & Charles Black, 1982, cloth, p. 2398.

J87.   "Wilson, Colin," in *A Guide to 20th Century Literature in English*, edited by Harry Blamires.   London: Methuen, 1983, cloth, p. 304.

J88.   "Wilson, Colin (Henry)," in *The Writers Directory, 1984-86*. Chicago: St. James Press, 1983, cloth, p. 1050.

J89.   "Wilson, Colin Henry," in *The International Who's Who, Forty-Seventh Edition, 1983-1984*.   London: Europa Publications, 1983, cloth, p. 1480.

J90.   "Wilson, Colin Henry," in *Who's Who: An Annual Biographical Directory 1983*.   London: Adam & Charles Black, 1983, cloth, p. 2436.

J91.   "Wilson, Colin Henry," in *Who's Who in America, 43rd Edition, 1984-1985*.   Chicago: Marquis Who's Who, 1984, cloth, Vol. 2, p. 3512.

J92.   "Wilson, Colin Henry," in *Who's Who in the World, 7th Edition, 1984-1985*.   Chicago: Marquis Who's Who, 1984, cloth, p. 1116.

J93.   "Wilson, Colin (Henry)," in *The Science Fiction Source Book*, edited by David Wingrove.   London: Longman, 1984, cloth, p. 265.

   b.   New York: Van Nostrand Reinhold Co., 1984, paper, p. 265.

J94.   "Wilson, Colin Henry," in *Who's Who: An Annual Biographical Directory 1984*. London: Adam & Charles Black, 1984, cloth, p. 2473.

J95.   "Wilson, Colin Henry," in *The International Who's Who, Forty-Eighth Edition, 1984-1985*. London: Europa Publications, 1984, cloth, p. 1529-1530.

J96.   "Wilson, Colin (Henry) (1931-   )," in *Encyclopedia of Occultism & Parapsychology: A Compendium of Information on the Occult Sciences, Magic, Demonology, Superstitions, Spiritism, Mysticism, Metaphysics, Psychical Sciences, and Parapsychology, with Biographical and Bibliographical Notes and Comprehensive Indexes, Second Edition*, edited by Leslie A. Shepard. Detroit: Gale Research Co., 1985, cloth, Vol. 3, p. 1445-1446.

J97.   "Wilson, Colin (Henry)," by John A. Weigel, in *Twentieth-Century Crime and Mystery Writers, Second Edition*, edited by John M. Reilly.   New York: St. Martin's Press, 1985, cloth, p. 911-913.

J98.   "Wilson, Colin," in *Encyclopaedia Britannica, Fifteenth Edition*. Chicago: Encyclopaedia Britannica, 1985, cloth, Vol. 12, p. 687.

J99.   "Wilson, Colin Henry," in *The Oxford Companion to English Literature, Fifth Edition*, edited by Margaret Drabble.   Oxford: Oxford University Press, 1985, cloth, p. 1072.

J100.   "Wilson, Colin Henry," in *Who's Who: An Annual Biographical Directory 1985*. London: Adam & Charles Black, 1985, cloth, p. 2088-2089.

J101.   "Wilson, Colin Henry (1931-)," in *Longman Dictionary of 20th Century Biography*, edited by Alan Isaacs and Elizabeth Martin.   London: Longman, 1985, cloth, p. 533.

J102.   "Wilson, Colin Henry," in *The International Who's Who, Forty-Ninth Edition, 1985-1986*. London: Europa Publications, 1986, cloth, p. 1619-1620.

J103.   "Wilson, Colin (Henry)," by John A. Weigel, in *Contemporary Novelists, Fourth Edition*, edited by D. L. Kirkpatrick.   London and Chicago: St. James Press, 1986, cloth, p. 891-894.

J104. **"Wilson, Colin (Henry),"** by John R. Pfeiffer, in *Twentieth-Century Science-Fiction Writers, Second Edition*, edited by Curtis C. Smith. Chicago and London: St. James Press, 1986, cloth, p. 801-803.

J105. **"Wilson, Colin (Henry),"** in *The Writers Directory, 1986-88.* Chicago and London: St. James Press, 1986, cloth, p. 1012.

J106. **"Wilson, Colin Henry,"** in *Who's Who: An Annual Biographical Directory 1986-87.* London: Adam & Charles Black, 1986, cloth, p. 1889.

J107. **"Wilson, Colin Henry,"** in *Who's Who in America, 44th Edition, 1986-1987.* Wilmette, IL: Marquis Who's Who, 1986, cloth, Vol. 2, p. 2996.

J108. **"Wilson, Colin Henry,"** in *The International Who's Who, Fiftieth Edition, 1986-1987.* London: Europa Publications, 1986, cloth, p. 1723-1724.

J109. **"Wilson, Colin (1931-),"** by T. E. D. Klein, in *The Penguin Encyclopedia of Horror and the Supernatural*, edited by Jack Sullivan. New York: A Promised Land Production, Viking, 1986, cloth, p. 465-466.

J110. **"Wilson, Colin, 1932- "** [sic], in *The Reader's Adviser: A Layman's Guide to Literature, 13th Edition*, Volume 1: The Best in American and British Fiction, Poetry, Essays, Literary Biography, Bibliography, and Reference, edited by Fred Kaplan. New York: R. R. Bowker Co., 1986, cloth, p.   .

J111. **"Wilson, Colin Henry (1931-),"** in *The International Dictionary of 20th Century Biography*, by Edward Vernoff and Rima Shore. New York: NAL Books, New American Library, 1987, cloth, p. 758.

J112. **"Wilson, Colin [Henry],"** in *Benét's Reader's Encyclopedia, Third Edition.* New York: Harper & Row, Publishers, 1987, cloth, p. 1068.

J113. **"Wilson, Colin Henry,"** in *Who's Who in the World, 8th Edition, 1987-1988.* Wilmette, IL: Marquis Who's Who, 1987, cloth, p. 1106.

J114. "Wilson, Colin Henry," in *The International Who's Who, Fifty-First Edition, 1987-1988*. London: Europa Publications, 1987, cloth, p. 1594.

J115. "Wilson, Colin Henry," in *Who's Who: An Annual Biographical Directory 1988*. London: Adam & Charles Black, 1988, cloth, p. 1921.

J116. "Wilson, Colin (Henry)," in *The Writers Directory, 1988-90, Eighth Edition*. Chicago and London: St. James Press, 1988, cloth, p. 1015-1016.

J117. "Wilson, Colin [Henry] (1931-)," by Judith E. Boss, in *The New Encyclopedia of Science Fiction*, edited by James Gunn. New York: Viking, 1988, cloth, p. 506.

J118. "Wilson, Colin Henry," in *The International Who's Who, Fifty-Second Edition, 1988-1989*. London: Europa Publications, 1988, cloth, p. 1624.

J119. "Wilson, Colin Henry," in *Who's Who in America, 45th Edition, 1988-1989*. Wilmette, IL: Marquis Who's Who, 1988, cloth, Vol. 2, p. 3328.

J120. "Wilson, Colin Henry," in *Who's Who in the World, 9th Edition, 1989-1990*. Wilmette, IL: Marquis Who's Who, 1988, cloth, p. 1245.

J121. "Wilson, Colin, 1931- ," in *Contemporary Authors: A Bio-Bibliographical Guide to Current Writers in Fiction, General Non-fiction, Poetry, Journalism, Drama, Motion Pictures, Television, and Other Fields, New Revision Series, Volume 22*, edited by Deborah A. Straub. New York: Gale Research Co., 1988, cloth, p. 511-515.

J122. "Wilson, Colin Henry," in *Who's Who: An Annual Biographical Directory 1989*. London: Adam & Charles Black, 1989, cloth, p. 1943.

K.

ABOUT THE AUTHOR

Other Materials

NOTE: I have not included here theses which were later published as books, and which are so noted in Section H, above.

K1.   **A Bit Off the Map, and Other Stories,** by Angus Wilson. London: Secker & Warburg, 1957, 193 p., cloth. [story collection]

    b.   New York: Viking Press, 1957, 193 p., cloth.

In the title story, the principal character, Huggett, is, according to Nicolas Tredell (in his book, *The Novels of Colin Wilson*), "...a satirical portrait of Colin Wilson" (p. 71, Vision Press edition).

K2.   **The Sound Barrier: A Study of the Ideas of Colin Wilson,** by Sidney Campion. 167 typewritten pages. A manuscript completed in 1963 as a companion to *The World of Colin Wilson*, but never published.

ANALYTICAL TABLE OF CONTENTS:
Chapter One: The Method of *The Outsider*. Chapter Two: Widening the Foundations. *Religion and the Rebel*; *Declaration* essay; *Age of Defeat*; Wilson's phenomenology; *Beyond the Outsider*. Chapter Three: Problem of the Modern Novel. *Ritual in the Dark*; *Adrift in Soho*; *Man Without a Shadow*; *World of Violence*; *Necessary Doubt*. Chapter Four: Philosophy and Imagination. Philosophical issues; *The Strength to Dream*. Chapter Five: Sex and the Problem of Consciousness. Study of murder; *Origins of the Sexual Impulse*.

K3.   **The Intellectual Hero: An Enquiry into the Theme of Colin Wilson's Novels Ritual in the Dark and World of Violence,** by

Dag H. Christensen. A thesis presented to the Department of English, University of Oslo, 1969.

K4. **Colin Wilson: A Singular Collection Offered by June O'Shea.** Los Angeles, CA: June O'Shea, Bookseller, 1981?, 52 p., paper.

A catalog of Wilsoniana offered for sale as a "singular collection," by a well-known California book dealer and Wilson fan (to whom the novel *Space Vampires* is dedicated by Wilson). The latest date mentioned in the catalog is 1981.

CONTENTS: Introduction, Manuscripts, Correspondence Files, Books by Colin Wilson, Books Co-Authored by Colin Wilson, Books Co-Edited by Colin Wilson, Book Appearances by Colin Wilson, Off-Prints by Colin Wilson, Periodical Appearances by Colin Wilson, Interviews with Colin Wilson, Books Spuriously Attributed to Colin Wilson, Books About Colin Wilson, References to Colin Wilson, Screenplay. The catalog reproduces some fascinating extracts from letters written by Wilson to O'Shea, and letters from Wilson's lawyer to a pornographic book publisher who used his name on two of their publications (see L2).

The entire collection was purchased by the Tomás Rivera Library, University of California, Riverside, for inclusion in their Special Collections Department (now the Center for Bibliographical Studies, University of California, Riverside).

L.

MISCELLANEA

L1. **LIBRARY COLLECTIONS.** The following libraries are known to have collections or archives of Colin Wilson manuscripts, letters, books, and other materials:

1. The Special Collections Department, Tomás Rivera Library, University of California, Riverside, now (since August, 1989) the Center for Bibliographical Studies, University of California, Riverside. Included are the materials purchased in 1982 from June O'Shea (for a general description, see K4 above): first-edition and reprint books, manuscripts, letters, and other materials. Items are available for viewing by appointment with the Curator of the collection.

2. Harry Ransom Humanities Research Center, University of Texas at Austin. Materials include: two Wilson notebooks from 1951 and 1952, manuscripts of the play, *The Death of God*, and several articles, and a few letters from or to Wilson and other well-known writers of the 1950s.

3. Humanities Library, Local Studies Section, Leistershire County Council, Libraries and Information Service, Bishop Street, Leicester, England. Includes roughly 107 items.

4. Cornwall County Library Services, Local Studies Library, Redruth Public Library, Cornwall, England. Includes about 40 titles.

L2. **SPURIOUS BOOKS.** The following titles were published under Colin Wilson's byline, but were not written by him:

1. *Daddy and Young Peggy.* San Diego (?), CA: Derby Adult Series, 1975, p., paper.

2. *The Nympho Teacher.* San Diego (?), CA: Derby Adult Series, 1975, p., paper.

L3. **SCREENPLAYS.** Two screen adaptations from Wilson's works are known to exist:

1. *The Glass Cage*, screenplay by Brian Phelan from Colin Wilson's novel. Second (and final) draft dated March 29, 1968, Paramount Pictures Corporation. Unproduced. A copy of the screenplay exists in the University of California, Riverside collection of Wilson's works (above).

2. *Lifeforce*, screenplay by Dan O'Bannon and Don Jakoby. Tri-Star, 1985. Directed by Tobe Hooper, music by Henry Mancini, special effects by John Dykstra and John Gant. Starring Frank Finlay, Mathilda May, Peter Firth, Steve Railsback, and Patrick Stewart. A very uneven adaptation from Colin Wilson's novel, *The Space Vampires*, featuring spectacular visual effects, but a markedly weak conclusion.

L4. **DEDICATIONS.** The following titles have been dedicated to Colin Wilson, in whole or in part:

1. *Jack the Ripper*, by Daniel Farson. London: Michael Joseph, 1972, 144 p., cloth. Also: London: Sphere Books, 1973, 157 p., paper. "To Colin Wilson, the most generous of friends and authors, and to the memory of Francis Camps."

L5. **PLAYS.** In addition to *Strindberg* (see A29), which was originally performed in 1971 as *Pictures in a Bath of Acid*, other Wilson dramas produced (but not published) include: *The Metal Flower Blossom: A Comedy in Three Acts* (1960; 85 pages), *Viennese Interlude* (1960), *The Death of God: A Play in Three Acts* (1966; 77 pages), and *Mysteries: A Play in Three Acts* (1980s; 96 pages). An adaptation of Wilson's novel, *The Mind Parasites*, was produced by Bauer Contemporary Ballet, January 8-17, 1986, at the Skylight Theater, Milwaukee, Wisconsin.

L6. **UNPUBLISHED WORKS.** Wilson has several notebooks containing early stories, including *The Last Betrayal*, about the Crucifixion, and which he considers to be "a turning point in my writing" (letter to Colin Stanley dated June 12, 1988). It must have been written in the late 1940s. He adds: "I would hate to see it published now, but I can still remember the kind of conviction with which I wrote it."

He also has various early versions of *Ritual in the Dark*, originally called *Ritual of the Dead*, plus several stories about a character based vaguely on Van Gogh. A school notebook, *Essays on the Life Aim*, still exists. This was "probably my first work." *The Quintessence of Shavianism* also exists as a "little notebook." Wilson believes that just two volumes of the *Manual of General Science* survive: "...the second one which contains the article on geology, as well as various others, and the last one, which was devoted mainly to mathematics. I suppose the others have got lost at various times."

Campion reprints in Chapter 23 of *The World of Colin Wilson* a 1952 "fragment from a notebook which appears to be an early sketch for *The Outsider*" (p. 245), entitled "The Possibility of a Poetic Burial" or "A Lover for Thais." In addition, Chapter 6 has extracts from Wilson's journals for March, 1950-February, 1951, and Chapter 9 quotes from April, 1951-July, 1951.

Campion also mentions Wilson's large novel, *Lulu*, pieces of which were penned beginning in the late 1950s, on pages 226 and following: "...It is a sexual analysis of the life-urge. The starting point, apparently, has been Alban Berg's unfinished opera, *Lulu*, based on two tragedies by Frank Wedekind; Lulu, for Wedekind, symbolises the life-urge; she is simultaneously completely innocent and completely destructive. Colin has commented several times that Wedekind seems to be the only writer who holds a view of sex close to his own; it remains to be seen how far Wedekind's conceptions will appear in the final version of the novel." When I queried Wilson about *Lulu* recently, he seemed to indicate that the project had reached a *cul-de-sac*. Whereas the manuscript was larger than *War and Peace*, it needed considerable work to make it publishable. At present he doesn't have further time to dedicate to it, and the book may never be completed.

Finally, Campion also mentions several unfinished plays: *The Power House* "...deals with his favourite theme: the relation between sanity and insanity. Its basic idea could be summarised as follows: in a Yorkshire mental home there is a madman who believes he is Rasputin..." (p. 225); and *Express to Nowhere*, "...begun but never finished...dealt further with the problem of absolute dictatorship" (p. 222).

L7. **CATALOGING DATA.** In the Library of Congress classification scheme, Wilson's main entry is "Wilson, Colin, 1931- ," his permanent literature number is PR6073.I44, and his bibliography number is Z8976.487.

QUOTH THE CRITICS

THE OUTSIDER (1956)

NOTE: The full text of all the major English-language reviews of *The Outsider* are reproduced in my book, *Colin Wilson, a Celebration* (Cecil Woolf, 1988) [see also H26].

"I feel a quickening of interest in this extraordinary book because I suggested *The Outsider* as the English title of M. Camus's *L'Etranger*, on which Mr. Wilson extensively draws.   He is a young man of twenty-four who has produced one of the most remarkable first books I have read for a long time, a blending of the philosophic approach with literary criticism reminiscent of Mario Praz or Mr. Aldous Huxley's didactic anthologies."

—Cyril Connolly

"What [Wilson] has so far published is a fine work of clarification. A strangely mature and subtle mind has produced a brilliant synopsis of the modern mind and spirit."

—Oswald Mosley

"It is an exhaustive and luminously intelligent study of a representative theme of our time—and what makes the book truly astounding is that its alarmingly well-read author is only twenty-four years old...Mr. Wilson's book is a real contribution to our understanding of our deepest predicament."

—Philip Toynbee

"It represents the search of a young man of great integrity and discernment for some higher purpose in life than mere living.   What makes his work still more unusual is that, unlike Sartre, Samuel Beckett, and other hypochondriac outsiders of the St. Germain school, he avoids glorying in his own ill-health and actually wants to get well."

—Kenneth Walker

"The book is in itself readable and seems to be not a blueprint, but a sincere and illuminating record of an individual's deeply felt experience in a particular field of reading. What is greatly to be admired is the author's enthusiasm and the doggedness, as it were, with which he holds on to his own piece of rope or thread. It is not a performance, but a genuine exploration."

—Rex Warner

RITUAL IN THE DARK (1960)

"It is a well thought out and original plot, and certain things in the book, for example the revelation of what Nunne's true intentions towards Gerard have been, come as excellent and subtle dramatic surprises, and make me think Colin Wilson could one day be a novelist to reckon with."

—P. N. Furbank

"...Mr. Wilson writing a novel for the first and, conceivably, for the last time..."

—Times Literary Supplement

ADRIFT IN SOHO (1961)

"What stands out in this novel and makes it not only readable but also worth reading, is the personality of Harry. He has a fund of intellectual energy, and a vigorous determination to extract the last ounce of meaning from any experience; more, he refuses to allow any experience to be meaningless. He sees to it that everything that happens to him has a didactic value, or at least starts a profitable train of thought. He is literary-minded, but with a sense of humour about liking life to imitate art. With all its faults *Adrift in Soho* makes one look forward to Mr. Wilson's next novel with great interest."

—Bernardine Bishop

"From the moment the story opens the reader is lost, spellbound, in pursuit of the young man who comes to London like Dick Whittington—a simpleton displaying, it is true, a certain bookwormishness. Mr Wilson has got outside himself. This is a small book—and in Mr. Wilson's work it may well prove to be a minor one—but it is surely a signpost to a distinguished career as a novelist."

—Times Literary Supplement

THE STRENGTH TO DREAM (1962)

"...I consider *The Strength to Dream* to be an important attempt to relate the purpose of literature to the purpose of life, and I strongly recommend anyone interested in religion, ethics, or the literature of the

248

imagination to read it as soon as they can. Colin Wilson gives us hope
of a way 'out of the maze'."

—Peter Russell

BRANDY OF THE DAMNED (1964)

"The liveliness of his mind and the sparks which come off it in show-
ers make stimulating reading."

—Times Literary Supplement

"There is very little that is dull in these pages, and they may encourage
the music-lover who thinks he knows the repertory to question some
of his preconceptions and explore a little further."

—British Book News

BEYOND THE OUTSIDER (1965)

"This book offers the general reader a useful survey of significant aspects of modern thought."

—British Book News

"This new book offers an argument which, if it is not quite adequately
sustained, is yet almost consistently referred back to and sometimes
carried forward, and which is both tenable and heartening."

—Times Literary Supplement

INTRODUCTION TO THE NEW EXISTENTIALISM (1966)

"This seems to me the best book Mr. Wilson has written; and certainly
his work never lacks interest...[He] has written a lively, provocative,
and readable introduction to the new existentialism, and he should now
go on to write a major exposition of the themes he here adumbrates."

—William Tonks

THE MIND PARASITES (1967)

"Mr. Wilson's appetite for knowledge has always been impressive, and
he succeeds in making this battle for the human spirit at once exciting
and plausible."

—British Book News

"This is a novel which, if it came from an unknown hand, would create all the old Wilson furore over again. Set in the future, and relating how man finally learned to confront and master the mental malaise that seems to grip him tighter and tighter with every decade of this century in which 'progress' has got the bit between its teeth and bolted, it is clearly at one level science fiction. But so is the best of Wells, and it is with him that the not unflattering comparison is to be made. In particular, the objectification of our social 'mental illness' as a real disease caused by a real micro-organism pays-off triumphantly both as a narrative and as a debating device."

—*Hilary Corke*

VOYAGE TO A BEGINNING (1969)

"Despite the author's youth, this autobiography is timely. It traces his philosophic development, reveals his restlessly inquiring mind and the sturdy independence of judgement which was already apparent in his essay on Adler, written at the age of twelve. The book will be of great interest to everyone interested in contemporary thought, in literature, and in human beings."

—*British Book News*

BERNARD SHAW: A REASSESSMENT (1969)

"This is certainly one of the outstanding books in the mounting pile on Shaw, written out of an exhaustive knowledge of the whole output of the man Colin Wilson ranks as 'the most important European writer since Dante'."

—*British Book News*

THE OCCULT (1971)

"[This] is by far and away his best work to date, and worthy to be placed on the same shelf alongside William James, F. W. H. Myers' monumental study on *Human Personality*, and Frazer's *Golden Bough*...In a review of a thousand words or so, one cannot do justice to a book of this calibre...It is an essential volume for every public and university library, as well as for readers interested in any way whatsoever in the wide spectrum of interrelated occult subjects which he discusses with such penetration and intelligence." [The full text of this review for *Books & Bookmen* is reprinted in *Colin Wilson: A Celebration* (London: Cecil Woolf, 1988) {see also H26}].

—*Alan Hull Walton*

THE SCHOOLGIRL MURDER CASE (1974)

"This novel is persuasive in its documentary aspects, a little less than hypnotic, perhaps, as a thriller. It grips because of a tantalisingly exact description of Scotland Yard procedures, and some rather touching human detail. But—Wilson's great, rare virtue as a writer has always been his interest in ideas, and even this slight work is instructive as a further glimpse into his remarkable mind."

—*Wilfred De'ath*

MYSTERIES (1978)

"The detail and wide range of the book defies analysis in these few pages. But each and every example and subject is described, probed, and weighed-up with such an eagle-eye that the volume immediately becomes 'definitive.' Moreover, the flow of writing is so natural and unaffected that nothing could be easier to read. There is, I think, only a single word which adequately sums up the qualities of this enormous opus of over 260,000 words—already a 'classic' in its own right—and that word is superlative." [The full text of this review for *Books & Bookmen* is reprinted in *Colin Wilson: A Celebration* (London: Cecil Woolf, 1988) {see also H26}].

—Alan Hull Walton

AFTERLIFE (1985)

"Still an unbeliever, I nevertheless find Mr. Wilson's approach stimulating and thought-provoking. Indeed, he is one of the few authors in this field who can sometimes make me wish that I had not lost my active interest in parapsychology many years ago."

—*R. C. Warwick*

"Colin Wilson provides clear descriptions of contemporary studies in out-of-body experiences and near-death experiences, and attempts to formulate a comprehensive theory covering all the data."

—*Renée Haynes*

RUDOLF STEINER (1985)

"I have no hesitation in commending this book, not only as the sole biography that is not hagiography, but also because it is well written for newcomer and scholar alike, sharing the liberating power of Rudolf Steiner's esoteric spiritual vision."

—Francis Treuherz

AN ESSAY ON THE 'NEW' EXISTENTIALISM (1986)

"[This] is a refreshing, lucid, succinct, and stimulating philosophical statement. It will be of great interest to all scholars of Colin Wilson's work and modern philosophy in general. At the heart of it is an attack on pessimism."

—John Rosewell

"In this new short essay Colin Wilson summarises in a succinct form the aims of three decades of his writing."

—Peter Wallis

ALEISTER CROWLEY (1987)

"This is an enjoyable introduction to one of England's most eccentric figures. I thoroughly recommend it."

—Grub Smith

SPIDER WORLD: THE TOWER (1987)

"Numerous comparisons will be made, especially to Tolkien, though Wilson spares us *The Hobbit* whimsy while acknowledging his debt. I detected echoes of H. G. Wells and Orwell's *1984*, but finally all such comparisons become pointless unless they prove how little Wilson owes to anyone. This is his own unique creation, and I believe it is his masterpiece. From start to finish, Wilson knows exactly what he is doing, and shares his enjoyment with the reader. Literary swots and pedants who have lost their youthful vision may hate this book, but there is no justice if this extraordinary novel fails to become a best-seller."

—Daniel Farson

JACK THE RIPPER (1987)

"Wilson's introduction is a concise and illuminating affair, as one might expect from such an expert on the pathological mind."

—Sean Thomas

THE MISFITS (1988)

"This exploration of pornography and sex crimes does contain quite a lot of interesting ideas, and offers some unusual perspectives on sexual behaviour."

—Roger Baker

"Like all his work, it is vigorous, vulnerable, and breathes the bracing ozone of autodidactism. The most heartening thing about all of the speculative works that Colin Wilson has written is their optimism. He believes that we have advanced beyond the Homeric heroes. You may be ready to rise above sex, but you will enjoy this strange book because it is very firmly about sex."

—Anthony Burgess

AFTERWORD:

INSIDE OUTSIDE

Reflections on Being Bibliographed

by Colin Wilson

When Edmund Wilson wrote *Thoughts on being Bibliographed* in 1943—he was 48 at the time—he spent most of his time reflecting sadly on the generation of his youth and the glories "of the days that were no more." When I began thinking about my own reaction to being bibliographed, I realized that I was completely free of any such nostalgia. And this is not just because I feel that the "Angry Young Men" and Beat Generation of my youth were not of the same stature as that generation of Joyce, Eliot, Hemingway, Fitzgerald and the rest. It is because I seem to lack Edmund Wilson's feeling of having come to "the end of a chapter." When I was twenty, I felt myself to be a struggling writer who was going to have a long and difficult task making his contemporaries understand what he had to say. Now I am fifty seven, I *still* feel I have a long and difficult task making my contemporaries understand what I have to say. I have certainly not succeeded in doing it yet.

What *do* I have to say? If I try to go to the heart of it, I recognize a deep conviction that the human race is close to some profound evolutionary change. at least as important as the change that occurred about five thousand years ago when the Sumerians first developed the art of writing. Of course, there had been a kind of writing long before then: our caveman ancestors had recorded the phases of the moon on pieces of bone. But the Sumerians learned how to record their everyday *speech* on clay tablets, and this was as revolutionary as the invention of the gramophone record. Before that, a man's experience died with him, except what he could pass on to his children or fellow tribesmen by way of oral tradition; writing meant that his experience could be passed on to all his fellow men. It was a kind of conquest of time.

I can remember making the same kind of discovery when I was sixteen. I was working as a lab assistant at my old school, and in theory I should have been ecstatically happy, since it had always been my ambition to be a scientist. But I had left school shortly after my sixteenth birthday—my father wanted me to earn a weekly wage—and spent some months working in a textile factory. This had made me so profoundly depressed that I spent my evenings and weekends reading poetry and escaping into a world of dream landscapes. Now physics and chemistry struck me as shallow and unimportant; they had nothing to say "to my condition." I experienced a powerful compulsion to write about the problem of life itself, about why we are alive and, above all, what we are supposed to do now we are here. Suddenly I was haunted by the image of a lone man confronting a universe that is full of darkness and mystery. In my earlier days of faith in science, I had seen this problem as a joint venture, being attacked by thousands of scientists. Now I had an appalling feeling that every man is alone, and that no one else can help him to solve his deepest problem.

One evening, I heard on the radio—on the BBC's new Third Programme, devoted to music and literature—a broadcast about the diaries of Samuel Pepys. Suddenly, I was overwhelmed by a powerful desire to *talk to myself* on paper. The next morning was a Saturday, and I had to work in the lab. When I left school, I went into a large stationary store next to my bus stop and bought a fat quarto-size notebook. That afternoon I went into my bedroom, put the date at the top of the first page, and began to write. I poured out my feelings as if talking to a sympathetic priest, all my irritation and misery and frustration. Frustration—that seemed to me to be a key word, the condition in which I spent most of my days and nights. And by about five o'clock that afternoon, I was amazed to find that all my frustration had dissolved away. Like Wordsworth at the end of his own classic expression of misery and frustration, the Ode: "Intimations of Immortality," I felt suddenly that "I again am strong." The writing had given me power over my own emotions, and I once again felt in control.

Of course, the frustration returned as soon as I got back into the lab, like the water leaking into a boat. But I had acquired myself a pump, and discovered the trick of writing myself back into objectivity and sanity. Within weeks, that first notebook was full, and I began a second. And I became obscurely aware that I had discovered a secret that was as important as the Sumerian discovery of writing. The Sumerians had only learned how to speak to one another through the written word: I had discovered how to speak to myself, and also how to use the writing to uncover an even deeper self. I was like a man digging for buried treasure.

Of course, I was far from the first to discover this trick—of using the diary as a kind of digging machine. Earlier diarists had merely recorded events; but from Goethe onward, they learned how to use it as a substitute for "Confession." Goethe's novel *The Sorrows of Young Werther* led the way in 1774, as its art hero poured out his heart about his delights and miseries. Writers like Amiel and Senancour used the journal form to express their real frustrations. And the result was the Romantic revolution that fascinated me so much: writers who felt again and again that they had achieved glimpses of heaven, or of a way of life that would be literally a *heaven on earth*. Of course, these "glimpses" had the ultimate effect of making them thoroughly unhappy, because they made the return to "everyday life" seem unbearably dull. This is why so many of them committed suicide or died of wasting illnesses: it was the spirit that was wasting away in a world it felt alien to it. Yet underneath all the misery and despair there was a strange underlying optimism; somehow, they *knew* that the truth of the world was "absurd good news."

When I was 28, I decided to write a book about this paradox; it was called *The Outsider*. It came out in May 1956, when I was 24, and, to my amazement, it made me famous; it became a bestseller in England and America, and was translated into a dozen languages within a year. The book was about romantic "Outsiders" like Van Gogh, Nietzsche, Dostoevsky, Lawrence of Arabia. I had been convinced that it would be either ignored or violently attacked—like Nietzsche's first book, *The Birth of Tragedy*, which had turned him into an academic outcast. Its success astounded me; it seemed that I was mistaken to think that I was living in a purely materialistic age. But it took only a week or so to make me realize that its success was all an absurd misunderstanding. The critics who praised it were not really interested in the problem of why we are alive and what we ought to do now we *are* here—only in literary fashions. It was symbolic that I should have achieved success in the same week as John Osborne, whose play *Look Back in Anger* had just caused a furore at the Royal Court, and which was basically a stream of satirical invective against the British middle classes. Osborne and I were soon labelled "Angry Young Men" (by J. B. Priestley), and regarded as rebels against the "Establishment." I didn't give a damn about the Middle Classes or the Establishment, although my girlfriend's middle class parents had behaved towards me in much the same way that Alison's parents behave towards Jimmy Porter in Osborne's play. I would simply not have felt it important enough to write about. So to be bracketed with Osborne and Kingsley Amis as some kind of a social rebel seemed as absurd as being bracketed with racing correspondents on the grounds that I had written about outsiders.

The tide turned fairly quickly; the critics and journalists soon got sick of the Angry Young Men, whose notoriety kept them constantly in the gossip columns. They were particularly tired of me because no one understood what I was trying to say, and the simplest way of evading this dilemma was to label me "pretentious" or muddled. And at this point, I must confess, I began to feel a helpless rage and frustration. I had spent years disciplining myself to ignore disappointment; I had taken to heart Shaw's dictum: Never lose your temper. Yet after my second book *Religion and the Rebel* had been torn to shreds by the critics who had hailed *The Outsider* as a "brilliantly intelligent contribution to our understanding of our deepest predicament," I found it hard not to grind my teeth with fury at their sheer stupidity. The truth was that I had been born into the worst possible country for a writer of ideas. In France or Germany or Scandinavia, I would have been accepted as a member of the European existentialist tradition. In America, I would have found a comfortable job as Writer in Residence and made a healthy living on the college lecture circuits. In England, where seriousness is regarded as bad taste, and the cricket score as the most urgent topic of the day, I might as well have been writing in Serbo-Croat.

Fortunately, I have never been given to self-pity; no one who has been dazzled by the vision of science at the age of eleven can ever again take his own emotions too seriously. Besides, I was more fortunate than most of the romantic poets and artists; at the age of 22, after an unsuccessful first marriage, I had met a girl who seemed to me to embody everything the romantics had dreamed about; she was serene, good-tempered, intelligent and physically attractive, and the first time I saw her, I was immediately possessed by the conviction that such dazzling incarnations of the eternal feminine were not for the likes of me. So I sternly suppressed my tendency to fall hopelessly in love. Then, as good fortune threw me into her company, I realized that she was quite unaware of how madly desirable she was; she was in the grip of a kind of innate modesty that may have had something to do with a strict middle class upbringing which had impressed on her the necessity of being, before all else, a well-behaved young lady. It began to dawn on me that she was taken in by me, and that my conviction of my own genius did not strike her as absurd. In what seemed an astonishingly short time, she had agreed to write to her fiance to break off the engagement, and to go to London with me instead. I felt a little alarmed; it seemed an awful responsibility for a "romantic Outsider" to drag a girl away from a respectable marriage to someone she had met at university and into the uncertainties of a bohemian existence in London. Her parents were outraged when they found out and did all they could to break it up. But for better or worse, we soon found ourselves totally addicted to one another. I often said jokingly that one day ours would be regarded as one of the great love stories, like Romeo and Juliet or Tristan and Isolde; but I must confess to an undertone of seriousness.

In London, she had trained as a librarian while I worked at odd jobs and slept out in parks in a sleeping bag to save rent. I was working on a novel called *Ritual in the Dark*, which was about "Outsiders." About a year after I met her, I decided to write a nonfiction book about Outsiders, and began writing it in the Reading Room of the British Museum in January 1955. I sent off its early pages, together with an outline, to a London publisher, and, to my amazement, he wrote back to say that he would like to read the rest of it. Before the year was out, he had accepted it. Then came the morning towards the end of May 1956 when Joy and I got up early and rushed down to the newspaper vendor on the corner to buy the two "serious" Sunday newspapers, the *Observer* and the *Sunday Times.* It was a staggering experience to find that both of them contained lead reviews of the book which hailed it as brilliant. Another London newspaper headed its review: "He's a major writer—and he's only 24." It was like stepping on to a merry-go-round which went faster and faster while the music became deafeningly loud. In America a year later, Kerouac and Ginsberg had much the same kind of experience when they were hailed as founders of the "Beat generation." And then, within weeks, non-stop publicity by popular journalists had caused a turn of the tide, and I found myself being dismissed as "pretentious" by idiots who would have found Batman intellectually taxing. I seemed to be faced with a blank wall of total misunderstanding. For all my "fame," I was as unknown as I had been when I was writing *The Outsider.*

At this point, Joy's parents caused further problems by turning up at my flat armed with a horsewhip and trying to drag her away forcibly. We were giving dinner to an old villain called Gerald Hamilton, the central character in Christopher Isherwood's novel *The Last of Mr Norris*, and he lost no time in rushing to the telephone and summoning half the reporters in Fleet Street. We made the mistake of fleeing from London, pursued by the press, and for the next few weeks, we were one of the main topics on the front pages. Even *Time* magazine came out with a full-page story about it. When we finally returned to London, my publisher gave me the best piece of advice he ever dispensed: go and live somewhere quiet in the country. The man in the next room had a Cornish cottage for rent; we took it and left London for the west country, where we have lived ever since.

It was therefore predictable that my second book, when it appeared, would be attacked by the critics; but even I was shocked by the violence of the storm. *Time* summarized it in a long report headed: "Scrambled Egghead." It had seemed bad enough to be dismissed by gossip columnists, but to face these howls of execration from the "intellectual" critics seemed unbelievable. I re-read pages of *Religion and the Rebel*, and felt again some of the excitement I had felt in writing it. Surely these morons could *see* that it was full of important ideas, that it carried the nihilistic existentialism of Sartre and Camus to a new and more positive level? But as the weeks passed, and the hostile reviews continued, it was obvious that no one *did* see. One critic, Marghanita Laski, sounded a sympathetic note when she wrote: "Never has a very bad book been so violently attacked." When I wrote to ask her why she thought it was so bad, she replied that she had not read it.

It was obvious that, where my work was concerned, I was in a far worse situation than I had been when I was sleeping out on Hampstead Heath. Now I was "known," yet in another sense, totally unknown. *Nothing* I could say or do or write could clear up this misunderstanding. And I was clearly at a crossroads. If I gave way to these feelings of frustration, and counter-attacked the critics, I would be wallowing in the same kind of negative emotions that irritated me so much in *Look Back in Anger*. But I only had to read a few pages of Nietzsche or Shaw to recognize once again the great unsolved problem of the 19th century, the problem that lay like a tree trunk across the road of intellectual progress. These "Outsiders" had died or committed suicide because they felt that life was a dream—or, worse still, a kind of fly trap. Hemingway expressed this pessimism when he wrote: "It would get you in the end." When I learned that Samuel Beckett had been given the Nobel Prize, it seemed to me a symbol of the sheer, swinish stupidity that has infected our civilization like a disease: that a man can spend his life moaning that life is meaningless and futile and that no effort is worth making, and be given a prize by a committee of idiots for his contribution to modern culture. Nietzsche had experienced the same rage about the imbecility of 19th century Prussian culture, and it had contributed to his mental breakdown. Suddenly, I saw with great clarity that I had to do better than these Outsiders of the 19th century. I had analyzed their problem and recognised that many of them were destroyed by an excess of self-pity. Yet within a short time of his death—even while he was still alive but hopelessly insane—Nietzsche's message had been understood. I had to learn to profit by that lesson. I had said that the Outsider has to learn to stand alone; now I had to live up to my own recommendation.

I have to admit that it proved to be unexpectedly hard work. I completed my novel *Ritual in the Dark*, and it sold well: but the critics determinedly ignored it. I completed my "Outsider cycle" with four more volumes, exploring this problem of romanticism and pessimism and carrying my analyses into new fields—for example, the psychology of sexual deviation in *Origins of the Sexual Impulse*. In *The Mind Parasites* I produced a parable of the dark forces of the mind that had destroyed so many Outsiders; the book became a science fiction classic and has remained in print ever since; in America it has even been turned into a ballet. But in England it was passed over in silence; nothing could ever again induce a British critic to mention my name in a list of contemporary writers. It was rather like dropping a stone down a well and hearing no splash. I continued to write, and my books continued to be published and translated; some countries, like Japan, published literally everything I wrote, even to essays and magazine articles. In the mid-1960s, I learned to my astonishment that I was the most widely read British author in the Middle East—although lack of copyright agreement with the Arabs meant I received no royalties. Yet as far as England was concerned I was writing in a vacuum.

If I had been living alone in a room, like so many of my Outsiders, I suppose I would have been tempted to beat my head against this brick wall of indifference. But by this time, Joy and I had moved into a house overlooking the sea—we bought it in the days just before the housing boom—and our first child, a daughter, had been born. Two sons followed. I found that I adored children, and that when I looked at them, the attacks or indifference of the critics no longer mattered. Shaw asked: "Is there a father's heart as well as a mother's?" and the answer was obviously yes. By writing a good deal—Robert Ardrey once told me: "Brother, you write too much"—I managed to make a reasonable living, although we were seldom out of overdraft at the bank. I made lecture tours—in America, the Middle East, Japan—and life was so busy that the sense of working in a vacuum no longer mattered. But when, on a visit to Tokyo, a Japanese student said to me: "In England you must be a famous as Charles Dickens?" I roared with laughter and replied: "In England few people have ever heard of me."

The problem, of course, is that in England we have no intellectual tradition. This may sound a strange assertion about the country of Shakespeare, Milton, Ruskin and Wells. But the English have never had the slightest interest in ideas; some of our best philosophical minds have been Irishmen and Scots. The French take an active interest in their intellectuals; in England, the nearest an intellectual comes to achieving public recognition is when he goes on a television panel. Even in America there is a desire to "keep up" with what the best minds are thinking, so that works like Jacques Barzun's *House of Intellect* find their way on to the bestseller list. But the English take a pride in their anti-intellectualism; they even prefer their famous composers, such as Elgar and Bax, to behave like country gentlemen and show an enthusiasm for cricket. I love to quote a story told by Berdyaev about Russia in the pre-revolutionary period. A group of intellectuals had sat up all night discussing religion and philosophy; towards dawn, one of them yawned and said he wanted to go to bed. Another replied: "But we can't go to bed yet—we haven't yet decided whether God exists!" In England, that would be dismissed as affectation. Carlyle once remarked: "If Jesus Christ were to come today, people would not even crucify Him. They would ask Him to dinner, and hear what He had to say, and make fun of it." As a Scot, he knew exactly what kind of people he was dealing with. That is why he also remarked: "Four thousand people cross London Bridge daily, mostly fools."

Once I had decided that this was so, I could see that there was not much sense in losing my temper about it. But that, in any case, would have been a failure to grasp my own most important insight. If

I was correct in believing that most of the great "Outsiders" died of weakness, an excess of self-pity, rather than of the sheer magnitude of their problem ("I see too deep and too much"), then I had no reason to complain. So long as they couldn't actually destroy me, or prevent me from making a living, the British literary establishment were an irrelevancy. I was only vulnerable so long as I entertained a desire to be "recognized." It was when I was writing a book on Wilhelm Reich that I suddenly saw the essence of the problem. Reich was, in many ways. a great scientist; but he was possessed by a craving for fame that finally drove him into paranoia. Of course, all scientists want to be appreciated; Einstein must have been delighted when his first paper on relativity earned him recognition and a professorship. But he was indifferent to fame; his only deep concern was trying to understand the universe. He derived total satisfaction from the work itself.

The solution lies in this recognition that, while all human beings possess a personality that thrives on recognition, we also possess what might be called an "Impersonality," which can become totally *absorbed* in the objective world. (And T. E. Lawrence remarked: "Happiness is absorption.") At about the age of 18, I had recognized that the essence of all art and science is "escape from personality," and that strange sense of freedom that comes as we leave "ourselves" behind. I had always been profoundly moved by that last line of Shaw's *Candida*: when the poet has been rejected by the woman he loves and walks out alone into the night, Shaw writes: "But they do not know the secret in the poet's heart." That secret is the great secret of the romantics: that human beings do not *need* "personal" satisfaction to be happy; true happiness consists in slipping past the barriers of personality into that strange realm of pure affirmation. In Hesse's *Steppenwolf*, as the hero sits in a restaurant and drinks a glass of Moselle, his fatigue and depression suddenly vanish and he becomes aware again of "Mozart and the stars." All art produces the same intoxicating effect on us by lifting us beyond the sense of personal identity into a far more exciting universe, in which "my" problems seem laughably trivial.

This explains my intense dislike of so many modern writers whose stock in trade is pessimism and defeat. The purpose of art is to give human beings glimpses of freedom. Shaw remarked that we judge the artist by his highest moments, the criminal by his lowest. So it follows that artists and writers who portray life as boring and meaningless are behaving more like criminals than artists. The Russian philosopher Shestov remarked of Chekhov: "Stubbornly, despondently, monotonously, during his entire period of literary activity...Chekhov did one thing only: in one way or another he killed human hopes." Of course, if an artist is great enough, then a little sadness and despair do no real harm; but if like Graham Greene or Céline, he spends his life assuring us that human existence is one long defeat, then his work ceases to convey glimpses of freedom, and becomes an ally of everything that is worst in our civilization. Watching one of those literary discussions on television recently, I was staggered when a publisher remarked that Beckett is one of the greatest modern writers; but it is a typical example of the way we have come to accept a borderline type of criminality—the killing of human hope—as a valid literary activity.

But the power of art to convey glimpses of freedom also enables us to understand the despair of the romantics. They discovered that these realms of the impersonal are not always accessible; the personality traps us like a prison. I recognized this clearly in my teens, when I would look forward to a weekend of reading poetry, listening to music (on the radio), and generally washing the dust off my soul. Yet as often as not, when I opened *Palgrave's Golden Treasury* on a Saturday morning, I found that my favorite poems left me indifferent; nothing I could do could bring that sense of "opening up," as if inner barriers are sliding back. I would often spend all weekend trying to recapture the magic, and only succeed in doing so at ten o'clock on Sunday evening when a return to work was only a few hours away.

The odd thing was that whenever I succeeded in achieving these "wider" states of awareness, this problem seemed utterly trivial; in a strange sense, I now felt that it didn't *matter* whether I achieved them or not. They were there, like the Himalayas, and if I couldn't find my way there today, I could probably do so tomorrow or next week; they wouldn't run away. All I had to do was to make a determined effort to increase my optimism and powers of resistance. My central problem, I could see, lay in underestimating my own *durability*. This was the same recognition that came to Marcel in *Swann's Way*, when he tasted the cake dipped in herb tea and suddenly experienced an overwhelming sense of ceasing "to be mediocre, accidental, mortal." And the source of this recognition was simply an intensely perceived memory of childhood, and the recognition that, in some odd sense, he stood *above* time.

But I had also noticed something far more important for the solution of the "Outsider problem"—that whenever we are faced with danger or crisis, our sense of weakness is seen to be an absurdity: suddenly we *know* that "if only" we could escape and "return to normal," normal life would be seen as unutterably delightful. Dostoevsky achieved this recognition as he stood in front of a firing squad, and he makes his Raskolnikov say that if he had to stand on a narrow ledge, in eternal darkness and tempest, he would still prefer to do that rather than die at once. The same recognition once came to me on a long train journey, when I was beginning to feel bored, and I switched on my portable radio and heard that hijackers were still holding a plane in the desert after several days, and that the temperature inside was over a hundred. Suddenly, I could see that my own boredom was simply a form of *spoiltness*, like a badly brought-up child. G. K. Chesterton expressed the same insight in *Manalive* when he made the hero point a revolver at the heads of "aesthetic" poets who claim that life is futile, and achieve the immense satisfaction of seeing them beg for their lives.

This insight I labelled the "if only" feeling, for it always brings the same certainty: that "if only" the problem would vanish, we would have no problem whatever in being permanently happy. I was much struck by a radio talk by Hans Keller, the BBC's head of music, in which he described how, in the late 1930s, he saw his friends disappearing into concentration camps (Keller being a Jew in Nazi Germany), and said to himself: "If only I could escape from Germany, *I swear that I would never be unhappy again.*"

This is clearly *the* basic answer to the "Outsider problem." We simply have to learn to maintain this level of insight to refuse to surrender to the spoilt child in us. It is as if all of us contained two people, like those little men who pop in and out of old fashioned barometers to indicate wet or fine weather; one a rational adult, the other a self-indulgent brat. What destroyed most of the romantics was not the unfairness of life, the malevolence of the universe, the futility of effort, but their inability to prevent their lives being dominated by the brat. The answer lies in directing all our effort and determination to un-spoiling the brat and turning him into a well-behaved child.

So what is it that stands in our way? Mostly an inborn tendency to lose heart the moment we experience a fairly low level of fatigue. Sheer determination and self-discipline can have a tremendous effect. But these are not the whole answer. No one emphasised the importance of self-discipline more than Gurdjieff, and his disciple Ouspensky. Yet both ended their lives as oddly disappointed men. Even the most rigid self-discipline left them short of their goal. Self-discipline *is* the answer; but not the complete answer. That lies elsewhere, in a deeper recognition. It was expressed by Robert Anton Wilson in an essay called "Multiple Realities" in *Cosmic Trigger*, in which he describes how, as an editor of *Playboy*, he smoked a great deal of marihuana. And one evening, when his wife was out, he made a "neurological discovery"—that most of the phenomena of self-hypnosis can be replicated on marihuana. "Instead of being an unplanned voyage into unexpected sensory thrills, pot became a deliberate program of sensory enrichment. One could turn music into colors, into caresses, into *tastes*; one could grow to gigantic size or shrink down inside one's own cells and molecules; one could *tune* one's nervous system like a combination microscope-TV set.

"Several extraordinary months of experiment soon revealed that one could do much of this without pot... and the shaken Materialist began at long last to understand what Freud meant by *projection* and Buddha by *maya*. It became clear as vodka that whatever 'reality' means philosophically, our everyday *experience* (the commonsense definition of 'reality') is almost entirely self-programmed. *This cine-*

matic editing occurs so rapidly that we are not normally aware of doing it (my italics); thus we add many things that aren't there at all (Freud's projection) and leave out millions of things that are there (Freud's censorship). Confusing the finished product with an accurate reflection of externality is exactly what Buddha meant when he said normal consciousness is delusion (*maya*)."

I suspect that by Freud he means Jung, and that by Buddha he means the *Upanishads*; but apart from that, this seems to me to be one of the most dazzlingly insightful passages written in the 20th century—particularly the recognition that the editing occurs so rapidly that we are not aware of doing it. This explains those emotional ups and downs that caused the romantics so much misery. The sun goes behind a cloud and we "sink" without even realizing that it is happening—still less realizing that *we are doing it ourselves*. And on a bright spring morning, we experience what Chesterton called "absurd good news" without realizing that this is yet another aspect of the cinematic editing which Husserl called "intentionality." When I receive a piece of good news—say an unexpected check in the post—it has the effect of reprogramming my subconscious mind so that the editing becomes positive, and everything I look at seems fascinating. Bad news causes a sinking feeling and a loss of inner pressure, exactly like letting air out of a tire; again, we are quite unaware that we are doing it ourselves by an unconscious process of rapid editing. When Hans Keller reflected: "If only I could escape from Germany I swear I would never be unhappy again," he had caught a glimpse of the fact that *we do it ourselves*, that *he* was in charge of his feelings, not "fate." When I feel happy, it is because I have *told* myself that I am lucky, that I have good reason for delight; and my invisible "rapid editor" makes sure that everything I see seems interesting and delightful. By recognizing his existence, Robert Anton Wilson had achieved some degree of control over the invisible editor.

We all know this unconsciously. For example, we all feel a certain contempt for people of low vitality, people who try to evade problems and allow life to get them down. If we really believed that life is futile—or at least, that it is "neutral"—we would not experience this contempt; it is a recognition that *we* are in control, and that a man who fails to recognize this is a fool and a weakling: that it is his own fault.

So the answer lies in a certain insight, an insight that demands a certain subtlety of understanding. Objectively speaking, human beings have every reason for tremendous optimism. If we could learn to stop being dominated by the "brat" (a condition I have labelled "upside-downness"), the mind would automatically live in a state of "positiveness," a kind of unending pleasant-anticipation—for most of our gloom and depression is due to unconscious negative editing. Immense inner forces would be unlocked, forces that are at present held imprisoned by a lifelong habit of negativeness. And once human beings had become accustomed to this new state of energetic optimism, the problems that seemed so appalling to the romantics would vanish like a dream, and life would become quite literally "heaven on earth." The human race would have reached a new and immensely exciting point in the story of its evolution.

ABOUT COLIN STANLEY

Colin Stanley was born in Topsham, Devonshire, England, in 1952, and was educated at Exmouth School. Beginning in 1970, he worked for several years for the Devon Library Services, before taking a position at the University of Nottingham Library. He recently completed his librarian's degree. The author of several books and pamphlets, he has also edited *Colin Wilson, a Celebration: Essays and Recollections* (London: Cecil Woolf, 1988), a noteworthy anthology of nonfiction pieces on Wilson's life and career. Stanley is the founder and publisher of Paupers' Press, which has published several original essays by and about Colin Wilson. *The Work of Colin Wilson: An Annotated Bibliography & Guide* is his first book-length bibliography.

TITLE INDEX

To Colin Wilson's Works

270

"Existential Criticism and the Work of Aldous Huxley," C9

"Existential Psychology: A Novelist's Approach," C54

"Existential Temper of the Modern Novel," C34

Existentially Speaking: Essays on the Philosophy of Literature, A93

Express to Nowhere, L6

Facolto Paranormali, A46e

"Faculty X," C65

"A Fair Hearing," C257

"Faith or Fantasy?" C191

"Families of Death," C144b

"Fantasy and Faculty X," C336

"The Faust Outsider," C24, A6

"Female Murderers," C121b

"Fertility Religion," C268

La Filosofia degli Assassini, A34b

"Finnegans Wake," E16

"Fire-Raisers," C122

"Flat Earth," C323

"The Flawed Superman," C214

"Foreword" [Behind God's Back], D43

"Foreword" [Cause of Death], D35

"Foreword" [Murderer's Who's Who], D29

"Foreword" [Perfect Murder], D61

"Foreword" [Positive Magic], D39

"Foreword" [Ritual Magic], D26

"Foreword" [The Aleister Crowley Scrapbook], D62

"Foreword" [The Dark Gods], D34

"Foreword" [The Essential T. C. Lethbridge], D33

"Foreword" [The Leap], D48

"Foreword" [The Life and Work of David Lindsay], D38

"Foreword" [The Power of the Pendulum], D22

"Foreword" [The Roots of Witchcraft], D14

"Foreword" [The Rosy Cross Unveiled], D32

"Foreword" [The World of Colin Wilson], D1

"Foreword" [Witch Amongst Us], D52

"The Forgers," C156

"Forgery," C156b

"The Former Life of Mrs. Smith," C64

The Fortress, A86bc

Frankenstein's Castle—The Double Brain, Door to Wisdom, A57

"The Frenchman," B2

"Freud, Reich, and Nietzsche," C72

"Friedrich Dürrenmatt: Heir of the Existential Tradition," C26

"The Fuehrer in Perspective," E87, E88

G. I. Gurdjieff: The War Against Sleep, A76

A Gaiola de Vidro, A17h

"Gangsters," C111

Garard Sorme Shi Na Sem No Nikki, A8j

"Gateway to Other Worlds," C249

"Gazetteer of British Ghosts, by Peter Underwood," E48

The Geller Phenomenon, A49

"Geller's Guru," C259

"The Genius of Ronald Duncan," C195

"Gentlemen Crooks," C177

"Getting Inside the Outsiders," C73

Geurimja Eom-Neun Yogmang, A8g

"Ghosts," C277

"Gin Doesn't Stain," E121

"Girl 20, by Kingsley Amis," E59

The Glass Cage, A17

The Glass Cage [screenplay], L3

Glass Noori, A17i

"Glastonbury," C269

"Glazunov, Alexander," C218

The God of the Labyrinth, A26

"God of the Labyrinth," B13

De God van het Labyrint, A26c

"Gog and Magog," C270

"Going into Europe," C40

"Going into Europe Again?" C71

"Good-Time Girls," C167

"Gorran," C94

"The Grand Tradition, by J. B. Steane," E89

"The Great Seducer," E120

"The Great Unrecognised," C36

275

SUBJECT INDEX
With Author/Title Index

285

293

Nakamura, Yasuo, A1o, A2q, A4n, A7g, A15b, A17i, A18e, A21d, A23f, A30d, A31l, A34f, A35e, A50f

Naked Lunch (Burroughs), A19

Napier, S., A50

Narziss and Goldmund (Hesse), A38

Nassauer, Rudolf, E92

Nausea (Sartre), A1, A15, A60

The Near and the Far (Myers), A15

Necessary Doubt (C.W.), A14, H12, H20, K2

The Necronomicon, A20, A42, D27

Necrophilia, A9

Needleman, Jacob, A31

Neil-Smith, Rev. J. C., C66

Neill, A. S., A63

The Neophiliacs (Booker), H8

Nero, A67

Neuburg, Victor Benjamin, A82

Neumann, Gustav, A12

Neurosis, A63, A69, A73, C69

New Atlantis (Amery), E96

The New Existentialism (C.W.), A73

New Pathways in Psychology (C.W.), A73, H12, H17

Newgate Calendar, A22, A67

Newman, Charles, A14

Newman, David, A5

Newman, Fred, A62, I54

Newman, James, E19

Newman, John Henry, A2

Newman, Paul, H27

Newton, Isaac, A58, A61

Newton, J., A23

Nicholas, Anthony, A8

Nicholas II, Tsar, A13, A67

Nicholls, Peter, E113, J66

Nicholson, John, A74

Nicholson, Mary, E38

Nicolson, Iain, A56, A61

Nieman, Gilbert, A1-A2

Nietzsche, Friedrich, A1, A9, A15, A19, A34, A72, A75, C72, C78, C227, E4, H22

Night Side of Nature (Crowe), A71, D54, G3

Nihilism, A14, C78

Nijinsky, Waslaw, A1, A18, E21

Nijinsky (Reiss), E21

Nim (Terris), E106

No Orchids for Miss Blandish (Chase), A19

Noble, Jeremy, A11

Norman, C. H., A6

Nostradamus, A31, A51

Notebooks of Malte Laurids Brigge (Rilke), A12

Notebooks, Vol. I (Coleridge), E6

Nott, Kathleen, A14

A Novelization of Events in the Life and Death of Grigori Efimovich Rasputin (C.W.), A91

Novels, A4-A5, A8, A10, A12, A17, A20, A23, A26-A27, A30, A42-A43, A50, A68, A74, A86-A87, A93

The Novels of Colin Wilson (Tredell), H20, K1

Noyes, John H., A9

Nye, Robert, A7, A20, A28

Oates, Joyce Carol, A23, A31, H26, I36, I40

O'Bannon, Dan, L3

Objectivity, A65, A67

Obregon, Enrique de, A43f

Obscenity, C31

Occult, A31, A35, A46-A49, A51-A53, A61-A62, A64, A69-A71, A73, A80, A83, A92, C64, C66, C76, C129, C224-C226, C233-C234, C246-C261, C330, D26, E86, I34

The Occult (C.W.), A35, A46-A48, A52, A59, A73, C65, C211

Occult revival, A35

Occult Science—An Outline (Steiner), A75

An Occultist's Travels (Reichel), D20

O'Connor, Gary, A29

Octaves, Law of, A59

Odell, Robin, A84, D29

"Odic Force," A31, A44, A52, A70

O'Donnell, D., A3

302

Praxis (Weldon), C327
Precognition, A31, A61
Preiswerk, Helen, A69
Prelati, Ricky, A5
"Preparedness," A33
Prester John, A67
Preston, Gregor A., A66
Preston, Harry, A5
Pre-vision, A13
Price, Harry, A31, A62
Price, R. C. G., A4, A8
Price-Turner, W., A27
Priestley, J. B., A1, A31, C37, C39, H1, H26
Printing, Invention of, A67
The Prodigy (Hesse), A38
Profumo, David, A90
Prohibition, A67
Prokofiev, Sergei, A11
Promiscuity, A9
Prophecy, A47, A61, A64, C286
Prostitution, E34
Prostitution in Europe and the New World (Henriques), E34
Protection rackets, C102
Protest (Feldman & Gartenburg), C14
Proust, Marcel, A28
Prurience, C338
Pryce-Jones, Alan, A10, C4
Psi power, A52
Psychedelic drugs, A31, A57
Psychic Detectives (C.W.), I58
Psychic powers, A46, A64
Psychical Research, Society of, A31, A70-A71
Psychoanalysis, A63
The Psychoanalytic Forum, Vol. 3 (Lindon), I26
Psycho-expansion, A70
Psychokinesis, A62
Psychological Types (Jung), A69
Psychology, A9, A14, A19, A33, A57, A77, A90, C47, C54, C69, C72-C73, C79, C85, C331, C333-C335, E75, F2
Psychometry, A52, A62, A64, A70, C129, C234

Psychopaths, A67
Ptolemy, A58
Publishing, C31
Pubs, A37
Puharich, Andrija, A52, A70, C258-C259
Punishment, A67
Purcell, H. D., H26
Pyramids, A61, C273, C282
Pythagoras, A31, A58
Quantum theory, A58
The Quest for Wilhelm Reich (C.W.), A44, C212
Quinn, Martin, E120
Quinton, Anthony, A4, A7
Rabelais, François, A26
Railsback, Steve, L3
Ramakrishna, Sri, A1, A28
Rambeau, James, E120
Rand, Ayn, A15
Rank, Otto, A9, A33
Rape, A67, C106, C140
Rapid Eye Movements, A52
Rasmussen, Elisabeth & Knud, A4k
Rasp, Renate, H26
Rasputin, Grigori, A13, A31, A46, A51-A52, A91, B15, L6
Raudive, Konstantin, E49
Rauschenbach, Emma, A69
Raven, Simon, A3
The Ravishing of Lady Mary Ware (Wheatley), E61
"Raymond," A71
Raymond, J., A13, A14, A16
Read, Herbert, E8
Reade, Damon, A17
Realism, A7
The Reappearance of Christ and the Masters of Wisdom (Creme), E104
Rebecca (du Maurier), A45
"The Recollections of Father Zossima," A1
Red Barn Murder, A22, A67
Redgrove, Peter, E98
Rees, Goronwy, A31
Reflexive Universe (Young, A.), A52

Welch, Colin, A67
Welch, Louise, E115
Weldon, Fay, C327
Wells, H. G., A1, A7, A14, A19, A21, A31, A35, A45, A54, A64, E77
Wenyon, Michael, A61
Werewolf, A64
Weschcke, Carl L., A50
West, Anthony, A4
West, Nathanael, A7
West, Paul, A4
West, R. H., A31
Westcountry Mysteries (Williams), D51
Weston-Smith, Miranda, C235-C236
Wharton, Will, A20
What Is Class Consciousness? (Reich), A63
Wheatley, Dennis, C66, E61
Whiskey, A37, C204
White Goddess (Graves), A31
Whitehead, Alfred North, A2, A14, A18
Whiting, John, C7
Whitman, Walt, A32
Whittemore, Reed, A21
Whittington-Egan, Richard, A15, A18, A84, E71, E92
Widmer, Kingsley, H6
Widower's Houses (Shaw), A21
Wilber, Ken, E116
Wilde, Oscar, A7, A15, E39
Wilgus, Neal, A23, A55, H17
Wilhelm II, Kaiser, A67
Wilhelm, Richard, A69
Wilkinson, Oliver Marlow, A51
The Will to Power (Nietzsche), A9
Williams, Michael, C238, D15, D51
Williams, Raymond, A1
Williamson, Henry, A15, C28, C36, E108, H21
Williamson, J. N., C336
Williamson, Malcolm, A11
Willingham, Calder, C327
Wilson, Angus, A1, A25, C4, H26, K1
Wilson, Bryan R., E81
Wilson, Colin, A25, C337, and Sections H, I, J, and K (generally)

Wilson, Damon, A21, A83, A86
Wilson, Edmund, A36
Wilson, Gahan, A23
Wilson, Glenn D., E84
Wilson, Joy, A25, I16, I37
Wilson, Robert Anton, I61
Wilson, Rowan, A86
Wilson, Sally, A86
Wilson, Tim, I31
Wine, A37
Wingrove, David, J93
The Wise Wound (Shuttle & Redgrove), E98
Witch Amongst Us (Bourne), D52
Witch Doctors, A64
Witchcraft, A31, A61-A62, A64, A67, A82, C103, D14, C283
Witches, A52, A64, A67, C76, D52
Wittgenstein, Ludwig Josef Johann, A2, A14
Wolf Man, A63, E63
The Wolf Man and Sigmund Freud (Gardner), E63
Wolfe, Gary K., A55
Wolfe, Jeremy, A10
Wolff, Antonia, A69
Wolleback, Per, A40
Woodcock, George, E66
Woodruff, Ura, A64
Woods, William, E86
Woolf, Cecil, C53, E25
Wordsworth, Christopher, H4
The Work of Colin Wilson (Stanley), D64, H28
The World of Colin Wilson (Campion), A1, D1, H4, K2
The World of Mathematics (Newman), E19
The World of Violence (C.W.), A23, A73, B10, H12, H20, I24, K2-K3
Worlds in Collision (Velikovsky), E86
Wreckers, A67
Wright, Giles E., A12
Wschlke, Carl L., A50
Wuthering Heights (Brontë), A72, C212
X-rays, A58